THE BRITISH CONSTITUTION NOW

THE
BRITISH
CONSTITUTION
NOW

Recovery or Decline?

FERDINAND MOUNT

HEINEMANN : LONDON

William Heinemann Ltd
Michelin House, 81 Fulham Road, London SW3 6RB
LONDON   MELBOURNE   AUCKLAND

First published 1992
Copyright © Ferdinand Mount 1992

A CIP catalogue record for this book
is held by the British Library
ISBN 0 434 47994 2

Phototypeset by Deltatype Ltd, Ellesmere Port
Printed in Great Britain
by Clays Ltd, St. Ives Plc

CONTENTS

CONTENTS

PREFACE

The reader will find this book a queer mixture: part history, part political theory, part contemporary polemic, with several spoonfuls of biography thrown in. The reader is entitled to an explanation for this unusual compote. Hitherto, after all, writings on the British Constitution have usually fallen quite neatly into one of three distinct categories: the historic-evolutionary (usually written by historians), the present-descriptive (reserved for political scientists) and the future-prescriptive (preferred by practising politicians).

The present essay is based on the view that it is futile to examine the British Constitution without attempting, however haltingly and inadequately, to combine all three approaches. I do not expect this combination to please everybody, or indeed anybody. It will be too sketchy for the historians, too literary for the political scientists, too theoretical for the politicians, too antiquarian for the futurists. But I can see no honest alternative, since we are dealing with a set of arrangements which (a) is historically rooted and determined, (b) has to be read by practising politicians as a set of rules which are, for the moment, binding and so ought to be coherent, and (c) is unmistakably under a variety of pressures which will lead to further evolution.

Accordingly, we begin by considering some of the assertions and evasions of our leading constitutional authorities, since it is they who have all too often blurred or distorted our understanding of the way we are governed. This is the burden of the first two chapters of the book. The third chapter examines, quite rapidly, our present practices and the main problems besetting them – or rather those features which have been identified in recent years as problematic – and some of the solutions proffered. The fourth chapter brings into consideration the outside pressures now bearing down on us. In the final chapter, some effort will be made to sketch a plausible future course of constitutional development – plausible in the sense of 'likely' as well as 'desirable' or 'practicable'. 'Will we?' is clearly just as important as 'Should we?' or 'Could we?' None of these questions can be sensibly answered unless we have a rough understanding of both the past history and the present state of our Constitution; and such an understanding depends on first cleaning our minds of old misunderstandings. To go in search of a constitution, let alone of *the* Constitution, we have to rummage in our mental past as well as probe into our political futures.

DEDICATION

The last book which attempted with any distinction to argue its way through the morass engulfing the law and the Constitution was the book of that title by Sir Ivor Jennings, first published in 1933. *The Law and the Constitution* was dedicated to Jennings's LSE colleague, Harold J. Laski, and bore the marks of Laski's own thoughts on the British Constitution.

This present book is dedicated to the memory of Laski's very different successor as Professor of Political Science at the LSE, Michael Oakeshott. Many of its pages bear the marks, no doubt sadly smudged, of Oakeshott's thought, and his seminal distinction between an 'enterprise association' and a 'civil association' runs through the argument. I hasten to add that this in no way purports to be the kind of book Oakeshott would have agreed with, let alone have wished to write. It is a poor engraving after a non-existent original.

I

DELUSIONS
AND DISCONTENTS

Swift's first failure

When Jonathan Swift was a young man, he lodged with his patron, Sir William Temple, the celebrated essayist and diplomat. William III, when afflicted with the gout, used to come down to visit Temple and would wander round his famous gardens at Moor Park, accompanied by Temple's petulant protégé (who was already discontented with his role as secretary on twenty pounds a year). The King took to the young man, who could be engaging when he wanted to be; he showed Swift how to cut asparagus in the Dutch manner and even offered to make him a captain of horse. Temple must have been gladdened by the sight of his secretary conversing so pleasantly with his king in the asparagus patch. A few months later, he thought of Swift's persuasive powers when he was trying to persuade William that there would be no danger to royal power in assenting to a Triennial Act.

Swift was sent to Kensington Palace. Buoyed by happy memories of the rambles in the vegetable garden, he bounded off on his mission, full of confidence, being, as he says himself in his *Autobiographical Fragment*, 'well versed in English History although he were then under three and twenty years old'. Unfortunately, the King was quite unmoved by Swift's brilliant arguments. Dutch William, 'who was a stranger to our constitution', remained stubbornly convinced that 'King Charles 1st lost his Crown and Life by consenting to pass such a bill.' Swift went home humiliated and bewildered: 'he told his friends that it was the first incident that helped to cure him of vanity.'[1]

Dr Johnson, notoriously obsessed by the vanity of human

wishes, records the incident in his Life of Swift with a good deal of relish. But he does not record the sequel. The following year, a Triennial Act *was* passed. William signed it reluctantly and apprehensively, but he had recognised that he had no choice in the face of an implacable Parliament. He was beset by Jacobite plots, short of cash and embroiled in foreign wars. It is a pity that he lived scarcely long enough to see how the advent of three-year parliaments served only to entrench the stability and popularity of the monarchy. Sir David Ogg tells us that 'The Triennial Act, opposed by many Tories in 1694, was acclaimed by nearly all of them in 1716 as one of the sacred things in the constitution.'[2] William had more cause to fear molehills than the mountain he made out of the Triennial Bill. When he was persuaded to sign it, it was entirely by force of brute political circumstance and not by the subtle and learned arguments of Jonathan Swift.

The cautionary tale is applicable not only to human vanity generally but to the specific type of vanity which afflicts constitutional reformers. It is an ever recurring fact of history that constitutions are made, amended and broken, not by the play of rational arguments deployed by clever young men in research institutes but by the harsh clash and grinding of the tectonic plates of power. It is the political struggle rather than the pursuit of good government which ultimately decides rulers and ruling classes whether or not to drive through or give in to proposals for reform; and it is the balance of forces rather than the balance of the arguments which dictates which side is to prevail.

To grant all or even some of this would be a dangerous concession for constitutional reformers to make. They would thereby be undermining those claims to pure rationality which are essential to their cause; they would be exposing themselves to the accusations that their programmes were no more than cynical manoeuvres for power decked in the bunting of high principle.

In reality, proposals for constitutional reform are often the poetry of the politically impotent. Accordingly, many such proposals lose their allure when power is gained or regained. There is nothing like the loss of office for concentrating one's mind on the iniquities of the System (use of the capital S is a sure sign of being

Out with a capital O). In the late 1970s, many leading Conservatives took up the cause of Proportional Representation as a bulwark
against the ideological blitzkriegs to be expected of extremist (that
is, socialist) parliamentary majorities. When the Conservatives
regained office, that campaign for Proportional Representation
melted in the pleasant sunshine of power – only to be succeeded in
the late 1980s by an equally high-minded Labour campaign for PR
to save the country from an eternity of 'extreme' Conservative
governments. In his famous Dimbleby Lecture (19 October 1976)
and later in *The Dilemma of Democracy* (1978), Lord Hailsham
waxed apocalyptic about the perils of 'elective dictatorship' and
called for a written constitution and a Bill of Rights, but this
anxiety seemed to recede somewhat as he and his party regained
office. By 1991, he was defending the flexibility of our unwritten
Constitution, pouring cold water on the idea of a Bill of Rights and
claiming that 'we are probably the most successful political society
that has ever existed'.[3]

Hailsham was by no means the first writer on constitutional
matters to allow a certain partisan gloom to cloud his ruminations.
In the 1930s, for example, during the interminable Baldwin years,
Sir Ivor Jennings, the author of *Cabinet Government* and an LSE
Fabian of the most principled sort, wrote in *The Law and the
Constitution* that ' "Parliament" means a partisan majority. A
victory at the polls, obtained, perhaps by mass bribery or
deliberate falsehood or national hysteria, theoretically enables a
party majority to warp the law so as to interfere with the most
cherished of "fundamental liberties".'[4] This danger remained
theoretical, he thought, so long as the democratic system continued to operate, but that qualification seems to offer scant
comfort, since he also thought that the democratic system itself
was protected from destruction only by the threat of revolution. In
other words, the whole edifice was extremely shaky. One cannot
help feeling that he would not have been quite so apprehensive if a
good Fabian government had been in power at the time.

But Jennings was positively optimistic compared with A. V.
Dicey, the leading constitutional theorist of the preceding generation. In the conclusion to the introduction to the eighth edition of

The Law of the Constitution (we shall hear more of this introduction, which was later to be suppressed), he wrote of 'the admitted and increasing evil of our party system' and of 'declining faith in that rule of law which in 1884 [the year when he was writing the first edition of his great work] was one of the two leading principles of constitutional government as understood in England'.[5] Change and decay in all around he saw, and this melancholy was not unconnected with the fact that the abhorred Liberal government had finally managed to pass an Act introducing Home Rule for Ireland – a calamity which he had been fighting against for thirty years:

> The sovereignty of Parliament is still the fundamental doctrine of English constitutionalists. But the authority of the House of Lords has been gravely diminished, whilst the authority of the House of Commons, or rather of the majority thereof during any one Parliament, has been immensely increased. Now this increased portion of sovereignty can be effectively exercised only by the Cabinet which holds in its hands the guidance of the party machine. And of the party which the party majority supports, the Premier has become at once the legal head and, if he is a man of ability, the real leader.[6]

Liberals of the period were liable to take much the same view. Morley thought that the Prime Minister's power was 'not inferior to that of a dictator, provided that the House of Commons will stand by him'.[7] Asquith said that 'the office of Prime Minister is what its holder chooses to make it'.[8]

Now this is precisely the discovery that, fifty years later, J. P. Mackintosh and R. H. S. Crossman thought they were making for themselves. The Prime Minister was no longer *primus inter pares*, but simply premier. They too, it should be noted, were writing like Dicey before them and Hailsham after them, from a position of political impotence, as Labour MPs during thirteen years of Conservative rule. When Crossman did enjoy power under Harold Wilson, he found (although he was somewhat loath to admit it, even to his diary) that the Prime Minister did not always get his way, that, despite Wilson's indefatigable manoeuvres, quite often the Cabinet blocked him; sometimes again, the Civil Service acted as a brake on the will of the Labour Party's majority; more often still, events took charge and dictated the development of policy.

At this stage, we do not need to try and establish when and to what extent the office of Prime Minister became rather more than first among equals. What needs to be noted here is the shortness of the constitutional historian's memory and his recurring tendency to be swayed by his own personal political hopes and fears. He is a creature of his times, and tends, perhaps more than he knows, to write for his times and addresses himself to the apprehensions and discontents of his contemporaries.

And when the constitutional historian turns constitutional reformer, he is often tempted to present as new-minted solutions to the problems of the day devices which he knows (or ought to know) have been on offer before. To an uncommitted observer, any such claim to originality always sounds a little implausible. The dilemmas or challenges which face us are unlikely to be wholly novel. Scotland, Wales and Ireland are not new neighbours to England. We can scarcely be the first generation to be exercised by the problems of creating or maintaining the unity of the kingdom. Yet a curious historical blankness appears to descend whenever constitutional reform is discussed, as though to examine the history of aborted or rejected reforms were to weaken the will of present-day reformers. Not many present-day advocates of federal arrangements for the UK choose to recall the agitation for 'Home Rule All Round' in the early years of the century. Not many enthusiasts for Proportional Representation hark back to the brief craze for PR among leading politicians such as Balfour and Churchill in the uncertain years after the First World War. And it is an inconvenient fact for the supporters of a parliament for Scotland that they have come closest to success so far when two quite unconnected things coincided: the maximum flow of North Sea oil into Scottish terminals and the need of the Callaghan government for the votes of the Scottish National Party. These contingencies in no way discredit either the theoretical or practical case for a Scottish assembly, but they do say something about the intensity of Scottish devotion to the cause and the sincerity of the English conversion to it – and hence they say something too about the chances of an enduring settlement arising out of such a conjunction.

Thus constitutional history and constitutional reform tend to merge into a single project, one usually carried out by unreliable and passionate partisans who have little or no commitment to establishing the true line of development in the past or to attempting any cool qualitative analysis.

We are told that the system is in decline, has been corrupted, has lost its old checks and balances. But if we enquire, 'Well, when was the heyday then?', we are unlikely to hear any clear or precise or agreed answer. Was there ever a moment at which it was possible to say in all honesty that some kind of general overall settlement of the principal constitutional questions had been arrived at? Can we identify and date the first appearance of the finished article?

'It is only within the last 50 years,' Mr Gladstone said in 1879, 'that our constitutional system has settled down.'[9] Seven years later, he was proposing the First Home Rule Bill, the most fundamental shift in the system certainly since the Great Reform Bill and arguably since the Act of Union nearly two centuries earlier. Even when Gladstone came to the Second Home Rule Bill, he was still looking for something like settlement: 'The plan that was to be proposed was to be such as, at least in the judgment of its promoters, presented the necessary characteristics – I will not say of finality, because it is a discredited word – but of a real and continuing settlement.'[10]

Bagehot, writing in the mid-1860s, speaks airily in *The English Constitution*[11] of 'former times, when our constitution was incomplete'. Now that the supremacy of the House of Commons had become a settled thing, Victorian Britain or England (for Bagehot was sloppy about these things and showed no great interest in affairs west of Bridgwater or north of Manchester) had come pretty close to political perfection. Alas, barely had he laid down his pen before the 1867 Reform Act smashed all his assumptions and left him trembling before the mob with scarcely more confidence in the future than a mere Tory like Lord Salisbury. In the preface to the second edition,[12] we are told of 'the

6

great difficulty in the way of a writer who attempts to sketch a living Constitution – a Constitution that is in actual work and power. The difficulty is that the object is in constant change.' And, therefore, can never be completed.

Between the wars, Sir Ivor Jennings was complaining that 'the British constitution is changing so rapidly that it is difficult to keep pace with it'.[13] In other words, that moment at which Mr Gladstone thought things had settled down at last was only the point of departure for a further series of seismic shifts: 'during the past sixty or seventy years the Constitution has been profoundly modified under the influence of collectivist ideas'.[14]

Nor was this untoward or unexpected. These continuing shifts were characteristic of our tradition. Jennings quotes with approval Baldwin's view that:

> The historian can tell you probably perfectly clearly what the constitutional practice was at any given period in the past, but it would be very difficult for a living writer to tell you at any given period in his lifetime what the Constitution of the country is in all respects, and for this reason, that almost at any given moment . . . there may be one practice called 'constitutional' which is falling into desuetude and there may be another practice which is creeping into use but is not yet constitutional.[15]

But can anything so slippery, so malleable and mutable be really thought of as a *constitution* at all? Tocqueville said bluntly, 'elle n'existe point' – which Dicey calls 'a dark saying', and translates as 'the English constitution has no real existence',[16] as if at least the poor thing could lay claim to some shadow-life. But the saying is not dark at all. It is a straightforward assertion that a phenomenon so changeable in both its details and its principles does not deserve the name of constitution. There is indeed something richly comic about Lord John Russell's assertion that the 1832 Act had attained the limit of desirable change. When he made the speech in 1837 that was to earn him the nickname of 'Finality Jack', he himself had yet to introduce no less than three further measures of parliamentary reform.

7

But is finality in our constitutional arrangements such a ludicrous or impractical aspiration? Is there something appropriate and natural about their open-ended, uncodified nature? Is this accumulation of statutes, conventions, customs and historical deposits, written down in a dozen different places and in no place at all, the only or the only desirable system for ensuing liberty, justice and good government?

English exceptionalism

The mainstream of constitutional authorities finds it congenial to say yes to all this. They are professionally subject to self-deception, sharing the belief, sometimes explicit, sometimes tacit, that the course of constitutional development has followed a providential, perhaps inevitable pattern. Marxist historicism and the Whig theory of progress are feverish intensifications of a state which may afflict the least ideological of historians in a milder form.

For this reason, it is even truer of constitutional history than of other types that 'history to the defeated cannot say alas or pardon'. Reforms that were aborted are treated with passing condescension or entirely neglected. Trevelyan's *History of England* barely mentions Cromwell's *Instrument of Government*, the first full-scale attempt at a written constitution for these islands and a forerunner of the sort of written constitution that now operates in a large number of modern democracies.

This inclination to treat British constitutional history as the outcome of the workings of a rational Providence has several further consequences. First, there is the temptation to draw the conclusion that this rational Providence has chosen to shower its blessings uniquely upon these islands.

At the beginning of *The Law of the Constitution*, Dicey quotes Burke and Hallam on the unrivalled beauties of our constitutional arrangements:

No unbiased observer, who derives pleasure from the welfare of his species, can fail to consider the long and uninterruptedly increasing prosperity of England as the most beautiful

8

phenomenon in the history of mankind. Climates more propitious may impart more largely the mere enjoyments of existence, but in no other region have the benefits that political institutions can confer been diffused over so extended a population; nor have any people so well reconciled the discordant elements of wealth, order and liberty.[17]

Seventy years later, Hallam's rhapsodic complacency would have sounded a bit naive, and Dicey hastens to disclaim the role of worshipper; the constitutional lawyer is 'called upon to perform the part neither of a critic nor of an apologist, nor of an eulogist, but simply of an expounder'.[18] This is, of course, a fraudulent pose. In no time at all, Dicey too is eulogising the marvellous flexibility of our institutions, the sturdy continuity of our parliamentary traditions, the unquenchable respect for the rights of the individual shown in our courts. How blessed we are to be free of the rigid legalism which blights the lives of the Americans, the Swiss and other peoples who have the misfortune to be ruled by federalism, which, he tells us over and over again, is 'a very peculiar sentiment'.

Nor is this defensive, propagandising way of writing about the British Constitution a quaint Victorian habit, long since shaken off by more clinical modern practitioners. Graeme C. Moodie, one of the few post-war political scientists to write copiously about the British Constitution, boasts, for example, that:

the British constitution is thus a continuously changing blend of the ancient and modern. One of its strengths has been that for the most part it has permitted governments to wield the power necessary to govern effectively without allowing them to rule for long in an arbitrary and irresponsible fashion, disregarding the wishes at least of the more powerful and articulate sections of the governed. Another source of strength has been that, on the one hand, no rigid constitutional or political orthodoxy has been able to ossify the institutions of government and, on the other hand, partly for this reason, it has not been necessary totally and swiftly to reorganise them at the cost of destroying established habits of thought, behaviour and sentiment.[19]

9

Here, not for the first or last time, we come across the familiar dichotomies between the British and the rest. Our arrangements are flexible, evolving, fluid, alive; theirs are rigid, static, ossified, dead and unable to respond to change. The particular features which our system has evolved turn out to be particularly suited to our needs. The two-party system, for example, is 'conducive to stable and mature government'.[20] We would be mad to abandon our flexibility. Dr John Gray, the most distinguished modern exponent of the British liberal tradition, asks almost incredulously: 'is it really being proposed that we exchange the inestimable advantages of a well-ordered constitutional monarchy for the rule-bound chaos of modern legalism?'[21]

Britain – or England (the two terms are indiscriminately used in the most surprising way) – is an exception. The beauties of our arrangements are unique and not to be seriously compared with those of other nations, and the continuous, unbroken, unending process by which we arrive at the present state of those arrangements is itself one of those beauties, and, in a curious way, one which ennobles us, for we are not simply dumb recipients of a given set of arrangements; we are its inhabitants, its conservers and creators.

But who are *we*? Can it seriously be argued that the inhabitants of Northern Ireland have been blessed by a long tradition of peaceful constitutional arrangements? The fundamentals of *their* Constitution have been turned upside down on half a dozen occasions in the past two centuries. In 1783, they were handed over to Grattan's Parliament. In 1801, the Act of Union brought them back again. Then came three Home Rule Bills, then the 1920 Government of Ireland Act establishing the Stormont Parliament, then the 1972 Act abolishing it again. Take a somewhat longer timespan from the Union of 1707, and Scotland's constitutional arrangements would scarcely appear to have enjoyed a much more exceptional degree of stability; and even if we accept, as Unionists from A. V. Dicey to Enoch Powell have accepted, that the Union of Parliaments was a monumental and irreversible act of statemanship rather than a confidence trick played on the innocent Scots (as Scottish nationalists like to imagine), we still have to recognise a persistent *jerkiness* in Scotland's government; the separate systems of legal and ecclesiastical government remind us of the earlier political separation and so bear witness to something that has been lost. I am not concerned at this stage to weigh the blessings of Union against the longing for independence, but there is no denying that the position of the Scots is at least of the same type as the position of the Bretons and the Catalans and the Flemings. There is not much exceptional about it.

Yet, as soon as we confine our exceptionalist charm to the English alone, we have muddled the purity of its outline, for we cannot help referring back to the struggle to extend the blessings of Englishness to the other inhabitants of these islands. Our history begins to look rather more like the history of other peoples – particularly other peoples who have struggled to impose unified rule on their less populous neighbours. Comparisons begin to be made.

According to S. E. Finer,[22] in the civilised world, every country bar two has some kind of constitutional document which enjoys a special entrenched status and can be altered only by following special procedures, usually of a complex and laborious kind. The two exceptions are the United Kingdom and Israel. Until its 1986 Constitution Act, New Zealand was a third. (The Home Office Minister, Mr John Patten, thinks it still is.[23] We shall return both to this interesting piece of legislation and to Mr Patten.) The arrangements in Israel naturally owe a good deal to the British tradition. But no other country, not even the countries of the old Commonwealth, has chosen to imitate Britain's abstinence from a written basic law.

Now this might be an historical accident, due perhaps to the prevailing fashion at the time when these arrangements were mostly drawn up. It might be that the British tradition, being older, had had the good luck to endure through the age of written constitutions and survived to offer a model of flexibility and adaptability to potential reformers around the world.

The remarkable thing is how few takers there seem to be for our model. One scarcely ever hears of reformers in these other countries yearning to get rid of their rigid arrangements; nor, in most cases, does there seem to be large-scale agitation to alter the main provisions of those arrangements. Rather, political animals, especially in the English-speaking countries, above all the United States, prefer to spend their time arguing – with a good deal of heat and expertise – about the correct interpretation of their constitutions. Further, they seek to extract new certainties and fresh principles on which to draw up laws to govern matters which never entered the heads of the Founding Fathers – abortion, experiments on animals and so on. Far from these written constitutions becoming dead-letter documents, seldom consulted and relevant only in extreme situations, their provisions steadily reduced to irrelevance by the weight of new statutes, constitutional analysts worry away at each clause and comma with ever greater intensity, seeking to extract still more exact rigidities. Nothing seems to shake their belief that their Supreme Courts and their armies of constitutional lawyers are quite capable of improving standards of justice and administration without large-scale constitutional reform. They seem to feel no sense of anachronism or frustration in this pastime.

I do not intend to romanticise the work of lawyers and politicians in written-constitution states. Many of their debates are clearly seeking to extract what is not there from documents which were written in utterly different circumstances. To spend one's life in constitutional interpretation of this sort may engender a kind of reverence which is just as 'irrational' as the adoration of a dynastic sovereign.

It is, indeed, often the case that, as Jennings argues at the beginning of his preface to *The Law and the Constitution*, 'a written constitution tends to obscure the fundamental changes which are taking place, and constitutional lawyers explain a political system which exists on paper and not in practice'.[24] The United States Constitution contains a good deal of material designed to distribute as clearly as possible the nation's war-making powers between the Congress and the Presidency. And yet it seems to have been possible for President Bush to pursue an offensive option against Iraq and dispatch nearly half a million men to the Persian Gulf before gaining congressional approval, leading Professor Michael

J. Glennon, of the University of California Davis Law School, to deduce the 'near-complete irrelevance of the law in the matter'.[25] But is this an example of irrelevance or merely desuetude? Or were the President's actions legitimate exercises of presidential authority (after all, Congress *did* eventually give authority for the actual waging of the war)? And, even if these actions do suggest that the original intentions of the Framers have become somewhat neglected, we should not overlook the ways in which Congress has limited the President's offensive freedom of action – for example, by the legislation on arms exports, by the Intelligence Oversight Act of 1974 and by the War Powers Act of 1973.[26] Geoffrey Marshall[27] points out that congressional actions may have halved the value of US arms sales to the Middle East from 18 billion dollars in 1983 to 9–10 billion dollars per annum in the later 1980s. More important still, the existence of the constitutional provisions leaves a standing opportunity for the Congress to reclaim what it believes to be its legitimate powers; the existence of these powers, even if they have been neglected, provides solid ground for a reasoned and sustained counter-attack by the Congress against an overmighty President. A constitution which consists in nothing but the body of prevailing practice offers no such ground for continuous and substantive argument. Thus it will not do for Jennings to dodge any comparison between the written and the unwritten by remarking in a world-weary fashion that 'in these days constitutions come like water; and even if they do not go like wind, strange things happen to them which were not contemplated by their framers.'[28] It may be true that the British 'constitution of today [1933] is only superficially like that of the Third Reform Act';[29] but the continuity of the constitutions of the US and other long-established written-constitution nations is an important fact which determines the nature of political life in those countries in a way which is foreign to the United Kingdom.

British exceptionalists must be able to muster a formidable degree of self-confidence if they are to dodge making some kind of serious comparison with the prevailing practice in those countries which are our most successful allies and rivals.

If all these nations are happy enough with their constitutional

13

status quo and, in one way or another, are remarkably prosperous, materially and socially, our own arrangements certainly deserve a rigorous (though not necessarily unfriendly) examination.

In particular, we can scarcely avoid noticing that there does seem to be some kind of disjunction in the British Constitution between the certainty, predictability and regularity which we aim for when we frame and administer new laws and the fluid and slipshod quality of the arrangements for their framing. When we look at a game like cricket or football, there seems to be little conflict of this sort. Not only are the rules of the game stable, regular and administered by more or less the same standards wherever the game is played; the rules for changing the rules also ensure long and detailed consideration and set a series of stiff hurdles before enactment can be secured. The same is true of the rules of most professional associations, trade unions, charitable organisations and the like. Thus the written-constitution states mimic, on a larger scale, the proceedings of most smaller human associations; it is the British tradition which stands out, not merely as an exception to other states but also as an exception to other rule-making bodies in Britain.

Nor is it any kind of mystery why we expect other rule-making bodies to provide a stable and clear set of rules which can be altered only by elaborate procedures involving prolonged scrutiny and often minimum majorities of two-thirds or three-quarters of the electorate. We want to be certain, first of all, that the rule-change commands very wide support and has not been pushed through to suit the whim or the self-interest of a faction which has temporarily mustered a majority. Second, clarity and stability ensure that the rules are familiar to all who will have to abide by them; not merely will ignorance of the rules be no excuse, it will be rare, not to say unknown, among the players or even the majority of the spectators; in a crowd of 100,000 football supporters, there will scarcely be a handful who do not understand the new offside rule, although it is by no means simple. Thirdly, the shared knowledge simplifies the task of the judge, umpire or referee; he may be accused of having made a mistake, but, in general, it will be his perception of facts that is attacked, not his knowledge or interpretation of the rules which provide the basis for his judgments. Thus there is far less scope for putting pressure on him to bend his judgments in this or that direction than there would be if the rules themselves were unclear or open to a variety of interpretations. Stability of the rules encourages stability of judgments.

Our political arrangements correspond only faintly to these desiderata. The rules can be changed in an afternoon in an atmosphere of panic and then left on the statute books for decades (the Official Secrets Act 1911 is the *locus classicus*). The rules change very frequently and often for no pressing reason. The innumerable changes in the system of local government finance over the past thirty years were inspired by no great social imperative; it would have been better to have left in place almost any one of the half-dozen systems that have kept local government in a state of constant turmoil. Thus the ground rules do not survive long enough to enjoy either familiarity or authority – which provokes unremitting political pressure to alter them yet again. And, because they accumulate so little respect, there is no deterrent to those who wish to exploit them to the maximum that the letter of the law will permit; the spirit of fair play has no room to breathe.

Nor is it entirely clear that an appeal to the antiquity and continuity of the British tradition will succeed in obliterating these misgivings. After all, traditional, custom-ruled societies are scarcely notorious for the heedless rapidity with which they change their arrangements. In any case, before making this appeal, we ought first to establish how accurate are these claims to antiquity and continuity. If a principal part of the claim of British exceptionalists is that we in this country stand on firm ground because it is in essence the same ground on which we have always stood, then we need to be sure of our geography. We have to show that our position has not unwittingly been shifted by erosion, subsidence or the prevailing wind.

The continuity myth

To maintain such self-confidence, English exceptionalists have to rely on a somewhat smoothed-down version of history. They, or their sources, must have a consistent bias towards emphasising continuity rather than descrying discontinuity. It is not simply that each development must be seen as part of a rational pattern. Reforms which are scotched or killed must be written off as doomed rebellions against the onward march of Our Constitutional Tradition; what is lost or never obtained must not be mourned over, nor the qualitative effects of its absence candidly assessed.

Sir David Lindsay Keir, for example, begins his *Constitutional History of Modern Britain* (1485–1937) with the usual hymn to continuity:

> Continuity has been the dominant characteristic in the development of English government. Its institutions, though unprotected by the fundamental or organic laws which safeguard the 'rigid' constitutions of most other states, have preserved the same general appearance throughout their history, and have been regulated in their working by principles which can be regarded as constant. Crown and Parliament, Council and great offices of state, courts with their judges and magistrates, have all retained, amid varying environments, many of the inherent attributes as well as much of the outward circumstance and dignity which were theirs in the mediaeval world of their origin.[30]

Let us pause briefly to note the crucial modifying phrases in this paean: 'the same general *appearance*' . . . 'principles which can be *regarded as constant*' . . . 'amid *varying environments*' . . . '*the outward circumstance and dignity*'. Already the ground is prepared for easy slithering between continuity in matters of form and continuity in matters of substance, between appearance and reality.

The Tudor monarchy, Keir hastens to tell us, was not a violent repudiation of the past, nor a period 'of sweeping constitutional innovation, but of a determined and successful attempt to make existing institutions yield their proper results'.[31] Resisting the temptation to point out how many other despots in less happier lands have tried to 'make existing institutions yield their proper results', one cannot help noticing that at least one institution has dropped off the list, namely the Church. Keir notes that 'the

Crown attempted to make innovation acceptable by maintaining at least the appearance of continuity',[32] but these efforts, like those of later Church historians, 'can have little or no meaning for the historian of the Constitution. For him the Reformation, despite all the efforts of the King or churchmen to suggest otherwise, must be regarded as a revolution.'[33] The whole rich corpus of Church property, canon law and doctrinal tradition – all swept away, obliterated from the English polity for good and all.

This is a fine example of the 'useful fiction escape clause', much employed by historians and propagandists from Burke, through Bagehot and Dicey, down to the present day.

Dicey says, for example, that appeals to precedent in the law courts are 'merely a useful fiction by which judicial decision conceals its transformation into judicial legislation'.[34] When we read Blackstone's account of the great powers of the Crown, 'we are in the midst of unrealities or fictions'.[35] And, Dicey adds, the damage done by such fantasies is that we remain in ignorance of the true extent of the powers of the Crown and the other parts of government. Jennings makes the same point: 'political changes in the United Kingdom are marked by our use of fictions. Institutions are rarely abolished; they continue in theory but shorn of their essential functions. Names remain in constant use, but they represent different things.'[36]

Yes, it will be conceded (for it cannot be plausibly disguised), there was a violent change here, and, yes, fictions were deliberately elaborated to disguise the violent and shocking nature of the discontinuity. The monarchy was not the same after 1688 as it had been before, but, Burke argues in *Reflections on the French Revolution*, the British people wanted it to be the same, and so ingenious public men like Somers told them it was the same. 'On that delicate occasion', the two Houses of Parliament 'threw a politick well-wrought veil over every circumstance tending to weaken the rights, which in the meliorated order of succession they meant to perpetuate'.[37] These exercises in fiction – these continuity substitutes – can be, indeed ought to be, regarded as just as good as the real thing. Our constitutional history can thus be walled off from the violent erratic course of real events. Any holes which may appear in the wall are likely to be sealed soon enough by the natural brevity of political memories.

The Tories of Queen Anne's reign forgot how fiercely they had opposed the Triennial Act only twenty years earlier. J. E. A. Jolliffe in *The Constitutional History of Medieval England from the English Settlement to 1485* (the companion volume to Keir) remarks on 'the absence of any sense of historical criticism as to the institution of parliament. The commons make statements as to what is the 'ancient use and custom of Parliaments' which could be contradicted by the memory of a normal lifetime, and no one cares to correct them.'[38]

Nor does one thing lead inescapably to another.

King or commons admit from time to time claims which seem to us, from our more experienced view, to presuppose wide principles of autocracy or parliamentary right, but pass them almost without comment. Things are done in one parliament which ought to set the precedent for a radical diversion of the line of constitutional progress, but are done without emphasis or debate and forgotten in the next.[39]

He was talking about the fifteenth century, but it is hard to see that much has changed.

For the constitutional historian who tiptoes into his own times, the continuity myth leads him along a path beset with puddles and pitfalls. For what seemed at the time of writing an immutable part of constitutional custom and practice may with little or no warning, after a sudden political squall or landslide, turn out to be extremely mutable.

Sir David Lindsay Keir, writing on the eve of the Second World War, suggested that basic facts had been recognised in the relationship between colonies and the mother country and this was 'one of the many reasons why the Empire has not again been broken asunder by such shocks as tore the Thirteen Colonies from the Britain of George III'.[40] Even the third edition of his *Constitutional History of Modern Britain*, published in 1946, contained a comforting prognosis: 'it may reasonably be hoped that ultimate community of interest . . . may inaugurate a period in which the necessity of reforging the links of Empire will seem more important than dismantling its formal unity'.[41] Little more than a year later, the great dismantling was under way. Nor are more recent constitutional historians immune from such embarrassing upsets. The third edition of Moodie's *Government of Great Britain*, published in 1971, contained the assertion that, although the UK Parliament possessed the right to pass any legislation it wished for Northern Ireland, including an Act to abolish the Stormont government, 'in practice, however, this is unlikely to happen'.[42] The Stormont Parliament was abolished in 1972.

Again, Mackintosh's *The British Cabinet*, published in 1962, in the course of describing the conventions of the modern British Constitution, asserts that 'it is almost certain that no future Prime Minister will be drawn from the Lords'.[43] A year later, Lord Home, somewhat in the manner of Birnam Wood coming to Dunsinane, sidestepped this convention by resigning his peerage. Even hindsight may turn out to be lacking in foresight – as in Harold Laski's remarks in *Reflections on the Constitution* that 'no-one dreamed in 1906 that Lord Salisbury would pretty certainly prove to have been the last peer to become Prime Minister'.[44]

But these are merely the pratfalls which anyone bold enough to attempt prophecy in any field risks as an occupational hazard. Much more serious is the glossing over of qualitative change, the refusal to recognise the magnitude of the alteration in our arrangements and attitudes over the centuries.

The disappearance of the Church from the British constitutional scene may seem a far-off event now, and of no practical relevance to the debates of a secular age. Indeed, the way we were taught history at school tends to encourage the view that the political pretensions of the Church were always an alien intrusion and that their shaking off by the Tudors, although motivated by coarse dynastic imperatives, was in some sense a recovery of the true English tradition.

This may be stirring patriotism, but it is poor history. Even the sketchiest consideration of the transition from the Plantagenets to the Tudors can scarcely avoid noticing the change from plural or shared sovereignty to monolithic or absolute sovereignty. The disappearance of the notion that the king's power was subject to

God's power, and the extinction, demotion or bypassing of the Church courts, represented enormous alterations to ways of thinking no less than to the administration of justice and the structure of politics. Intertwined with the rise of secular absolutism comes the decay of the hierarchical pyramid of the feudal system, its foundations less deeply dug in England than elsewhere perhaps but none the less a powerful agent for the dispersal of power throughout the counties and lordships and multifarious other subdivisions of the land.

In its heyday, 'Far from being a single community at the disposal of the king's agents, the county was a patchwork of administrations, some where the king had all, some where a greater or less degree of privileged right prevailed, and much of which it could be said, *ibi domino Regi nihil accrescit* – "here the lord king has nothing".'[45]

Well, it will be said, all this was long in the past and in a country which is foreign to us. But the continuity myth asserts that it was not foreign to us, that it is from this particular acorn that the beloved oak, still standing outside our window, really did grow. Thus Dicey begins Chapter IV of *The Law of the Constitution* with the grand claim that:

> Two features have at all times since the Norman Conquest characterised the political institutions of England.
> The first of these features is the omnipotence or undisputed supremacy throughout the whole country of the central government. . . . The second of these features, which is closely connected with the first, is the rule or supremacy of law.[46]

This claim is the vital underpinning to the whole Diceian theory of the absolute unfettered sovereignty of Parliament which, we are to understand, took over – whole, undiluted and undamaged – the old royal supremacy.

True, in theory, these derivations ought to be regarded as irrelevant, since Dicey is wooing us in the guise of a lawyer–scientist: 'the kind of constitutional history which consists in researches into the antiquities of English institutions, has no direct bearing on the rules of constitutional law'.[47] Yet he himself finds it useful to bolster his arguments with large assertions like 'England has, at any rate since the Norman Conquest, been always governed by an absolute legislator.'[48] And Dicey's own arguments are peppered with appeals to the manners and traditions of the country and the feelings of true Englishmen. No less than Hallam and Freeman, Blackstone and Coke, Dicey relies on a continuous unwavering English tradition. And he himself endures to this day. The preface to a recent compendium of essays on the Constitution begins with the gloomy but incontestable observation that 'Dicey's shadow still dominates British constitutional law and political theory. . . . Dicey's word has in some respects become the only written constitution we have.'[49]

And if Dicey's assertions about the single, literally monarchical nature of the English system before the Reformation are a ludicrous misdescription of that dappled world with its ever shifting boundaries of power between King, Parliament, feudal magnates and the Church, they are also woefully incomplete as a description of post-Reformation England. What Dicey and, indeed, many more recent writers on the Constitution fail to describe is the *thinning* of the system. Not only do we see the gradual whittling away of rights and privileges of outside institutions – whether local, professional or clerical – by the prerogative claims of central governments. We also see the simplification and streamlining of the group of central institutions. Parliament, originally seen as an external check on royal power (indeed, it first met outside the boundaries of the royal palace), becomes internalised. 'Parliament and the King', so to speak, becomes 'Parliament-in-the-King' and then finally, after the struggles of the seventeenth century, 'the King-in-Parliament'. And then over the succeeding two centuries, the House of Commons itself becomes a monolithic power, as the House of Lords drops down to become an assistant, subordinate chamber. This in turn may be ridiculed as a potted caricature of the complex realities, but it is no more of a caricature than the Dicey version which has held sway so long.

In recent decades, it is true, certain restive stirrings have been noticed. Non-historians like Lord Scarman have become discontented with the caricature as it applies to the subordination of the courts to Parliament. In his 1974 Hamlyn Lectures, *English Law: The New Dimension*, Scarman harks back, somewhat wistfully, to days when judges were not so compliant, such as the declaration of Chief Justice Coke in *Doctor Bonham's Case* (1610) that 'the common law will control Acts of Parliament, and sometimes adjudge them to be utterly void'. Scarman records, too, the verdict of Sir Frederick Pollock that 'the omnipotence of Parliament was not the orthodox theory of English law, if orthodox at all, in Holt's time.'[50] Indeed, in the celebrated case of *Ashby* v. *White* (1701), that would seem to be a pale reflection of Chief Justice Holt's view, at least if the legend current in the nineteenth century is to be believed. The case concerned the intervention of the House of Commons to protect a corrupt returning officer for Aylesbury from a lawsuit brought by Ashby for failing to record his vote. According to the legend, which obviously reflected the general drift of Holt's opinion, while the case was pending, the Speaker of the House of Commons in full state, accompanied by his retinue, appeared in Holt's court and threatened to commit him to jail. In reply, Holt is said to have told the Speaker to begone, or he would commit *him* immediately, 'had he all the House of Commons in his belly'.[51]

From the point of view of public debate, these strands in English constitutional history are now almost forgotten. Coke, after all, is now remembered in the orthodox history as a defender of the right of Parliament against the Crown, not of the rights of the judiciary against Parliament. Scarman has, of course, an ulterior motive for reminding us of them. The gleam in his eye is for a new constitutional system of checks and balances: 'I would hope that a supreme court of the UK would be established (we already have its embryo in the judicial committees of the House of Lords and Privy Council) with power to invalidate legislation that was unconstitutional and to restrain anyone – citizen, government, even Parliament itself – from acting unconstitutionally.'[52] This is in no sense a new dream. Scarman himself quotes Cromwell's belief that 'In every Government there must be somewhat fundamental, somewhat like a Magna Carta, which should be standing, be unalterable. . . . That Parliaments should not make themselves perpetual is a fundamental. Of what assurance is a law to prevent so great an evil, if it lie in the same legislature to un-law it again.'[53]

Now Cromwell is not an authority likely to overwhelm the hearts of traditionalists. We have been educated to regard him as an awful warning rather than a harbinger of enlightenment. What is more important to Scarman's case is to convince traditionalists that he is advocating 'a return to earlier attitudes',[54] resurrecting an ancient, not inventing a new tradition of constitutional law; Cromwell, for his part, was trying to crystallise the correct relationships between legislature and judiciary as they had been before the Stuart perversions and presumptions.

It may be argued that neither Cromwell nor Scarman is fully successful in his contentions. At this stage, I am concerned only to note a reluctance, never wholly suppressed by the prevailing orthodoxy, to accept the untrammelled omnipotence of Parliament. Every now and then, a certain resentful feeling is observable; a suspicion is voiced that the main line of constitutional historians have not been telling us the whole story. In the interests of the continuity thesis, they have been peddling their own useful fictions, and we ought to be wary of them.

The Radcliffe underlinings

As our national myths begin to lose their old self-confidence, it is no longer simply those who are out of power or, like Scarman, out of sympathy with the government of the day, who begin to question those myths and fictions. I do not mean that politicians and constitutional theorists have only now become conscious of the fragile underpinnings of our institutions. Mr Gladstone, after all, was well aware that the British Constitution 'presumes, more boldly than any other, the good faith of those who work it'.[55]

What we begin to notice is a certain loss of confidence in that good faith. Recourse to that ancient arbiter, 'the good sense of the British people', no longer seems as secure as it did. This is, I think, a comparatively recent development. During the war and for some years afterwards, it was axiomatic that, whatever the short-comings of this or that government, they would be corrected in good time by the combined gumption of people and Parliament. The character of the British people buttressed and sandbagged any weak points there might be in our constitutional defences. Yet, even then, there were already one or two sceptics.

The other day, at the back of a filing cabinet, I came across a tattered little red paperback. It was a copy of *The Problem of Power*, the 1958 version of the 1951 Reith Lectures delivered by Lord Radcliffe, the celebrated High Court judge and chairman of many a royal Commission and public enquiry. The lectures he gave are of a characteristically melancholy turn. Power, that dangerous, combustible, but unfortunately indispensable substance, could be safe only under certain conditions and in certain hands. These conditions were increasingly unlikely to be found in Britain, although Radcliffe had not yet reached the conclusion to which he was later driven – that the British people had become 'ungovernable'.

The book is a more extended statement of the doubts about the wisdom of unfettered parliamentary supremacy which have come, now and then, from leading judges from the days of Coke and Holt. Between the wars, Lord Chief Justice Hewart in *The New Despotism* (1929) questioned the wisdom of Parliament in so blithely showering unlimited discretion on Ministers. His particular target was 'the Henry VIII clause' which permitted the Minister 'to do any other thing which appears to him necessary or expedient for bringing the said provisions into effect'.[56] This is a quotation from the Rating and Valuation Act 1925, but it could just as well have come from half-a-dozen other Acts of the day which conferred similar discretion, amounting in Hewart's view to the stealthy introduction of 'administrative lawlessness'. In his famous denunciation of the trend, he declared,

> Much toil, and not a little blood have been spent in bringing slowly into being a polity where the people make their laws, and independent judges administer them. If that edifice is to be overthrown, let the overthrow be accomplished openly. Never let it be said that liberty and justice, having with difficulty been won, were suffered to be abstracted, or impaired in a fit of absence of mind.[57]

Hewart's attack was on a narrower front than Scarman's fifty years later but was directed at the same enemy – the ability of the executive with a tame parliamentary majority to push through unfettered extensions of arbitrary ministerial powers. Radcliffe's lamentation comes somewhere between the two, both in time and in scope. Taken together, these three lawyers, ranging in temper from the caustic reactionary Hewart to the eirenic liberal Scarman, constitute a formidable challenge to the constitutional orthodoxy.

My little red book is underlined, sometimes in pencil, sometimes by a ballpoint pen, in a lush, even sweeping hand. The underliner has chosen the most Cassandra-like of Radcliffe's pronouncements, the passages in which he enunciates with the most solemn gravity the ways in which the British Constitution has been debased and corrupted in our own times. For example:

'In the true middle-age, *absolute power would have been an impious as well as an impossible conception.* It was impossible because the feudal system itself diffused power and made of the King less a sovereign than a chief among his barons, who in some countries actually elected him. . . . But it was impious because men did genuinely believe that there was all the difference in the world, or all the difference in the next, between *what you could do* and *what you ought to do in political life.* . . . "*The King is under no man, but he is under God and the law.*" That is Bracton speaking, an English lawyer of the thirteenth century. . . .'[58]

On the principle of the organised party in political life: '*carried to its logical conclusion, Parliament is turned into the instrument of power, instead of being its holder.*'[59]

Of the independence of judges: 'By the beginning of the eighteenth century they had been placed in a position that made them free from interference by Crown or Parliament, and *Parliament had not then begun the practice of passing statutes that give the executive a safe conduct through the ordinary law.*'[60]

On the separation of powers: Madison 'starts, of course, with the same assumption as they all made, that *the very definition of tyranny consists in accumulating all powers in the same hand* and that it makes no sort of difference for this purpose whether the hands are hereditary, self-appointed or elected. . . . Power is of "*an encroaching spirit*" and the legislative department, he notes, is "everywhere extending the sphere of its activity and drawing all power into its impetuous vortex." Madison and Hamilton both saw that faction, by which they meant "self-seeking" party, can wreck any constitutional theory, since it used the *forms of the Constitution to defeat the Constitution's purpose.*'[61]

On individual rights: 'Thus an American *can know that he has certain individual rights which stand above ordinary laws*, things that he cannot be made to submit to by any law. . . . *It is the mediaeval doctrine over again, a supreme law that overrules the law-making of men*, but with the written word of the Constitution in place of the uncertain theories of Natural Law.'[62]

'The British have formed the habit of praising their institutions, which are sometimes inept, and of *ignoring the character of their race, which is often superb*. In the end. they will be in danger of losing their character and being left with their institutions: a result disastrous indeed.'[63]

On the general will: '*It seems to me that Rousseau's "general will" got crossed with the principles of the Utilitarians, and that it was Bentham, not Rousseau, who broke the older shape of things in England and built up the new structure of majority rule*.'[64]

On citizens' rights: 'Those rights are said to have this peculiarity, that they have been, in the main, won in the courts of law; they have been upheld by judges as rights which exist by the im-memorial *custom of the country under the common law and they have not been created therefore by any deliberate act of constitution-making*. No doubt that could be said quite truly when it was said by Professor Dicey towards the end of the last century. But there are qualifications upon what he said that make it less important than it may seem. Firstly, *these great victories in the law courts were won against the power of the Crown, the executive, upon whom the common law, the ancient custom, always did impose limits*. There was no English tradition that gave an arbitrary power to the King or his servants. *But such victories could never be won against the force of anything sanctioned by Act of Parliament, because that is final law in our courts and every judge must give effect to it*.'[65]

'It is only sensible to see that with what is, practically, single-chamber government and with executive and legislative combined, *the security of what used to be called constitutional rights is a frail thing.*'[66]

'Under our system ideas and attitudes are unusually fluid, at any rate towards this sort of subject, and great words such as *constitutional rights, liberty and the rule of law seem to change their meaning even while one looks at them.*'[67]

'The old glories of the liberal tradition, the passionate belief that political liberties are the essential condition of the greatest liberties of thought, speech and action, have shrunk to a meaningless constitutionalism which *asserts that anything is all right if it is permitted, nothing is all right if it is forbidden, by an Act of Parliament.*'[68]

'It is hard to forgive the long tradition of the Whig historians, which has left us *the mystique of parliamentary supremacy with no comparable assertion as to its purpose.*'[69]

'*It is the vulnerability of the modern democratic society that is our abiding danger. . . . It is enervate of soul, an abdication of personal responsibility of judgment, that we have to fear. . . . Constitutional forms and legal systems are very well in their way, but they are the costumes for the men who wear them.*'[70]

There are many more such underlinings, but the general drift is clear. The underliner is deeply struck by Radcliffe's suspicion of a parliamentary majority's claims to untrammelled supremacy; the underliner takes very much to heart Radcliffe's anxiety that the character of the British people is no longer sturdy enough to support and defend their flimsy institutions; and the underliner is also much impressed by Radcliffe's reminders of earlier traditions in which Parliament and, before Parliament, the monarch were subject to the law of God or nature and by the way the American Founders translated this ancient check on power into their written Constitution.

Now the underliner was Margaret Thatcher. This was her copy of *The Problem of Power*. The hand is hers and she gave the book to me, commending in particular the passages she had marked. I mention all this, not simply to demonstrate the intensity of Mrs Thatcher's affection and admiration for the United States and its constitution but to demonstrate that the most robust Tory of our times shared the same unease as so many of her political opponents during the same period (that is, between the late 1950s when the paperback was printed and the early 1980s when she gave it to me). The staunchest defender of the sovereignty of our Parliament against the intrusions of Continental federalists was painfully aware of how vulnerable our institutions were and of how the old checks and balances, rudimentary and informal as they might have been, had been eroded and debased.

I do not mean to argue from this that Mrs Thatcher therefore was or is a covert supporter of a written constitution or the introduction of a supreme court. Nor is there the slightest contradiction between the wish to retain maximum national independence and a simultaneous unease about the durability of the institutions which express that independence. There are other ways than a written constitution of reintroducing or at least re-emphasising a greater separation of powers and of entrenching the basic principles of our parliamentary democracy; we have got this far without a written constitution; a little ingenuity, it could be argued, might enable us to repair the damage of the last century or so without losing its more desirable achievements.

At this point, all that needs to be stressed is that defence of our existing institutions is in no way inconsistent with a biting anxiety about their future. Allegiance to the principles of the status quo does not entail complacency. In private conversation, where candour costs nothing politically, most people with any degree of intellectual honesty or seriousness will admit to some unease about the prospects for our Constitution as it now is. That indeed must be my defence for recording the Radcliffe underlinings at such length – that they indicate, more clearly than any public speech could afford to, how the most uninhibited modern defender of the constitutional arrangements which we have inherited acknowledges that, as a system of fortifications for liberty and justice, they are inferior to the work of the Founding Fathers of the American Constitution. It may be that we shall choose different remedies from theirs (later on, we shall explore some of the available choices), but it is stupid and blind not to acknowledge the durable merits of their achievement and the vulnerability of ours.

We shall, no doubt, discern a difference in tone and interest between critics of our arrangements who come from the left or centre-left and those who come from the right. The former tend to be indignant and to be predominantly concerned with the supposed infringement or abridgement of civil liberties. Those from the right sound more apprehensive; they tend to be primarily anxious about the repair of our institutions so that they may once again command the kind of respect they used to command. These differences may lead to differing remedies being proposed; it would be a mistake to exaggerate the shared enthusiasms among constitutional reformers of different political views. And yet there is some common ground; there are recurring questions and dilemmas which honest observers of all parties and none have to offer some sort of answer to. And there are, besides, formidable external pressures which have firmly placed constitutional reform on an agenda which cannot be shelved; the European Community, the international market and the human rights movement will not leave us alone.

But, first, we need to become aware again of the old parts of our constitutional machinery which have been left to lie rusting in disuse in the corner of the field. The old doctrine of the separation of powers has never recovered its full vigour after Bagehot's onslaught on 'the fatal division of powers incidental to a presidential government'. The idea of judicial independence has faded to such an extent that many modern politicians and journalists, thinking to respond to the desires of their voters and readers, see nothing wrong in demanding that a Lord Chief Justice should be forced to resign because of a bad mistake.

After the release of the Birmingham Six, in March 1991, more than 140 MPs – over a fifth of the House of Commons – called for an address to be presented to the Crown petitioning for Lord Lane's removal. Leading articles in many newspapers demanded his resignation; so did Mr Bernard Levin in *The Times*. None of these outbursts included more than a passing nod to the constitutional considerations; in one of the *Independent*'s two leaders demanding Lord Lane's departure, the separation of powers was mentioned as a desirable thing, but not so desirable, it was implied, that it should impede the will of the outraged people. Only a few old lawyers such as Lord Hailsham could be found to point out that such a hue and cry was 'unconstitutional', and even they were slow to find words to describe precisely why it was unconstitutional. The fact that no judge had been removed in this way since the Act of Settlement, which provided for such removals, was either utterly forgotten or regarded as trivial. Even those commentators who defended Lord Lane, such as Mr Louis Blom-Cooper QC, tended to defend his conduct in the case rather than to expound the constitutional invulnerability of the judiciary. Mr Blom-Cooper came under attack from Mr Ludovic Kennedy in the *Observer*, who enquired with high indignation whether Mr Blom-Cooper believed 'that constitutionally the Queen in Parliament is supreme and if so who else is to judge the judges but Parliament?'[71] But the whole point of the independence of the judiciary is that no other organ of government is to judge their performance *as judges*. If Mr Kennedy, who has been a close student of the law for thirty years, cannot grasp this simple basic principle, there is little chance that most of his fellow citizens are fully aware of it either. The immense labour of past centuries which had gone into securing the independence of the judiciary seemed to have floated off into oblivion. It was argued in some quarters, in the columns of *The Times*,[72] for instance, that, while Lord Lane should not be dismissed, he should, after a proper interval, do the decent thing and resign of his own free will. This seems a distinction without much of a difference. Once a judge who makes a bad mistake is subjected to pressure so intolerable that he feels obliged to cut short his natural term of office, then such pressures are likely to happen more frequently and with greater intensity to other judges, so that judges may come to feel a considerable reluctance to speak out with the boldness that doing justice often requires. Indeed, the informal pressures, if they came to be a regular part of public life, might undermine the independence of the judiciary more effectively than the occasional, once-in-a-century removal of a judge by the formal procedures provided for by the Act of Settlement. The informal pressures would be much easier to apply.

The case of Lord Lane is worth rehearsing because it shows so clearly the intellectual thinness of the public debate in Britain, as opposed to, say, the US and the reluctance to engage seriously with constitutional questions, even a question which presents itself in such unmistakable terms as this one does. For in considering the dismissal of judges, we are not dealing with a trivial custom expressed in some obscure or transient convention. The question is central to the rule of law; it was settled by statute nearly 300 years ago; and it has stayed settled. Yet in the early months of 1991 the public argument was still being conducted as though the question were, if not open, at least one that could be played with quite freely.

As Nevil Johnson pointed out a decade ago, 'there has over a fairly long period been a retreat from constitutional ways of thinking in Britain'.[73] We suffer from 'the atrophy of any language in which we can talk of constitutional issues, of rules or of the principles of public law'. Accordingly, 'we are left floundering in a world of pure pragmatism, in which those who should know better turn to the business or management consultant for advice on how to design or re-jig the institutions of the polity.'[74] Anyone who thinks this verdict too severe should consult the recent polemic by Lord Beloff, not the least distinguished of post-war Gladstone Professors of Government and Public Administration, against all agitation for constitutional reform; the character of the piece may be judged by its rounding off with Pope's specious old couplet:

> For forms of government let fools contest;
> Whate'er is best administered is best.[75]

We have deceived ourselves into thinking that this preference for pragmatism, for muddling through, is the age-old British way of doing things, when, in fact, it has really grown up only during the past 100 years and is a symptom of decadence rather than continuity. In the past, our history was shaped, at least in large part, by the influence of great system-builders who could hold their heads up in company with the authors of *The Federalist Papers* (those authors themselves being, of course, offshoots of our tradition, too).

Not only does the present understanding of our constitutional arrangements seem thin and blurred; we also show an apparent reluctance or inability to recognise the ways in which those arrangements remain strong and well founded. We are not only strolling about in a fog; we also seem unaware of the vicinity of large solid objects. The natural consequence is that we are easily led to pay attention to the weaknesses of the Constitution as it now is, which are real enough, without taking much heed of its equally real strengths.

We lose the ability to distinguish between the weaknesses of the Constitution and the weakness of our understanding of the Constitution; thus our intellectual self-confidence is undermined as well as our political self-confidence. In much modern discussion of the British Constitution, there is a tentative, uncertain tone, occasionally shooting off in shrillness, not unlike the half-broken voice of an awkward adolescent. Whatever the advantages of flexibility and unwrittenness, it ought to be admitted that a price has to be paid for the resulting uncertainty.

This enfeebling of belief in or understanding of judicial independence is only part of the general thinning out of our constitutional beliefs. The House of Commons waxes indignant when peers offer principled and thoughtful opposition to the War Crimes Bill and sends the Bill straight back again, without a moment's hesitation or any pretence at amending it. As for local government, it is hard to interest most MPs in the historical continuity of the boroughs and counties; indeed, to offer that continuity as a reason for caution in undertaking yet another reform of the structure is held to show a misunderstanding of our constitutional arrangements which, it is argued (and Dicey argues this particularly strongly), make no distinction between subordinate legislatures, whether they be the government of Imperial India, the corporation of Manchester or the London and North-Western Railway Co. with its power to issue by-laws forbidding passengers to travel first-class on a second-class ticket. The Constitution, we are told, is parliamentary supremacy and nothing but parliamentary supremacy; it admits no considerations of natural law or human rights, just as it admits no powers for subordinate or external law-making bodies, except in so far as Parliament has defined and granted such powers. And Parliament itself is a thinned-down version of what it once was, the threefold bundle of King, Lords and Commons having given way to a single all-powerful body impeded only faintly by the incrustations of tradition.

Mr John Patten, in the fullest defence of the status quo to come from a government Minister in recent years, has argued that it is a fallacy to assume that single codified documents automatically serve to protect the civil rights of citizens: 'such documents are meaningless unless they exist within a country which has a political culture that renders them viable. . . . The greatest protector of citizens' rights in the UK are citizens themselves. . . . The protector of freedom in the end is the political culture, not some document, however weighty.'[76] Now this is clearly true, so far as it goes. In Radcliffe's terms, constitutional forms and legal systems are only costumes for the men who wear them; it is no use putting your trust in British institutions if the character of the British people has become too spineless and corrupt to uphold those institutions.

But 'political culture' in turn depends on, is nourished and defined and instructed by, those institutions; it would be hard, if not impossible, to imagine a healthy political culture which did not possess and inhabit a robust and coherent system of institutions. And the sad truth is that the terms in which Mr Patten proceeds to discuss our political culture do not suggest that it has endowed him with that understanding of the British Constitution which would have come as second nature to a highly intelligent youngish politician of an earlier generation. He argues, for example, that to incorporate the broad provisions of the European Convention on Human Rights into UK law would be unnecessary, because 'our laws – common and statute – secure the freedom and rights set out in the Convention' (why then, if our own laws are already sufficient protection, is the British government so frequently 'convicted' in the European Court of breaching the human rights of its citizens?) and 'the generality of the terms in which the

Convention is drafted would make interpretation highly problematic and confer upon independent judges the responsibility for the first time for developing public policy in this country. It is better for Parliament to decide upon these issues.' But, of course, the judges do already take the European Convention into account in framing their judgments – judgments which, on a huge range of issues, cannot help 'developing public policy'. What emerges from this and other passages is Mr Patten's distaste for entrusting any determination or protection of rights to 'necessarily and properly isolated judges. To transfer such power to judges is to transfer power to too few; to transfer power directly to everyone, through the medium of a referendum, is to transfer power to too many.' 'All power to Parliament' is thus Mr Patten's cry, faintly but unnervingly reminiscent of Lenin's 'All power to the soviets' – and not without the same fraudulence, since both slogans mean in effect 'All power to the government or governing party'. What seems alien to both Lenin and Mr Patten is the idea of *dispersal* of power to a variety of institutions – whether parallel, independent or subordinate.

In a remarkably revealing passage, Mr Patten argues that 'over time, Britain has developed a strong and balanced political culture. The balance is one between effectiveness – the capacity of government to govern – and consent – maintaining popular support for the political system.' This is a bizarre conception of balance, one which, I suppose, might apply just as well to any populist Third World regime – led by a Peron, a Menem or some relatively benign African leader – in which the regime, operating on no fixed principle except that of survival, yields as and when it deems prudent to popular indignation or apprehension. Life under such regimes may be more or less tolerable, but it is not the same as life in a constitutional system which is governed by stable principles and in which power is dispersed to independent, though here and there overlapping, institutions. When talking about balance, our political tradition has normally had in mind something quite different – the balance between different parts of the polity: between monarchy, Church, barons and Commons; or between government, Parliament and judiciary; or between the

Presidency, the Congress and the courts. By contrast, this coarse monolithic governmentalised conception of balance surely demonstrates an alarming impoverishment of constitutional thought – and one which, I fear, is more hopelessly stuck in far less thoughtful heads than Mr Patten's.

I do not propose to approach the present state of our arrangements in a mood of unrelieved melancholy. We may choose to chalk up a greater or lesser part of the alterations of the past century as gains or losses for liberty, democracy and effective government. But what we cannot deny is the bold and dramatic *simplification* of those arrangements.

Bagehot recognised this, with his quick, bright, coarse mind: the efficient part of the English Constitution, 'at least when in great and critical action, is decidedly simple and rather modern'. In the mid-1860s, that was a cause for pride. We had demonstrated our modernity by junking the labyrinthine paraphernalia of former times; we were simple, direct, modern.

Now we have been taught by the succeeding century to fear the 'terrible simplifiers' and to treat all claims to total power, in whatever name it is to be exercised, with deep distrust. Yet we seem somehow inhibited from considering, candidly and without politesses, the simplicity of our own Constitution. It is as though we feared that the restraints of custom, which alone prevent that simplicity being corrupted and abused, were so frail and powdery that they would crumble to nothing if we touched them.

That period of tactical discretion is now coming to an end. English exceptionalism will not endure much longer against the external forces now pressing in on it. If we are to rebuild the structure, if we are to restore some of the old complexities, get some of the old checks and balances back into working order, we need to start without delay.

To talk of 'rebuilding' and 'restoring' has, of course, a certain political charm. It is the way reformers in this country have traditionally reassured those who were suspicious of reform; at all costs, the new measures had to be depicted, however improbably, as old-fangled. Yet, in the present case, there is a little more to be said for going about matters in this way. For there really are elements which we have lost and which other modern constitutions have discovered or conserved. It is, indeed, noticeable that in recent tracts and manifestos by would-be reformers, such as Lord Scarman and Charter 88, there is an honourable groping towards tradition. It is the task of this book to assist that groping.

The first question we have to answer is: why has our understanding of our Constitution become so thinned and simplified? What is the origin of this seemingly inexorable tendency to get rid of the old checks and balances, to peel off the ancient gnarled bark and hack away the tangle of intertwining and overhanging branches? The natural place to look for some sort of answer is in what are grandly called 'our constitutional authorities', that assorted band of academics and journalists who have caught the public fancy in their day and survived to be quoted by their successors in search of something to hang an argument on.

Now academic good manners require that we should ignore, as far as possible, the personal temperaments and political views of these authorities. Indeed, if our gaze strays too long from their pages to their grave and thoughtful visages, we may run the risk of ceasing to regard them as authorities at all. They may come to look to us suspiciously like creatures of their time, not only fallible and quirky like the rest of us, but indelibly coloured with the aspirations and panics of the years in which they sat down to write their best-remembered works. Given the famous flexibility of the constitutional system they were writing about, how could it be otherwise? How could they not be concerned to promote this or that device or tendency or to defend some exposed or crumbling part of the great rambling habitation?

There is a great deal to be said for academic good manners. They are infinitely preferable to the bad manners of those Marxists and deconstructionists who pretend, no less implausibly, that everything on the page can be explained away by the material interests and the historical situation of the writer.

But the simplifying tendencies of British constitutional thought over the past century have been so dramatic, so overwhelming that we cannot and should not avoid considering the principal figures in the evolution of that thought not only as thinkers but as actors, or would-be actors, too.

The conventional technique in these matters is to refer, but only *en passant*, to the character and views of the leading authorities. Dicey, for example, is often referred to as 'a robust Unionist'; Bagehot's friendship with Gladstone may be mentioned; so may Sir Ivor Jennings's conversations with his fellow Fabians at the LSE. These references often have a jocular tone; Jennings, for example, in a footnote quips that 'what Dicey said in 1913 (when he was more than usually disturbed by the threat of Home Rule) is not evidence!'[77]

I think we need to take this political background somewhat more seriously and, without falling into the crass opposite extreme of attributing all these constitutional doctrines to personal partisan motives, try to trace some of the influences which, refracted through these works, have produced such a remarkable alteration in the understanding of our constitutional arrangements.

Bagehot offers us a high-Victorian liberal interpretation; Dicey a late-Victorian and Edwardian Unionist's; Jennings, together with Harold Laski and, later, R. H. S. Crossman, offers a Fabian or Labour version. These must be examined in turn to identify continuities as well as differences. We need not only to separate out their individual political colourings but also to examine what each has contributed to the overall tendency towards simplification and why.

The obvious answer is that the coming of mass democracy imposed its own agenda, which was, above all, a simplifying agenda, dedicated to ensuring that the popular will was implemented in a direct and unimpeded fashion. The parties – and their constitutional experts too – were carried along on the tide, sometimes uttering squawks of protest, sometimes deluded into imagining that they themselves were in control of events.

But this may be a lazy answer. After all, in other nations popular democracy has taken very different and often quite complex shapes in which mediating institutions, whether judicial or local or extra-parliamentary, are far more powerful, both in theory and in fact. We need not have ended up where we have, for good or ill. And the character of our major constitutional thinkers is not irrelevant and should not be immune to our enquiries.

2

THE THREE SIMPLIFIERS

Walter Bagehot and the efficient secret

If ever there was a writer for men of the world, it was Walter Bagehot. There is a manly common sense about every line he ever wrote; often witty, very often charming, he is never silly, never, never naive. The delight of his conversation was much remarked on by his contemporaries, from Gladstone and the great men of the City of London to his adoring family and his neighbours down in Somerset. One feels at ease with Bagehot. He makes his readers comfortable; despite his learning, in his early literary essays he asks the sort of questions ordinary chaps ask about literature: how much money did Shakespeare make? Was he really religious? and so on. In tackling the world of books, one inevitably comes up against queer, impractical coves who are anything but men of the world – drunks, drug addicts, bankrupts, loafers, especially loafers – and it is comforting to come up against them with Bagehot at one's side, so down-to-earth, so cheerful and so full of sensible advice, too. The poet Clough, a friend and associate of Bagehot at University College, London, took the strenuous counsels of Arnold and Newman 'too much to heart': 'He required quite another sort of teaching, to be told to take things easily . . . to go on living quietly and obviously.'[1] Bagehot's biographer, Alastair Buchan, rightly points out that 'it is obvious that Bagehot is writing not only about Clough, but about himself'.[2] Bagehot's bright, high, confident manner was dearly bought; his health was poor throughout his short life; he was constantly afflicted by chest infections, migraines and dizzy spells which affected his sight. And always at the back of his busy, conscientious mind lay the shadow of his feeble-minded half-brother Vincent Estlin and that of their mother, who needed to be watched too. When Bagehot was writing the last chapter of *The English Constitution*, he had to rush down to Langport from London, because his mother had suddenly started breaking all the windows in the family bank and had had to be taken off to the asylum again. For all Bagehot's charm and worldly wisdom, there is no doubt that, as Buchan says, 'the process of steeling himself to live in the real world had involved the atrophy of his sense of tragedy'.[3] He had a fear of pushing too deep beneath the surface and a distinctive aversion from the tragic in literature and life. And he seems to wish to turn the reader's head away from any spectacle or thought that might prove distressing.

We can, I think, detect in Bagehot a certain reverence for strength, for the hearty undisguised enjoyment of potency, and a corresponding impatience with weakness and ineffectiveness. I do not mean to suggest that he was an unkind or inconsiderate man (he was anything but), still less that he is to be lumped in with the Social Darwinists of his day (Buchan defends him very well against the over-interpretation of certain stray remarks in *Physics and Politics*); Bagehot does not believe that might is right, but he does believe that might has its rights and this renders him somewhat insensitive to and incurious about the balances and restraints which are at the heart of constitution-making. We shall meet the same psychological disposition (born out of an even more remarkable effort of the will to overcome physical weakness) in the next section.

In Bagehot's literary essays, one sometimes feels that he is occupied more in reassuring the reader – and himself – that the notorious agony of this or that writer's life was largely unnecessary, rather than in attending to the writer's works. How reassuring to know, for example, that William Cowper had no real reason to be unhappy: at Westminster School, he 'does not, on an attentive examination, seem to have suffered exceedingly'.[4] As for Cowper's days as a young lawyer, 'A reverend biographer has called his life at this time, "an unhappy compound of guilt and wretchedness." But unless the estimable gentleman thinks it sinful to be a barrister and wretched to live in the Temple, it is not easy to make out what he would mean. . . . The outward position of Cowper was, indeed, singularly fortunate.'[5] And when Cowper sank into extreme melancholy and made a series of tragi-comic botched attempts to kill himself, Bagehot thinks he could still have been jollied out of his gloom 'if only he had not fallen into the dangerous company of that Low Church fanatic, the hymn-writer John Newton'.[6] Like Clough, what Cowper required was 'prompt encouragement to cheerful occupation, quiet amusement, gentle and unexhausting society', rather than 'back-breaking parochial toil and a pernicious concentration on sinfulness'.[7]

Well, so no doubt Cowper did, and if it is a blessed relief to stroll the unnerving twisted lanes of literature with such a sensible fellow as Bagehot, must it not be even more pleasant to be guided by him through the labyrinth of our Constitution? Pernickety *littérateurs* who complain that Bagehot is a little *too* commonsensical fully to grasp every nuance of the life and work of a poet like Cowper ought surely to admit that, in dealing with the world, the best guide must be a man of the world rather than an innocent academic with no experience of affairs. Better to listen to a man who was consulted by Gladstone on the Bank Notes Issue Bill (and had his views incorporated in the eventual legislation) than to a mere theoretician. Bagehot's weaknesses as a literary critic can be nothing but strengths in a constitutional analyst.

But are they? It is easy enough for a modern reader to see the congenital failings of Bagehot as a critic: he consistently misses the point and imposes the wrong criteria; if he was assessing the work of Ernest Hemingway, he would spend a page or two on speculating how much Hemingway really knew about bulls and bull-fighting; the same if he was discussing the graphic work of Pablo Picasso. He seeks always a practical handle to get a grip on subjects which have in their essence no connection to that practice. He will not approach the work on its own terms, enter into its own realm.

And, in a strange way, this seems to me the comparable fault of *The English Constitution*, that alluring, sprightly, unfailingly entertaining work. It is a man of the world's guide to a realm which is essentially alien to him and to which Bagehot's favourite question

'How much?' cannot hope to provide all the answers. The trouble
is that this is the only question Bagehot knows how to ask. He deals
and can deal only in the coinage of power – who holds it and how
much he holds. For Bagehot, the purpose of any worthwhile guide
to a nation's constitution must be to identify and explain its
'efficient secret'. The rest of it is mere legal technicality to be sorted
out by the lawyers. What and who make the engine tick? That is
what the practical man of affairs wants to know. Everything else is
meaningless sham and ceremonial to him. All that stuff is merely
wool to pull over the eyes of the unlettered clods who make up the
vast majority of the population.

Those who have not previously read *The English Constitution* or
who come back to it after a long gap will, I think, be startled by its
relentless snobbery, its obsessive contempt for the mental powers
of the Great Unwashed (Bagehot's manner draws one to employ
such phrases). His famous distinction between the Dignified and
the Efficient parts of our Constitution pales into secondariness
beside the far sharper distinction he draws between the Knowing
(his readers) and the Unknowing (those who would not dream of
reading such a book, probably could not anyway and would be
shocked by its daring, cynical tone if ever they tried).

'The masses of Englishmen are not fit for an elective government,'[8] we are told. We need a visible symbol of authority because
'the fancy of the mass of men is incredibly weak and can see
nothing without it'.[9] A lord of ancient lineage is more likely to
awaken the sensation of obedience in 'the coarse, dull, contracted
multitude'.[10] Adult suffrage would be a calamity, for 'the rich and
wise are not to have, by explicit law, more votes than the poor and
stupid'; the members for the town districts would include
representatives not merely of the artisans – 'a select and intellectual
class' – but of 'the common order of workpeople'; such latter
representatives 'I may call "the members for the public-houses".'

It is for this reason that we must preserve the mysterious glow of
royalty; 'we must not let daylight in upon magic',[11] for fear of
undeceiving the mob. The mass of men can understand only
personal government, and so they must be conned into believing
that they are governed by a queen; otherwise they would not suffer

themselves to be governed at all. 'The lower orders, the middle orders, are still, when tried by what is that standard of the educated "ten thousand", narrow-minded, unintelligent, incurious.'[12] It is for their benefit that all this pageantry and show must be carried on. As a good progressive *Economist* man, Bagehot could not contemplate the possibility that some of the educated ten thousand might themselves also respond to the pageant of monarchy and that they too found its existence a heart-touching symbol of their shared history and culture and hence saw it not only as the focus for their allegiance but as the legitimate authority which was entitled to demand their obedience. For Bagehot, the educated ten thousand demonstrated their superiority by the very fact that they could see through the whole charade.

This is not simply a rhetorical distinction to flatter the readers. It is quite clear that Bagehot genuinely believes that this is how the system is maintained: middle-class men of the world like himself run the show according to the commonsensical principles of middle-class men of the world, and the lower orders, dazzled by the glitter of the flummery, go along with it. A visitor from Mars might suspect that this looked more like a precarious confidence trick than a durable constitution. And it would not be long before such suspicions would turn out to be justified.

Two years after *The English Constitution* began to be published in the *Fortnightly Review* over eighteen months, the 1867 Reform Bill was passed (the work's publication as a book coincided with the Bill). Rarely can the comfortable premises of a thesis have been so swiftly overturned. Bagehot never revised *The English Constitution*, but he did write a preface for the second edition of 1872. And what a remarkable transformation of attitude we find in it. Gone is the cheerfulness of the high-Victorian age; all at once, we find ourselves in the apprehensive, ever thickening gloom of the later Victorians. Bagehot's own high colour and high spirits seem to have faded overnight. He falls into line with those sages painted by Watts, whose pale, sad faces still remind visitors to the National Portrait Gallery of the melancholy long withdrawing roar of Christianity on the ebb. While Arnold and Tennyson pondered on a world without faith, Bagehot was suddenly forced to contemplate a world in which the lower orders, instead of being content to cheer the royal carriage from the roadside, were all at once in the driving seat of a motor in which the brake pads were quite worn away.

He was not ashamed to say what no MP could say, that 'I am exceedingly afraid of the ignorant multitude of the new constitution.'[13] It was a delusion to suppose that they would be 'more able to form sound opinions on complete questions';[14] the new class of voters needed 'to be guided by their betters' more than the old class had.[15] Alas, the reverse was likely to happen: 'In plain English what I fear is that both our political parties will bid for the support of the working-man; that both of them will promise to do as he likes if he will only tell them what it is; that, as he now holds the casting-vote in our affairs, both parties will beg and pray him to give that vote to them.'[16] The happy days of sound government by educated men were gone, perhaps for ever.

As a matter of fact, Bagehot's description of the way the system worked in his day had never been entirely accurate. The publication of Queen Victoria's letters, for example, was to reveal that the monarchy had not yet come to accept such a modest view of its powers and duties (that view was not entirely accepted until the reign of George V). Victoria was capable, as late as 1886, of attempting quite energetically not to send for Gladstone, claiming that she had thought he was eager to retire from public life – to which Gladstone replied with delicate irony, saying that he was 'very grateful for your Majesty's gracious consideration for his declining years'.[17] Thirty years earlier, she had been more thrustful still, claiming after Palmerston's dismissal in 1851 that 'she must reserve to herself the unfettered right to approve or disapprove of the choice of a foreign secretary'.[18]

Sometimes, her interventions were merely comic, as when she reproved Gladstone in 1886 for speaking outside his constitutency, especially at railway stations.[19] Sometimes, they were really scandalous, as in the 1886 case when she teamed up with the Opposition and had conversations with Salisbury which were flagrantly designed to keep Gladstone out and get Salisbury in until the Redistribution Act could take effect[20] – shades of James

Callaghan in 1969–70. It is hard to disagree with Jennings's verdict on the early years of Victoria's reign that 'the lesson of the Reform Act had not yet been learned. It was still not understood that the powers of the government rested on the vote of the electorate, not on the "confidence" of the Queen. The Queen herself did not understand the situation.'[21] It is equally hard to decide when, if ever, she did come fully to understand it. But what are we to say of a constitution which is not only unwritten but not even understood by its monarch?

All the same, these caveats aside, there is no reason to quarrel with Dicey's verdict that 'Bagehot was the first author who explained in accordance with the actual fact the true nature of the Cabinet and its real relation to the crown and parliament'.[22] Bagehot does, most of the time, succeed in bursting through the veils and masks of the useful fictions which have concealed the dramatic alterations in the disposition of powers.

The trouble is that this is all he does. He leaves us with no qualitative judgment or insight on the changes that have taken place; apart from a few derisive references to the United States, he essays little comparison with other types of constitution; he does not try to enquire whether the checks and balances which have eroded or disappeared may be or should be repaired or recovered.

The truth is, of course, that Bagehot was delighted that the Constitution had lost (if he thought it had ever possessed them, which is not quite clear) what he called, in the title of Chapter VII, 'Its supposed checks and balances'. Had not the US Constitution, with its elaborate division of powers and its reservation of so many vital powers to the states, lately proved itself unable to deal effectively with such a prime question as slavery? 'Policy is a unity and a whole,' Bagehot believed: 'The interlaced character of human affairs requires a single determining energy; a distinct force for each artificial compartment will make but a motley patchwork, if it live long enough to make anything. The excellence of the British Constitution is that it has achieved this unity; that in it the sovereign power is single, possible and good.'[23] God had looked down upon these islands and blessed their Constitution.

We can almost hear Bagehot huzzaing at this lack of

impediment. He is like a general who has found his *Schwerpunkt*, the place to mass his overwhelming force for a decisive break-through, or a businessman who has picked the market he can dominate, where the competition is at its puniest and the profit margins at their fattest. The approach is entrepreneurial; the concentration almost exclusively on government as a driving force; for Bagehot the Constitution is an engine, not an edifice; he thinks – is perhaps the first person to think – of the polity as 'Great Britain Ltd', although he would not be vulgar enough to use the phrase.

But no government – totalitarian, five-year-planning govern-ments included – ever works quite like that. Every polity, even one driven along by the crassest and most hectoring and brutal of governments, retains the architectural traits of what Oakeshott called a 'civil association', in which the rules are designed, or from time to time revised, in order to reconcile, compensate and balance conflicting interests, aspirations, customs, professions and classes. In seeking only for the 'efficient secret' of the British Constitution, Bagehot is making a category mistake. It is like looking for the efficient secret of South Kensington. The life of a city, or even of a suburb, cannot be reduced to that of a clockwork toy.

It may be said that a candid description of the principal working parts of the machine was achievement enough. Bagehot's analysis is so bright, so acute, so winning that to ask for more would be greedy. But the drawback of *The English Constitution* is that within its very brightness and acuity lies a dreadful intellectual and moral laziness. Having taken us on this delightful whirlwind tour behind the scenes, Bagehot leaves it to other, more ponderous spirits to brood on the purpose of the drama. He has achieved his prime object, to explain who runs the show and how they do it. And this is the only kind of information that men of affairs want or need to know. Anyone who has ever been asked to brief a leading industrialist or politician will know how quickly their eyes glaze once this essential information has been provided, how little interest they have in questions of theory or structure and how anxious they are to press on to other topics to gain more 'power facts'. Those who remain puzzled as to what is wrong with

46

Bagehot's treatment can only be recommended to read *The Federalist Papers* to see how constitutional theory can remain profoundly theoretical and profoundly practical at the same time. The greatest charge that can be levelled against Bagehot is that, at the most delicate and precarious moment in the development of the Constitution, he lowered our sights and, such was the impact of his bright breezy brilliance, they have stayed lowered ever since.

As Nevil Johnson rightly points out,

> the weakness of Bagehot's analysis lay in his relative lack of interest in the terms on which even the efficient parts of the Constitution rested. He was anxious to describe what happened, but more or less indifferent to the problem of making sense of this by reference to the principles guiding the actors. One long-term consequence of this was, of course, that the very pragmatism of that analysis helped to prepare the way for the weakening of the understanding of constitutional categories.[24]

Constitutional writing in this country since Bagehot has had a prosy, commonplace lack of ambition about it. And it is not, I think, coincidental that our understanding of our Constitution has become both attenuated and atrophied over the same period. Bagehot is the first of the great simplifiers of the British Constitution; he is not the least pernicious.

The peculiar sentiment of Albert Venn Dicey

'Dicey's word has, in some respects, become the only written constitution we have.' What a remarkable testimony to Dicey (and it is by no means a unique one) to hear a century after the first publication of his *Introduction to the Study of the Law of the Constitution* – the work on which that claim largely rests. What an extraordinary man Albert Venn Dicey must have been to have left a legacy so enduring. And so indeed he was, but not perhaps the sort of man one might have imagined to have bequeathed a reputation for thumping certainties.

Far from being a square-rigged, mutton-chop-whiskered

Victorian thunderer of formidable mien, Dicey was an elongated, shuffling near-spastic. A muscular weakness – according to family tradition, dating back to an obstetric error at the time of his premature birth – left him an invalid all his eighty-seven years. His sight was poor, in later life he was very deaf; his handwriting was so illegible that, when being examined for a fellowship at Trinity College, Oxford, in 1860, he received permission to dictate his answers. On the morning of going in for his first university examination, Jowett, the Master of his college, Balliol, told him 'your tie is very badly tied'; Dicey's effort to retie it were so futile that in the end Jowett tied it himself. In youth, he suffered continuously from bronchitis and had to wear a respirator. He had great charm and courtesy; his long sad face bore a distinct resemblance to that of his first cousin Sir Leslie Stephen (and was not unlike the faces of Stephen's daughters Virginia and Vanessa).

Such a person, when as intellectually gifted as Dicey was, might perhaps have been expected to become an aesthete of the Swinburnian sort; he and Swinburne were, indeed, fellow members of the Old Mortality Club at Oxford, the name for which was chosen on the ground that 'every member of the aforesaid society was or lately had been in so weak and precarious a condition of bodily health as plainly and manifestly to instance the great fragility and, so to speak, mortality of this our human life and constitution'.[25]

But it was at Oxford that he developed a taste for political controversy and first showed his characteristic ferocity in argument. As his best biographer so far, Richard Cosgrove, points out, 'he worked best in sorting out propositions into categories of black and white, for he never accepted the many shades of grey in public affairs'.[26] At first, his enthusiasms were religious – inherited from his Clapham sect forebears (the Venn in his name came from John Venn, the famous Rector of Clapham, whose daughter had married Dicey's uncle). He denounced bigots and watered-down liberal Christians like Jowett with equal venom. This single-mindedness he carried with him into the political causes to which he dedicated his later life, summoning up every available ounce of his fragile energies to curse, for example, 'the demoralising and degrading kind of government under men like Asquith who seem to be developing all that is worst in party government'.

It is less clear that he devoted the same passionate commitment to scholarship, although he held the Vinerian Chair of English Law at Oxford for twenty-seven years. As we have already seen, his references to English constitutional history can be dubious (he professed a certain contempt for history), and his knowledge of constitutional law in other countries was decidedly sketchy. His description of *droit administratif* in France was generally thought to be out of date and inaccurate by the time *The Law of the Constitution* was published. Dicey's misapprehensions were only rather skimpily corrected in later editions; his treatment was subsequently torn to pieces by Sir Ivor Jennings in *The Law and the Constitution*. But his failings are not restricted to a negligent or wilful use of the relevant material or even to a failure to do his research properly; again and again, his work shows a certain lack of reflective or absorptive power and an absence of intellectual humility. Dicey is always *debating*, as though he had never quite left the Oxford Union where he had shone so brightly and had so marvellously triumphed over the illness and ridicule that had blighted his early youth. He is, in short, a fighter rather than a scholar, a hard-driving campaigner rather than a judicious authority.

And the campaign he chose to fight in the early 1880s was to save the Union between Britain and Ireland. At the outset, when the agitation for some kind of Irish parliament began, Dicey was prepared to consider a range of possibilities. In a letter to his Oxford friend Bryce, he once mused: 'I think that a *bona fide* attempt to treat the Irish members as the persons entitled to decide on Irish legislation may turn out the best way out of our difficulties.'[27] Even in 1886, he was willing, in private at least, to consider a federal solution as an alternative to the stern unbending Unionism to which he was publicly wedded. He wrote to Bryce:

. . . I agree with you in the opinion that the constituencies will support the government [that is, Home Rule. . . . But] If it were possible and in accordance with English habits I should have first [that is, before the election] a plebiscite with the simple question of an independent Parliament for Ireland or not. Were there a vote in its favour I would then have a constitutional convention to draw up a constitution fairly carrying out this popular vote, and the Constitution itself I would then submit to the people, aye or no. . . .[28]

But outwardly his views had already hardened into a certainty which they were never again to lose. For the next forty years, he fought against Home Rule for Ireland with a vigour and tenacity rivalled by no fully fit man in the British Isles. And even when that cause was lost, he turned, right at the end of his life, to save the Union of England and Scotland from the agitation for 'Home Rule All Round' which surfaced after the First World War. To say in passing that 'Dicey was a diehard Unionist,' as though this was merely one facet of his temperament and tastes, on a par with an enthusiasm for Staffordshire china or fly-fishing, is grotesquely to underestimate the all-consuming nature of his commitment. Apart from the unceasing round of speeches he gave all over the country, he wrote a whole book against each of the three Home Rule Bills – *England's Case against Home Rule* (1886), *A Leap in the Dark* (1893) and *A Fool's Paradise* (1913); he also wrote, in conjunction with his friend and biographer R. S. Rait (who did most of the research), *Thoughts on the Union between England and Scotland* (1920). In each of these works, he hammered home the same message: a separate parliament for Ireland or Scotland would be a catastrophe that would destroy the United Kingdom. Federalism was a 'very peculiar sentiment' which might do for the Americans or the Swiss, but it produced weak government, and it was 'as a matter of history absolutely unknown to the people of England'.[29] To introduce any kind of federal system into these islands would be 'a revolution far more searching than would be the abolition of the House of Lords or the transformation of our constitutional monarchy into a republic'; the supposed precedents of Grattan's Parliament in Ireland or the century between the Union of the Crowns in 1603 and the Act of Union in 1707 were not precedents at all. 'Turn the UK into a federal state, and parliamentary government, as we know it, is at an end.'[30]

According to Dicey, it was the untrammelled power of Parliament which was the secret of England's power and glory; he venerated that power with an intensity that was almost mystical; it was as though its sheer concentration was infusing his own frail body with something of its unrestrained force. 'Under all the formality, the antiquarianism, the shams of the British constitution, there lies an element of power which has been the true source of its life and growth. This secret source of strength is the absolute omnipotence, the sovereignty of Parliament.'[31]

It is, I think, advisable to seize the opportunity of this first encounter with Dicey's celebrated idea of sovereignty to try to establish a rough working definition of what has become the key word in the British debate about European unity. The simplest approach may be to waylay the word as it enters the language of politics in its modern sense, during the struggles of the sixteenth and seventeenth centuries. The tradition of a natural law in which the only true sovereign was the divine order begins to fall apart under the battering of the Reformation; the hierarchical view of authority which had characterised the Middle Ages is swept aside by the unqualified absolutism of the Renaissance. It is the insatiable will to power that Hobbes describes in Chapter 11 of *Leviathan* which becomes the sovereign: 'in the first place, I put for a general inclination of all mankind, a perpetual and restless desire of power after power, that ceaseth only in death'. Desire of ease and sensual delight, or desire of knowledge or the arts of peace, or fear of oppression might dispose men to huddle together and obey a common power. But that desire of power was only quiescent, not snuffed out once for all.

The sovereign will cannot be irrevocably extinguished or relinquished; it can be lent, shared or parked for reasons of sentiment or convenience; but its recall remains an eternal possibility. This applies at every level – individual, corporate, tribal, religious, national. A person may re-exercise his sovereign will by deserting his tribe or nation and transferring to another; if forcibly prevented from doing so, he may go into 'internal exile', denying the allegiance of his conscience to the state in which he dwells. Similarly, a tribe or nation may swear allegiance to some larger entity – a state or federation – but however long that allegiance may be maintained, whether out of inertia, weakness or even positive enthusiasm, the inherent sovereign right to forswear that allegiance remains unblemished.

What Dicey denies (as do modern British nationalists) is the possibility of overlapping consents to different authorities or of a subordinate national loyalty coexisting with a sovereign allegiance. Like a spoilt child, a genuine national will must, sooner or later, demand the right to have it all. For this reason, a federalised United Kingdom, like a federal Europe today, is an unsustainable fantasy. There was no halfway house; if the Irish (or the Scots) were given their own parliament, the hungry appetite for sovereignty would soon drive them to demand complete independence.

We need not stop here to enquire how far the existing European Community (which seems to rub along) can fairly be described as 'federal'; we have enough trouble on our hands as it is. As for the difficulties of sustaining a federation which comprises different languages, races or religions, these are familiar enough – although it is worth recalling that the greatest of all civil wars was fought in a predominantly homogeneous country: the United States.

For the moment, all we need note is the appalling difficulty created by assuming this unappeasable sovereign will to be the all-important fact of political life. Far from buttressing the more modest and entirely correct claim of Parliament to be the supreme law-making body in the land, it immediately – and, as we shall see in Dicey's case, tragically – *undermines* the authority of Parliament. Why? Because behind the sovereign Parliament lurks the menacing, insatiable sovereign will of the people – the id to Westminster's ego. Parliament, we are told, might legislate in a way that would be and ought to be unwelcome to the people; and, when that happened, the people had a right to overturn that legislation by any means which came to hand. Thus, as we shall see, even by Dicey's own theory, parliament was not, could not be, sovereign after all.

The Irish, Dicey conceded, might not wish to be governed by the English; they might have many genuine grievances against the Imperial Parliament; but if they could not be reconciled to British rule, then in the long run he was prepared to say that Irish independence might be a lesser evil than Home Rule. In any case, the unhappiness of Irishmen was less important than the constitutional satisfaction of Englishmen. 'The varying forms of the English Constitution have, on the whole, possessed the immense merit of giving at each period of our history political authority into the hands of the class, or classes, who made up the true strength of the nation. Right has in a rough way been combined with might.'[32] The genuine grievances of the Irish ought to be accommodated – Dicey was not a heartless or unkind man – but the poorer and less numerous part of the nation must in the last analysis accommodate itself to the interests of the stronger majority. It was beyond Dicey's myopic sight to imagine how the powerless minority might acquire the means to inflict injury upon the majority; the terrorism of the late nineteenth century must have seemed to him a trifling inconvenience, certainly as compared with what he saw as the final disaster – the undermining of the sovereignty of Parliament.

By the time of the Third Reform Bill, his passion has become ungovernable. *A Fool's Paradise* – the third of Dicey's anti-Home Rule books – contains passages so bizarre that, even now, nearly eighty years later, one blinks unbelievingly and reads them again slowly to make sure one has gathered the sense correctly.

Already, twenty years earlier, in *A Leap in the Dark*, Dicey had prepared a fallback position if the opposition of the House of Lords, albeit prolonged to the last ditch, was not enough to save the nation from the grisly fate of a Home Rule Act. If the peers had to cave in, Dicey urged that they should at least tag on to the Bill a clause insisting on a referendum to secure the approval of the majority of the electors of the United Kingdom: 'This course, it may be said, is unconstitutional. This word has no terrors for me; it means no more than unusual'[33] – so much for the glories of our great constitutional tradition – 'and the institution of a Referendum would simply mean the formal acknowledgement of the doctrine which lies at the basis of English democracy – that a law depends at bottom for its enactment on the assent of the nation as represented by the electors.' The sovereignty of Parliament is ultimately subordinate to 'the sovereignty of the nation'. The crudity and coarseness of Dicey's thought are stripped bare in the extremities of his anxiety for the Union. Any notion of checks and balances, of due process of law or of the separation of powers flies away in the face of his desperate need to secure a majority somehow, somewhere against Home Rule.

But it is not until the Parliament Act of 1911 has finally destroyed the blocking power of the House of Lords that Dicey takes the final step and recommends, albeit in a periphrastic, weaselly fashion, actual insurrection. In *A Fool's Paradise*, remarkably subtitled 'A Constitutionalist's Criticism on the Home Rule Bill of 1912', Dicey asserts that, without a dissolution of Parliament, any Home Rule Act will 'lack moral authority',[34] because it had not been put to the people at the preceding general election.

Jennings argues that this doctrine of 'the mandate' had been invented by Conservatives solely in order to justify the House of Lords putting up a fierce opposition to Liberal measures.[35] It was merely part of the 'political cant', a stick used by the Opposition to beat the Government. Without endorsing its invocation on this or any other particular occasion, one may feel that Jennings's own prejudices are showing a little here. If the wish of the majority in the Commons is to carry all before it, on the grounds that it is the sole legitimate representative of the nation – and this is the basic proposition of modern British constitutional thought, to which Jennings no less than Dicey subscribed – then it is reasonable to ask that the legislative programme of that majority should, in fact, be the one that was placed before the nation at the preceding general election. It was certainly not good constitutional law to deduce from this proposition, as Dicey did in 1913,[36] that the king could dismiss his Ministers in order to ascertain the will of the nation. Even in 1913, that was understood by all except diehard Unionists as an improper use of the royal prerogative. Similarly, the doctrine of the mandate may not, strictly speaking, be part of constitutional law, but it is quite logical that, over the past century of mass democracy, it should have emerged as at least a useful political principle to which a successful government will pay some attention.

'If the government availed themselves of the Parliament Act to force the Bill through,' Dicey persisted, 'it will be in form of a law but will lack all constitutional authority and the duty of Unionists will be to treat it as a measure which lacks the sanction of the nation.'[37] In general, loyal citizens had a predominant duty to obey the law of the land, but 'such obedience can be due only when a law is the clear and undoubted expression of the will of the nation',[38] and even then 'there may exist acts of oppression on the part of a democracy, no less than of a king, which justify resistance to law, or, in other words, rebellion. It is idle to suppose that the existence or non-existence of these conditions can be determined by merely technical rules.'

Accordingly, 'moral resistance . . . will, from a constitutional point of view, be fully justified. I do not even assert that it may not rightly be carried by Ulstermen to extreme lengths.'[39] How extreme? Dicey dodges and hedges: 'I will not give, because I have not found, any certain opinion as to the right course to be pursued should the British electorate sanction the monstrous iniquity. . . . What are the limits within which the tyranny either of a king or of a democracy justifies civil war is not an inquiry on which I will enter.'[40]

While stifling our gasps at these remarkable sentiments, as inflammatory as they are evasive, as brutish as they are cowardly, we ought to note that even the approval of a referendum or a general election would not apparently remove this right to rebel against 'the monstrous iniquity'.

Any ambiguity that may linger in the pages of *A Fool's Paradise* was dispelled by the action Dicey took to demonstrate his readiness to support armed resistance to legal compulsion. He signed the Ulster Covenant. In all this, he had the support of his Warden at All Souls, the equally eminent constitutionalist Sir William Anson, the author of *The Law and Custom of the Constitution*.

Anson had once stated the orthodox doctrine that 'Parliament therefore is omnipotent to change, but cannot bind itself not to change, the constitution of which it forms a part.'[41] But as Professor Heuston of Trinity College, Dublin, puts it so nicely in his elegant and indispensable *Essays on Constitutional Law* (1961): 'he too was aghast at the prospect of being taken literally by a parliamentary majority composed of the sons of nonconformist manufacturers and Irish peasants',[42] and from the safe distance of his All Souls study egged on the rebels: 'If the covenanters meet [the Home Rule Act] with armed resistance, I for one believe, with a conviction which no results of a referendum or a general election can alter, that they are justified in their resistance.'[43]

Thus even the most robust theorists of parliamentary omnipotence do not take their own doctrine seriously when it conflicts with the feelings of their heart and gut.

By now, Dicey's notion of constitutional government seems a faded and tattered thing, bearing an unnerving resemblance to mob rule. It seems extraordinary that such an erratic and violent thinker could ever have achieved such monumental status as a constitutional authority. Nor has his most monumental work escaped the contagion. For to the eighth edition of *The Law of the Constitution*, appearing on the eve of the Great War, Dicey appended a new introduction, nearly a hundred pages long, in which he released virtually every bee that had been humming in his bonnet for the previous thirty years.

He blasted off yet against the iniquities of federalism, now exercising dangerous hold over the minds of Scotchmen too. After all, Mr Asquith had said during the passage of his Home Rule Bill, 'I think Scotch sentiment will also demand that whatever body is created there shall go by the name of "Parliament" and recall such traditions as are venerable in the institution which was extinguished by the Act of Union.'[44]

In this curious introduction, Dicey also had a crack at the evils of Proportional Representation, another new-fangled device which was not to his taste. On the other hand, the referendum once more received somewhat favourable treatment, on the grounds that it might 'keep in check the inordinate power now bestowed on the party machine'[45] – by which, of course, at that date he meant the party machine of the fiendish Asquith: 'I think one can't exaggerate the extent to which this Ministry is lowering the tone of public life.'[46] And, perhaps oddest of all, he included in the introduction to this supposedly authoritative guide to constitutional law a reprise of his diatribe against votes for women. Supporters of female suffrage were, whether they knew it or not, urging 'the absolute political equality of the two sexes' and demanding, by implication, seats in Parliament and in the Cabinet for women; 'it means that Englishwomen should share the jury box and should sit on the judicial bench. It treats as insignificant for most purposes that difference of sex which, after all, disguise the matter as you will, is one of the most fundamental and far-reaching differences which can distinguish one body of human beings from another.'[47] The conservative argument against votes for women 'conforms to the nature of things'.[48] He had said all of this, and more, twenty years earlier in *Letters to a Friend on Votes for Women* (1893). This little work contains riper stuff still. Nearly every man, so Dicey declared, was of the belief that 'women of pre-eminent goodness are often lacking in the virtues, such as active courage, firmness of judgment, self-control, steadiness of conduct, and, above all, a certain sense of justice maintained even in the heat of party conflict, which are often to be found in Englishmen even of an ordinary type'.[49]

If women had the vote, they might insist on the making of an ignominious peace, against the wishes of their more tenacious and courageous and far-sighted menfolk. No one dreamed that women ought to be police officers, governors of jails or coastguards. 'Nor can it be forgotten not only that women are physically and probably mentally weaker than men, but that they are mentally, as a class, burdened with duties of the utmost national importance, and of an absorbing and exhausting nature, from which men are free'[50] – those maternal duties from which, incidentally, Mrs Dicey, also a congenital invalid, was free too. Through all these ramblings, which now read so absurdly, it is not, I think, fanciful to detect further spasms of Dicey's worship of strength and his unwillingness ever to see strength curbed in response to the plaintive mewings of the weak. Although Dicey is no more than Bagehot to be lumped in with the Social Darwinists of his time, one sees repeatedly in his work a disinclination to linger over the protection of minorities or over those checks and balances which, however ramshackle and imperfect they may be, have afforded some defence against the strong on the rampage. Nor is it too curt an abbreviation of his thought to describe Dicey as being primarily interested in explaining the governing principle of power rather than in setting out the constitutional system as a whole. He devotes little or no attention to the complex and diverse local and national bureaucracies, both inside and outside the governmental system, which had already become a feature of British life. His description of the rule of law covers only the rudimentary personal rights of free speech, habeas corpus, freedom of assembly and so on; the intricacies of property law and trade union law were beyond his ken, and not accidentally so either, since these aspects of law tended to preserve the devolution and dispersal of power, while Dicey's aim – like Bagehot's – was to concentrate our attention upon the centrality and omnipotence of Parliament. He set out to simplify our understanding of the way we are governed and, as his panic about the Union increased with the years, he coarsened that understanding until, by the time of the Third Home Rule Bill, his panic became a monomania from which any notion of constitutional principle had almost vanished.

But this leaves us with the question only partly answered as to *why* Dicey became so obsessed with the maintenance of the Union. True, it was the central political question of his day. Governments rose on the promise of a solution to it and fell when that solution failed. It is not unreasonable that the maintenance of the Union, in one form or another, should have considerably coloured Dicey's work, whether or not we agree with his persistent belief that a federal outcome would have been a catastrophe. But why did his belief become a monomania?

There is at least a partial defence of Dicey's obsession (though not necessarily of his solution). It could be said that, in all his political work, he was laying bare what in reality has always been a central difficulty in the governance of these islands and which, in more tranquil periods, we (and here I mean we the English) have pretended was a trivial and secondary problem which lingered on into our own time only as a vestigial relic of old tribal conflicts.

Modern historians are increasingly inclined to trace a long pedigree for this self-deception and to reinterpret much of our civil conflict as a result. Conrad Russell has reinterpreted the Civil War as a 'War of the Three Kingdoms', in which religious and national aspirations were more important than class conflict; Jonathan Clark has delineated the growth of the doctrine of unfettered parliamentary sovereignty – in contrast to the mixed and qualified sovereignties of Continental states – as a response to the ever-recurring problem of keeping down or keeping in the Scots, the Welsh and the Irish (*Times Literary Supplement* 29 November, 1991). Thus constitutional developments which have been interpreted in the past as responses to clamours for democracy by newly emergent classes may, in fact, have been driven, at least partly, by the requirements of *national* unity. From Henry VIII onwards, the question that the ruling elite had to ask itself first was often not 'How can we pacify the merchants (or the bourgeoisie or the proletariat)?' but 'How do we pacify the Scots (or the Welsh or the Irish)?' It is arguable that Dicey was at least asking a question more central than many of his contemporaries or his successors knew, even if his 'path of safety' was not necessarily the right one.

In fairness to Dicey, we ought to make an effort of the historical imagination (the kind of effort to which he was himself congenitally disinclined). In the 1880s, the period when his belief that the path of safety was a unitary one hardened into unshakeable conviction, unitary government must have seemed a demonstrable source of strength. The only large-scale federal state then in existence, the United States, had, within Dicey's own memory, undergone the most bloody of all civil wars to date; Britain ruled the roost in Europe; Bismarckian Germany was still in the process of formation and seemed, politically and even industrially, still to have some ground to make up before joining the modern world.

Today, the balance of advantage seems more unclear, to say the least. In the free world, the USA and Switzerland have been joined in the ranks of powerful independent federations by Canada, Australia and Germany; Britain, France, New Zealand and Japan can scarcely claim to field a superior team for the unitarians. There is also – a less noticed phenomenon – a certain amount of traffic in both directions. New Zealand has become a unitary state; Spain seems to be finding that a solution to the problems of Catalonia and the Basque country lies in a step-by-step progression towards a federal state; will South Africa follow the same path?

Modern experience suggests several possibilities, none of them congenial to Dicey: that national minorities may be reconciled by a genuine reconstitution of the state into a federation; that such reconstitutions may be accomplished without either weakening the power of the state to make its writ run at home or weakening the nation's power relative to other nations; that federations are not, by the fact of being federations, weaker diplomatically, economically or militarily than unitary states, that the connection between England's greatness in Dicey's time and the exact nature of her system of government was at best unproven (a dozen other factors would have to be examined, such as the tradition of freedom of enquiry, the puritan ethic, the security inherent in being an island, plentiful coal reserves, and so on).

I certainly do not mean to suggest the contrary: that the introduction of a federal system tomorrow would promote the UK to the top of the international league; or that federations are, *ipso facto*, more stable and harmonious than their constituent nations would be as separate states (the examples of Yugoslavia and the Soviet Union are before our eyes). There is all the difference in the world between a voluntary and a coerced federation. Even those federations which were so benignly engineered by the Colonial Office for Africa and the Caribbean have tended to collapse in no time under the pressure of tribal or insular rivalries and suspicions. At this stage, it is sufficient to argue that Dicey's whole thesis is a chronic case of *post hoc, ergo propter hoc* and that his reading of constitutional history was not only warped but warped in a bad cause.

Yet there remains a certain emphatic sonority and an appealing clarity about the way he delineates parliamentary sovereignty. These qualities help to explain why his popularity has lasted so long and why *The Law of the Constitution* has run through so many editions. It was only kindness to Dicey's memory that when E. C. S. Wade, himself one of the foremost constitutionalists of his day, came to edit the ninth edition (1938), he dropped Dicey's embarrassing 1914 introduction which had hung, a putrid albatross, around the neck of the book for the intervening quarter of a century. By the late 1930s, Ireland was a free state, the flappers had the vote, and people were worrying more about Hitler than about Proportional Representation. In the constitutional sphere, too, other things had changed, and Wade could not help pointing out, in an equally long introduction of his own, that many of Dicey's statements about the uninhibited sovereignty of the Imperial Parliament no longer applied. The 1931 Statute of Westminster had in effect conferred a kind of quasi-sovereignty upon the Dominion parliaments: in theory, Parliament could repeal Section 4 and reclaim the power to legislate for the Dominions without their request and consent; in practice, sovereignty had been transferred.

Before we leave the subject of sovereignty, we should perhaps say a word or two about the development of the idea from Dicey's day to our own. The truth is that there has been little or no development. Dicey's orthodoxy – the monolithic nature of all constitutions likely to endure – still mesmerises an influential group of politicians and political commentators in Britain, for much the same reasons that it mesmerised Dicey: the fear of the internal crack-up of the United Kingdom, reinforced in recent years by the fear of alien incursion from and eventual take-over by the European Community. Yet even now in the early 1990s, just as in Dicey's day, there remains a strange incompleteness about the argument, an incompleteness all the more striking because Dicey's writings on the subject were so voluminous.

It is significant that the actual process of alienating sovereignty is seldom subjected to close examination from those who set most store by sovereignty as a unique, irreplaceable treasure, the loss of which makes, or ought to make, the losers inconsolable.

At what point precisely does a nation lose sovereignty? And at what point, if any, does that loss become irreparable? Is the abdication of sovereignty the same thing as renouncing self-government, and does it therefore occur at the same moment? Such questions tend to receive confusing or conflicting answers. For example, Mr Enoch Powell has always argued to the effect that something very terrible happened to the British in 1972 when the European Communities Act was passed. That 'surrender of Britain's self-government' was not irrevocable (we might yet come to our senses and reclaim our ancient right to govern ourselves), but there was no doubting the fact that we had given away a most precious possession. But was it sovereignty that we had given away?

Not according to one of Mr Powell's most eloquent disciples, Mr Noel Malcolm: 'Each time we delegate the exercise of important areas of our authority to "Europe", we do not lose sovereignty or become less sovereign; we merely become more likely to lose our sovereignty. We come closer, that is, to the moment when our constitution can be remodelled into a sub-ordinate part of the constitution of a federal state.' (*Spectator*, 16 November 1991). Sovereignty means 'constitutional independence'; we can, therefore, suspend what might be called our 'executive independence' in favour of all sorts of supranational bodies, such as NATO, GATT, the UN and even the European Community, without forfeiting our sovereignty; even the contro-versial question whether such supranational bodies should take their decisions by unanimity or by some type of majority voting is a secondary one, since ultimate authority can always be reclaimed and so our sovereignty remains intact.

On this view, sovereignty-loss does not occur until the moment at which the government of a nation-state formally signs on as a member of a federation. But in the real world, even a formal signature to a federal constitution may well not be the final end of the matter. If the federal union turns out badly, the nation-state may wish (no doubt after holding a referendum) to give notice, equally formally, that it intends to leave the federation. The constitution or treaty may explicitly provide for this. Article 17 of Stalin's new constitution of 1936, for example, proudly stated that 'The right freely to secede from the USSR is reserved to each constituent republic' (the entire constitution of this 'voluntary union' was reproduced, no less proudly, in Sidney and Beatrice Webb's *Soviet Communism: A New Civilisation*). Other, genuinely voluntary treaties of union, such as the Treaty of Rome, do not so provide; but that did not prevent the UK from holding its referendum on the continuation of British membership. There is no doubt that had the result gone the other way in 1975, the UK government would have begun negotiating to disentangle itself from the Community. And the same surely would happen if the UK were to form an intention to disentangle from the more intensely federated body of today. What of the Community of

2002? It is surely a reasonable bet that any discontented member state would still retain the effective power to leave.

Whether or not members of a federation are permitted to exercise such a power without hindrance remains a matter of brute historical contingency: Stalin and Abraham Lincoln were prepared to use force to stop secession; Gorbachev and Trudeau were not so prepared, although dedicated to the strenuous discouragement of any breakaway. This distinction between a federation which permits secession and one which doesn't is not only all-important to unhappy citizens of member-states in coerced federations, such as Yugoslavia or the Soviet Union; it also suggests that sovereignty may be *reserved*, even by members of a federation. To put it bluntly, if you go in voluntarily, well aware that you can get out again if you don't like it, can you really be said to have ceded sovereignty? Is it not the voluntary, dissoluble character of a community which is the crucial mark of its conformity to our ideals of democracy and self-government, rather than whether the arrangements are most accurately to be categorised as an association of nation-states or a federation?

The scope and whereabouts of sovereignty may be formally and specifically stated in any treaty or constitution, but even such statements are by no means uniform in their claim to permanence or in their relation to reality. The claim to sovereignty over Northern Ireland in Articles Two and Three of the Irish Constitution is at present inoperative (if not quite as inoperative as the King of England's long enduring claim to be also King of France); on the other hand, the Queen's sovereignty over Northern Ireland appears to be somewhat qualified by the proviso variously repeated in successive Northern Ireland Acts to the effect that 'in no event will Northern Ireland or any part of it cease to be part of Her Majesty's dominions and of the United Kingdom without the consent of the majority of the people of Northern Ireland voting in a poll' (the wording of the 1973 Northern Ireland Constitution Act).

None of this is to argue that sovereignty is a meaningless or empty concept. But we must be wary of that sleight of hand which bundles together all the attributes of national power and independence and then labels them 'sovereignty'. Sir Geoffrey Howe's jibe about sovereignty not being like virginity – something which either you possess or you don't – may have been a little saucy, but, on closer examination, the degree of sovereignty which any particular nation enjoys in practice does begin to look more like a point on a spectrum, comparable to the spectrum between chastity and promiscuity; one passes through celibacy, marriage, and the occasional infidelity on the way.

True, in the governing of any state or confederation of states there must exist what we might call 'a supreme set of arrangements'; otherwise, chaos and conflict are likely, if not inevitable. But these arrangements need not all be encoded in the same document (they never have been in the British Constitution). Nor need the powers conferred by these arrangements be all located in the same body. Thus a body may be supreme in one field – the making and revising of laws, say – but possess no competence in another, such as the arrest and punishment of offenders. This brings us to a further sleight of hand, often to be observed in the arguments of constitutional historians: we are often told that there must in any state be one single supreme authority – it may be a person like a Czar, or a body (perhaps a multiform body like the Queen-in-Parliament), or a document like the US Constitution. And because there can only be one of it, the supremacy (or sovereignty) enjoyed by the person/body must be the same kind of supremacy as that enjoyed by the document.

But this claim of 'necessary oneness' obscures the vast difference, both of kind and degree, between a person or body legitimated to exercise power and a document or set of documents laying down rules for the distribution and exercise of power. The fact that these two instances of supremacy share the quality of oneness conceals the far more important fact that the edicts of the person/body are undetermined and fluid, while the precepts laid down by a document are fixed and known. In any case, this trumpeted oneness pales beside the category difference: who would wish to say that the captain of a cricket team and the Laws of Cricket were the same kind of authority, merely because there could only be one of each?

This category mistake which we have come up against here is at the heart of the matter; and its purpose is a scurvy one, to conceal the real difference between a monolithic and a plural state. A rulebook is a rulebook, and a ruler is a ruler. It is only the sovereignty-obsession of the unitarians which could muddle the two.

Yet we shall find the same muddle, sometimes wilful, sometimes not, persisting into those modern accounts of the Constitution which still parrot the Dicean doctrine of sovereignty with an unstinting reverence normally accorded only to documents of divine origin.

These accounts do not swallow Dicey whole. Dicey's indifference to the whole world of administration, in contrast to what Maitland called the 'showy parts' of the Constitution – Parliament, Crown and High Court – had come to seem a little quaint by the 1930s. A new version was needed to reinterpret our constitutional arrangements to a modern audience.

Sir Ivor Jennings and the Fabian version

With Sir Ivor Jennings, we enter into a world which is familiar to us. *Cabinet Government* (1936) and *The Law and the Constitution* (1933) describe the kind of politics we are used to, and describe it, moreover, with a dry wit and a wealth of examples which are as appealing in their way as Dicey's resonance – for Jennings is no exception to the rule which has obtained at least since Hallam's day that constitutional theorists who wish to hold our attention must charm as well as instruct; this is not so, I think, in other countries where great constitutionalists may be dry as dust and still be respected as authorities; it is as though a certain literary agility is indispensable for those wishing to catch hold of our own elusive arrangements.

It is, above all, the fluidity, the incessant evolution of practice, which Jennings exposes so brilliantly. He has no illusions about the stability of any particular pillar of the Constitution; indeed, to use the language of pillar and portico would be alien to him; his discourse has the quality of that school of modernist architecture which emphasises not only the functional but the provisional; walls, staircases, floors, ceilings – all can be raised, lowered, added, removed – indeed , not only can be but must be, for politics is a purposive, goal-oriented activity in which rigidity has no place.

His reproach against the immediately preceding generation of constitutional writers, notably Dicey, for Dicey was the most notable, was that, while they might catch something of the fluid, evolutionary character of the British Constitution, they were too immured in their time and class fully to understand what it ought to be fluid *for*. Their class interest was itself a kind of rigidity which prevented them from seeing the world as it was and as it was about to be.

The burden of Jennings's complaint was that Dicey and his kind were Liberals of an antiquated sort, more concerned with liberty than with justice, more dedicated to the protection of property than to the protection of the poor. They had no conception of the scale of duties incumbent upon a modern government which was properly concerned for the welfare of all its citizens: the improvement of health, the provision of education, the stimulation of industry, the wellbeing of agriculture, the smooth running of transport, and so on and on. It was not simply that Dicey had failed to identify or engage with the considerable administrative apparatus which had already been built up in his own day; Dicey would not have known – or, we are led to infer, cared – much about what it was all for. For Dicey, so long as habeas corpus was maintained and the courts of law saw to it that Englishmen could still speak their own mind without fear, then the British Constitution was safe.

For Jennings, this view of the Constitution was wholly inadequate; it was the brainchild of an Oxford don who had no real understanding of the modern world and its demands upon political systems (I put the matter more brutally than Jennings does, but this is his drift). Not merely did Britain already possess a system of administrative law quite as elaborate as the French *droit administratif* (which Dicey claimed rested upon ideas 'alien to the conceptions of modern Englishmen'), but we could not possibly have got along without one. Jennings's attack on Dicey's false distinction between the French and the English system is so celebrated and so unanswerable that we are in danger of ignoring a more interesting phenomenon: Jennings's general complaisance about the growth of all bureaucratic mechanisms. I do not mean that he pays scant attention to the devices by which the citizen may obtain review of unjust acts of the administration; he encompasses with his usual competence certiorari, mandamus and the other remedies which enable the aggrieved citizen to gain access to the courts and which went on evolving well into the 1950s. Naturally, the new bureaucratic growths on the body politic had to be subjected to traditional ideas of justice and individual rights.

But Jennings does not at any point question the growths themselves. There is no brooding sense of danger such as we find in Hewart's *New Despotism*, written at much the same time. For Jennings, these growths were benign, and, within the limits of good sense, to be encouraged to grow further, as part of the 'modernising' of the British Constitution. Indeed, their right to grow was a matter of some urgency if Britain was to maintain a leading role among the world's democracies.

He begins *The Law and the Constitution*[51] with the awesome thought that 'Today, the individual is but a unit in a vast system of production and distribution whose limits are fixed (perhaps only temporarily) by the stratosphere.' A constitution was only an organisation of men and women. A lawyer had to possess more than a knowledge of his books: 'I would assert that no lawyer understands any part of the law until he knows the social conditions that produce it and its consequences for the people who are governed by it.'[52] Thus constitutional law shades into social administration, and the lawyer becomes something more like a social worker. 'A general and progressive reform of all the public services'[53] had altered everything. What Dicey had called 'the period of collectivism', Jennings declared, 'has changed the constitutional organisation, the practice of government, and the principles of political action'.[54]

The Constitution had so evolved under the pressures of collectivism, according to Jennings, that consultation with outside corporate bodies had become a constitutional convention: 'the

Home Office would not think of producing a new Factories Bill without consulting the General Council of the Trades Union Congress . . . no substantial measure dealing with local government would be passed without consultation with the association of local authorities'. Hesitating briefly after these remarkable assertions, Jennings does wonder whether perhaps this 'may not yet be a constitutional convention, but an administrative practice which is slowly changing into a convention'.[55] But for Jennings, this is only a quibble about timing; it does not strike him as in any way a constitutional enormity that consultation which is not provided for in legislation with a body which has no constitutional standing should become constitutionally mandatory by creeping acceptance.

There is a kind of unashamed bureaucratic slurring of all barriers, structures and distinctions in Jennings's description of the modern Constitution. Sometimes the slurring is between the party-political and the legal, as in his acceptance of the doctrine of the mandate as a constitutional convention (a convention which elsewhere, as we have seen, he was to dismiss as part of the Conservatives' 'political cant'): 'it is now recognised that fundamental changes of policy must not be effected unless they have been in issue at a general election'.[56] As innumerable examples before and since show, this supposed limitation upon government and upon Parliament itself is rather patchily observed, however desirable it might be.

Sometimes the slurring is between the legal and the administrative; 'no line can be drawn between functions which ought to be exercised by courts and those which ought to be exercised by administrative tribunals and administration'.[57] Indeed, since unified, ultimate control rested with Parliament, it didn't really much matter. 'So long as the major principles of policy are determined in Parliament the application of those principles to current problems can be left to administrators.' If injustices occurred, MPs could be relied on to kick up a fuss. 'The safeguard against bureaucracy or tyranny lies not in a precise delimitation of functions, but in democratic control through an elected House of Commons in which the Party system makes criticism open and effective.'[58]

We must, I suppose, make allowance for the clammy corporatist ethos of the era in which Sir Ivor was writing, the 1930s. And yet, after making such allowance, we cannot help noticing the total absence of any kind of rigour in the thought, the lack of aspiration to clarify principle or discern any sort of logical structure in the arrangements that confronted him. On the contrary, he seems eager to intensify the obscurity, to mix up things that, in reality, either were not mixed up together or need not have been. Consultations with the TUC and the local authority associations – unless specified by Act of Parliament – never at any time approached the status of constitutional conventions. Far from courts of law and administrative tribunals having melted into one bureaucratic morass, the tendency has been to extend the avenues of appeal from such tribunals to the High Court, so to speak, to 'legalise' them and separate them off from what we ordinarily mean by administration.

The collectivising process was not nearly as smooth and painless as Jennings implies. The terms of compulsory purchase of property were a scandal for several decades; the rights of ordinary individuals, no less than of large corporations, were generally agreed to have been systematically abused without proper redress being made available. State intervention in every sphere gave rise, as it always inevitably does, to a host of grievances among those it was intended to benefit, from farmers to social security claimants. I am not concerned here to argue the overall merits or demerits of such interventions. What needs to be pointed out at this stage is that to describe such actions as 'constitutional conventions' is a huge misnomer; they were legislative actions, many of a type which had been familiar for decades, if not centuries; only the scale of intervention was novel. Constitutionally, the questions which arose were ones of bringing such legislation into line with common law notions of equity, natural justice, fair play or whatever other term one wishes to use for much the same thing.

Towards the end of *The Law and the Constitution*, Jennings declares that 'to say that a new policy is "unconstitutional" is merely to say that it is contrary to tradition'.[59] Now that is familiar wisecrackery of the sort which is our peculiar English heritage.

Even Austen Chamberlain permitted himself to remark that ' "unconstitutional" is a term applied in politics to the other fellow who does something that you do not like'.[60] But Jennings goes further. At times, in *The Law and the Constitution* he seems to be saying: '*The constitution is what the government has got into the habit of doing.*' He goes beyond the widespread British view that the Constitution is the word which describes the principal rules underlying the governance of these islands; when he talks about political changes and constitutional change, he appears to elide the two, so that there is no meaningful difference between the two: 'the notion of the functions of the State has changed, and the balance of the Constitution with it'.[61] What, as we have seen, he really appears to mean is that the balance of the relationship between private, individual or corporate activity and state activity has changed; but a change in that balance is entirely compatible with an utterly unchanged Constitution. President Roosevelt could have set up a Tennessee-Valley-style Authority in every state without altering the United States Constitution. All that Jennings is really saying is that, in his day, the state had assumed powers over our lives to a far greater extent than in the days of Dicey and Bagehot – which is a banal statement but a highly interesting one to find placed so centrally in a work on constitutional law, since it shows how far Jennings had come to think of constitutional theory as the measurement of power – 'Who's got clout?' – rather than the analysis of structure.

This is only a mutation of the Bagehot tradition. The 'efficient secret' of Bagehot's day has become the clout count of Jennings's. Because power seemed to have accumulated in these new bodies – the civil service, the TUC, the local authorities, even the BBC – anyone who wished to know the 'real constitution' of the 1930s ought, in Jennings's view, to look at the behaviour and composition of such bodies and at their links with government. Now a 'clout network' theory of this sort has lasted well into our own day, being crystallised in such works as Anthony Sampson's *Anatomy of Britain* and, more recently, Jeremy Paxman's *Who Really Runs Britain?* It is the staple of television documentaries and provides the underpinning to the conspiracy theories of the left. Alas, whatever its uses as an explanation of contemporary political facts, it is wholly disabling for anyone who wishes to examine constitutional structure.

The writings of Ivor Jennings are beguiling and scholarly. In his attacks on the wilder statements of Dicey which, until Jennings, had been regarded by the political world as authoritative, he was deadly. It is ironic that Jennings should have fallen victim to the same type of bad faith, although in a different cause from that for which Dicey was willing to deviate from scholarly impartiality. Under the terrifying threat of Irish Home Rule and the break-up of the UK which Dicey thought was bound to follow, he was willing to undermine his own doctrine of the sovereignty of Parliament. Jennings, in his benevolence towards the rise of corporatist collectivism, was eager to embrace each new bureaucracy as at least a probationary member of the constitutional club; the new Fabian institutions had to be embedded in the British way of life, and how better to embed them than to label them as fresh constitutional conventions – the latest evidence of the irrepressible vitality which enabled the British Constitution to renew itself in each generation?

Is a certain confusion between fundamental constitutional rules and ordinary pieces of legislation inevitable under an unwritten or at any rate uncollected constitution? Are Bagehot, Dicey and Jennings merely unwitting agents of an intellectual degeneration which was inbuilt? Or have they gently nudged us along the downward path, so that, if we understand either the spirit or the letter of our constitutional arrangements less well than our great-grandparents, they must bear at least some of the blame? It is difficult and perhaps unrewarding to disentangle cause and effect. All that needs saying is that they certainly have not helped and that our understanding of what a constitution is has certainly not improved since the days of Canning and probably not since the time of Cromwell.

The collectivist urgency is not quite as pronounced in Jennings's work as it is in the memorable notes appended by his LSE colleague, Professor Harold Laski, and by Ellen Wilkinson, the fiery MP for Jarrow, to the report of the Committee on Ministers' Powers of 1932 (the Donoughmore Committee). Here the completion of the government's programme is declared to be a pressing priority, to which the antique procedures of the House of Commons ought immediately to give way. The House should content itself with a Second Reading of a general Bill, with the details of the legislation farmed out to committees of experts.

In her note, Ellen Wilkinson[62] argued that the Committee should not have given the impression that delegated legislation was a necessary evil: 'I feel that in the conditions of the modern state, which not only has to undertake immense new social services, but which before long may be responsible for the greater part of the industrial and commercial activities of the country' – now *there* was a glint in the eye – 'the practice of Parliament delegating legislation and the power to make regulations, instead of being grudgingly conceded, ought be widely extended, and new ways devised to facilitate the process.' Laski was right behind her; delegated legislation was 'the only way to grapple with the functions now performed by modern governments'; the unwieldly and cumbrous Committee stages simply could not cope with the flood of legislation that a modern government – we are to presume either a socialist or Tory government, for form's sake, although the dream is essentially a socialist one – would be undertaking.

In *Reflections on the Constitution*, his final work (published posthumously in 1951), Laski repeated his loathing of the 'irresponsible' Hewart's 'notorious' pamphlet, *The New Despotism*, which he denounced as part of 'a dramatic rearguard action that has been fought for many years now against a phantom army of bureaucrats lusting for power which has never had any existence outside the imagination of those who warn us of impending doom and disaster'.[63] Delegation of powers to Ministers was both inescapable and desirable, and Laski would 'think it lamentable if the content of those powers were subject to judicial scrutiny'.[64] To allow administrative tribunals and the like to fall under the control of the judiciary would have the effect of making the judges what they had become in the US – effectively a third chamber of the legislature, something which was obnoxious to someone like Laski, who was 'a strong believer in a stable executive with sufficient authority to drive an important and substantial programme through the House of Commons in the lifetime of a Parliament of five years'.[65] For this reason, he was fiercely opposed to any innovation, such as Scottish devolution or Proportional Representation, which might hamper or weaken the driving force of government. Never was the doctrine of elective dictatorship more proudly trumpeted than in those post-war years. Elective dictatorship had won the war; it was bound to win the peace too.

Laski never abandoned the belief put forward nearly thirty years earlier in *The State in the New Social Order* that 'We have . . . to free the general legislative assembly from the task of intimate and incessant supervision.'[66] And it was with a certain glee that he reviewed the political dramas of 1931 in *The Crisis and the Constitution*: 'our Government has become an executive dictatorship tempered by the fear of Parliamentary revolt.' After all, 'the thesis of Parliamentary government is that the party which can command a majority in the House of Commons is entitled to govern in terms of its will'.[67] Rather than succumbing to Ramsay MacDonald's corruption by power, Labour 'will need the kind of religious enthusiasm for its ends which Russian Communism displays'.[68] This driving will, this religious enthusiasm was all that was required of Parliament, for the tendency 'has become inevitable to make Acts of Parliament a conveyance of general powers to Whitehall, the precise details of which will be filled in by order in Council or departmental regulation'.[69] And 'there is no need, as the purists do, either to regret the fact of this development, or to regard it as the outcome of a "conspiracy" by civil servants, greedy, like any bureaucracy, for an increase in power'.[70]

In the first days of the Socialists' return to power in France in 1981, something of the sort was actually tried, a general nationalisation Bill being brought before the National Assembly (leaving the nationalisation of individual industries to be dealt with by committees). The helter-skelter abruptness of this proposal would have been anathema, I imagine, to the sage and sceptical mind of Sir Ivor Jennings. And yet the view that government is an *enterprise* which must press on if it is effectively to encompass and manage every aspect of the nation's life was not wholly foreign to him. He and Laski were, after all, comrades in the driver's cab.

The proposals he offers in *Parliament Must be Reformed: A Programme for Democratic Government* (1941) are far less sweeping than Laski's; yet he shares Laski's overriding concern that the thrust and scope of government should not be inhibited by delay or complication, such as might follow from devolution or Proportional Representation. He piously affirms that the legislative process should not be skimped. And yet, time and again, he assumes that there need be no debate on the technical details which raised no political questions. The British administrative machine 'had produced a civil service whose quality can (for once) be truly described by the hackneyed phrase that it is the envy of the world; it has avoided that conflict between executive and legislature which is the base of most democratic systems'; so long as the details were left to its expert mercies, everything would continue to run smoothly.

Within Jennings's quizzical acceptance of the fluid, ever-changing practices of the British Constitution, we find something resembling a set of political views; within the flowing motions of the soft tissue, we come upon something harder, bonier. I am not concerned here with whether we think of Jennings as a social democrat, a Fabian or 'left of centre', as the *Dictionary of National Biography* describes him. What matters for our present purpose is to identify his view of the British Constitution, which has been an enormously influential one.

Jennings, like all constitutional writers, was a man of his time, and his time was a time of managerial government. The managerial imperative spread through all parties and movements; to think of the 1930s as the last gasp of laisser-faire is a travesty. Modern-minded men in all parties – Harold Macmillan, Harold Laski, Oswald Mosley – saw government in terms of what Michael Oakeshott would have called an 'enterprise association' – or 'Great Britain Ltd'. The Cabinet was the board of directors of a giant conglomerate business, or, if you preferred, the national executive of a huge general trade union comprising workers in all sorts of different industries in the same sense that today Mr Tony Benn tells us that 'a constitution is like an engine that requires steam to make it work – even the most perfectly designed engine will not move without it'.[71] Naturally, it had to operate within rules – articles of association, Companies Acts, Weights and Measures Acts – but it was essentially a purpose-driven association, an engine for moving people and things in a chosen direction, and its purposes and destinations could naturally expect to enjoy priority over private purposes and destinations.

By contrast, a 'civil association' is an association of persons who agree to subject themselves to a set of common rules and to a common government in order to pursue their own diverse purposes. Circumstances may, of course, intimate to them that they should join together in some common enterprise, to defend themselves against an external threat, such as war or famine; but these shared enterprises are not the prime purpose of the association.

The constitution of the civil association – that is, the set of agreed rules – has no purpose beyond that of keeping the association in being and enabling its members to pursue their own interests and aspirations unhampered as far as may be humanly possible. It is a building, a place to dwell in, and not an engine for going places.

Oakeshott's elegant and eloquent formulation of the dichotomy is an ideal model, and, as with many statements dividing the world into two classes, the two classes are neither mutually exhaustive nor exclusive, and are not really intended to be so. But it cannot help striking the observer that one of the great political changes of the past century has been the gradual transition from a civil-association to an enterprise-association view of government. This has not simply been a transition from laisser-faire to collectivism – a transition partially reversed in many countries over the past decade – it has also, in Britain at least, represented a change in the way we think of our Constitution.

The transition is a subtle and partly masked one. Looked at from a distance, so to speak, the process of evolution may seem to go on following the same lazy, meandering course. Only the fluidity permitted by its unwrittenness remains constant. And yet I think it is possible to trace a difference between our understanding of this fluidity as it was a century ago and as it is today. Then, constitutional change was regarded as an occasional and disagreeable necessity which had to be made the best of and which was best disguised and draped with the ivy of assumed antiquity as quickly as possible; if stability and finality were not in practice attainable, at least in the immediate future, it was possible to declare and to believe that they were both desirable and achievable. In certain respects, it was possible to demonstrate (perhaps by a somewhat doctored version of history) that they had been achieved for considerable periods in the past and therefore we had every prospect of achieving them again. Rule stability was a normal condition, as it is for most human civil associations. It is this very rule stability which permits many such associations – sporting and social clubs, professional and learned associations – to require two or three annual or special general meetings (and thus a couple of years or more) before confirming any such rule change.

Now that kind of procedural stateliness remains typical in written-constitution states too; rule stability in most such states remains the normal expectation. It may be that, in practice, administrative activity and bureaucratic regulation have intensified in those states too, as they have in Britain; the United States has been subject to a flood of regulation from the New Deal onwards. But this constitutional steadiness has, I would argue, at least impeded the advance of the enterprise-association conception of politics. Not everything is in flux, and therefore not everything is vulnerable to the driving will of the political sovereign.

This steadiness of the constitutional arrangements is all the more remarkable – perhaps all the more essential – in a nation so dedicated to mobility as the USA. The pursuit of happiness may be specified in its constitutional preamble, but the rest of the Constitution is designed to prevent politicians taking over control of the chase. When the driving will is nakedly on view, as it is in the Laski–Wilkinson programme, its pretensions are unmistakable, simultaneously threatening and comic in their disproportion to what most people actually want of their governments. The enterprise association may be more seriously alarming when it is modulated through the tempered ironic discourse of Sir Ivor

Jennings and of his Fabian successors. We are accustomed to the argument that the fluidity of our arrangements and the omnipotence of parliamentary sovereignty leave us open to a species of elective dictatorship; Jennings, too, deals with this danger and leaves us with no greater solace than his predecessors did. But what Jennings does not deal with, and could not, because he is himself part of the problem, is our vulnerability to a headlong enterprise-association view of politics which denies us any prospect of stable constitutional arrangements and undermines the worth and independence of our private purposes. Because our government can do anything that its Commons majority will let it do, we are drawn helplessly, without really knowing how to argue to the contrary, towards the proposition that the government is ultimately responsible for everything, that there are, so to speak, no occupations reserved from this particular national effort. Once the nation has made its claim on some aspect or sector of private life, to withdraw that aspect or sector back into private life is an arduous business for which those involved may have irreparably lost the theoretical and rhetorical equipment.

These assertions may seem exaggerated, even fanciful. But one has only to examine the long aftershadow left by the state's incursions during the Second World War to see something of what I mean. For nearly half a century, the wartime imperative of 'Dig for Victory' continued to impose upon farmers a whole host of national obligations, fainter but still irksome reverberations of the edicts which had compelled them to farm their land as the Ministry wanted, on pain of confiscation. More indirect, less intentional were the effects of the 1944 Education Act, which licensed, though it did not instruct, local authorities to provide schools for all their children and, in so doing, eventually destroyed the independence and pride of many if not the majority of maintained schools. The success of the enterprise-association view deprived farmers, parents and teachers of the principles on which to found a defence of their independence. It is true that many such Acts made provision for appeals against unjust acts of administration. There was even limited scope for 'opting out'; for example, the 'education otherwise' clause permitted parents with strong educational views to educate their children as they wished. But there was no opting out for a working-class parent who simply wanted a school that taught the traditional things and inculcated the traditional values and dismissed incompetent teachers in the traditional manner. There was no appeal against the principles underlying the system, because there was no overarching justiciable set of rights on which to base any such appeal.

Now you will not usually find such matters dealt with in Jennings or in the works of other constitutional lawyers; they are not considered germane; they go beyond the province of mere constitutional law (for constitutional lawyers like to avoid awkward questions by an affectation of humility).

But we can see quite easily that, in fact, such matters are germane, since they are often covered in conventions of human rights which form part of the constitutions of other countries. And a brief study of such conventions will show that they have a general import, beyond the protection of a list of specific human rights concerning the right to privacy, the right to belong to a trade union and so on. Such conventions habitually assert the existence of a private field of action, interest and right; this field, moreover, is not a small patch at the back, somewhat resembling the peasant's little private plot in a communist country. The private field includes the most significant, intimate and abiding aspects of human life. By comparison, government is, in Burke's words, a mere contrivance for satisfying human wants, and in its efforts must respect those rights.

The importance of such conventions, however clumsy or windy their phrasing, is not only, or not even primarily, that they protect this or that individual human right against overweening governments (they are often quite ineffective in that regard, since governments have usually inserted clauses defining critical exceptions to those rights). What they do achieve is to state the subordinate, secondary and instrumental role of governments. They support written constitutions in *putting government in its place* and thus help to restore the understanding of society as a civil association.

Like all devices, they are liable to misuse by zealots, who

immediately adopt the conventions themselves as new enterprise-association agendas and then set about turning all social and political conversation into the battleground of a human-rights crusade. But, outside the American campus and the committee rooms of the British Labour Party, this perversion of the human-rights convention is as yet a relatively minor nuisance. It is worth mentioning here only because Fabians are now foremost in the effort to embed the European Human Rights Convention into English law but, in many cases, for just this wrong reason: that they wish to launch a new enterprise programme rather than to restore the old space and freedom of civil assocation. All constitutions, whether written or unwritten, are vulnerable to overworking; any statement of right or duty, however carefully phrased, can be pressed to the letter of its phrasing and beyond by legal and political activists. But a constitution which is properly articulated and generally understood will suffer, at worst, surface damage from the campaigners' probes; the majesty of the US Constitution – with all the space and civil certainty it confers upon its citizens – is not much impaired by, for example, enthusiastic over-interpretation by campaigners for and against abortion on demand. Some of the celebrated constitutional conflicts of recent years – that between civil-rights campaigners and the states-right defenders of the South – provided useful exercise for the ancient principles involved. The rights of both the states and the individual voter were more clearly understood as a result of the argument. Similarly, the Charter 88 movement in Britain can only be beneficial in so far as it provokes judges and politicians to brush up and articulate the relevant aspects of both common and statute law.

But as we embark on this process of re-educating ourselves in our constitutional arrangements, as a prelude to determining how they might be strengthened and improved, it is important to appreciate how much we have forgotten. We come at the end of a long degeneration of constitutional thought; the thinning of the system itself has been accompanied by a coarsening of its analysis. The original idea of describing a magnificent structure, delicately yet powerfully stressed and balanced, has given way to a crude diagram of a simple electrical circuit in which the concept of resistance is scarcely recognised. By coincidence, it seems, the three most noted constitutional analysts represent each of the three main political tendencies – Bagehot the Liberal, Dicey the Unionist, Jennings the Fabian. Yet all of them are ultimately Whiggish in their obsession with power rather than principle, their interest in movement rather than structure.

For that reason, we shall find them unhelpful guides when we come to consider the principal problems of the present day, for these are predominantly problems of architectural relationship rather than the maximisation of power-flow; of installing or replacing checks and balances rather than of giving effect to the will of the people. In this task, we are more likely to find assistance from the subtle and reflective constitutional theorists of the eighteenth and even the seventeenth century, from Montesquieu and Madison rather than Bagehot and Dicey. 'Constitutional reform' does not mean to us what it did to our great-grandfathers. The problem is no longer how to express the popular will (that we have succeeded in, beyond the wildest hopes and direst fears of the nineteenth century); we are now in search of the old pluralism which was the admiration of foreign visitors two centuries ago. Having oversimplified, we need to recomplicate. The grand simplifiers have had their day and served their purpose.

It has, until recently, been quite difficult to break free of the climate of thought which bred this tendency to dynamic simplication; we have ourselves, often at best half-consciously, been prisoners of that climate. But, looking back now, we can perhaps begin to discern some of its prime elements and their malign interaction: the anxieties engendered by the competition in national greatness, the vulgar-Darwinian obsession with 'development' and hence the impatience with any notions of structural permanence, the Marxists' simplification of class warfare – all these tending together to concentrate the mind on Power.

This idea of Power had such an insistent, menacing unity. It was something to be possessed whole or not at all; not only a zero-sum game, but the only game in town, a game which, if lost, meant that everything was lost; all the ancient conceptions of pluralism, of hierarchy, of duties and rights as overlapping and mutual, the whole cat's cradle which had constituted our public universe from the Middle Ages onwards – all that vanished from our minds and our vocabulary for the best part of a century. Burke's repeated insistence on complexity, on modulation, on qualification, above all on *difficulty* seemed to be part of a dead language, quaint, antique, irrelevant.

These melancholy reflections belong in a proper history of ideas; they are published here only to suggest that there is nothing coincidental about the similarities of timbre and method to be observed between our constitutional authorities, despite their party-political differences. Nor is that undercurrent of stifled panic merely a coincidence of personal temperaments; Bagehot, Dicey and Jennings, in their very different ways, were all distinguished representatives of a ruling class which was terrified by the sights and sounds and smells of industrialisation; their acute sensitivities vibrated to the eruption of seismic social forces in the neighbourhood; they lost interest in the local architecture and were only counting the minutes until the fire brigade arrived. Such a mood, though understandable, is unsuitable for the framing or repairing of durable political arrangements.

A sketch of the old spirit

If our understanding of the British Constitution has been attenuated or atrophied over the past century, if its outline is now vulgarised or simplified in most people's minds, what ought that outline to look like? What are the general principles which ought to guide our understanding? It may be useful at this stage to offer a sketch of what was traditionally thought to be the spirit breathing through our constitutional arrangements. In describing a set of arrangements so notoriously fluid and imprecise, a sketch is all that can or should be attempted. Even to outline firmly anything which can be dignified by the name of structure is to invite attempts to subject its girders to stresses which they were not designed to withstand.

Indeed, the first principle is that no principle should be overstressed or pushed to its limits. It is precisely the royal absolutism of the Renaissance which, renewed and tranformed into parliamentary absolutism, has destroyed our capacity for constitutional thought by asking over and over again the same question, 'Who ultimately has the sovereign power?' and insisting on an answer. Serious constitutional thought recognises that this is by no means the only question that needs to be asked and that the answer to it may, in any case, be misleading. Suppose one returns the standard answer: 'In Britain, the House of Commons.' If then, instead of declaring the question closed, as Bagehot, Dicey and even Jennings do, one goes on to ask: 'So if the House of Commons passes a Bill to slay the first-born in every family and overrules the resistance of the House of Lords to that Bill, does that Bill then become the law of the land? Would the monarch be justified in refusing to give her or his assent?' We shall then be told that this is a silly question and that public opinion would not permit such a Bill and morality (or equity, or conscience, or the natural law) would justify wholehearted resistance to such a law. But these considerations seem to erode somewhat the idea of untrammelled parliamentary sovereignty; the efforts of Dicey to make a distinction between the 'legal sovereignty' of Parliament and the 'political sovereignty' of the people only make the question more confusing. Again, Jennings says that parliamentary sovereignty is so far-reaching that even the traditional wisecrack that 'Parliament can do anything, except make a man into a woman' is an understatement; if Parliament passes a law to that effect, then *for the purposes of the law* a man is a woman. But the only effect of using these absurd examples is to lay bare the absurd nature of the idea of absolute sovereignty.

It does not, in truth, take much expenditure of effort to knock the props from under the more grandiose definitions of parliamentary sovereignty. What we are soon left with is the more modest principle that Parliament is the supreme law-making body whose legislative acts override those of the courts or of subordinate legislations. But, we must add, Parliament would not be acting properly, in accordance with law, if it interfered with the judgments of the law courts, or with the administration of justice in other tribunals, or with public administration generally other than by impartial and agreed procedures. In other words, Parliament, like the king of old, is subject to law, even if means may not always be available to enforce that subjection (although the potential disobedience of those affected by some lawless action of Parliament does constitute a considerable deterrent).

Jennings argues that the importance of the separation of powers is much exaggerated. But the fact that the powers cannot be wholly separated from each other does not mean that *some* degree of separation is not vital. And this separation derives its vitality, not from the ingenious clauses of a constitutional blueprint, but from the idea of an overarching law which must govern the actions of every public official in the fashion appropriate to his profession. Lawyers must conform to the proper standards of court etiquette, civil servants must be impartial and honest, and so on. If it is the constitutional duty of all public servants to act as responsible moral agents under the law (which it is, the duty often being stated in their oath of office or terms of employment), then they and the institutions to which they belong cannot be merely servants of a single power. The idea of justice itself helps to separate the powers. Neither logic nor history supports Bagehot's ineffably complacent assertions that 'the interlaced character of human affairs requires a single determining energy' and that 'the excellence of the British Constitution is that it has achieved this unity; that in it the sovereign power is single, possible, and good'. It is precisely the interlaced character of human affairs which makes a single determining energy so dangerous to them.

Bagehot's sweeping dismissal of the notion of 'supposed' checks and balances in Chapter VII of *The English Constitution* is equally unsound. The fact that checks and balances may be partial, informal or self-imposed does not entail that they are trivial or ineffective. The Lower House may have the ultimate power to impose its will under most modern constitutions, but that does not mean that whatever powers of restraint or delay may be given to the Upper House cannot act as a powerful inhibitor.

If we turn to individual rights, as opposed to the machinery of government, we shall notice that British constitutional history in no way shies away from enshrining high declarations of human rights, from Magna Carta to the Bill of Rights. It may be seen by posterity as an historical accident that our most recent subscription to such declarations has been confined to international declarations. There is, in principle, nothing unBritish about the UN or European declarations; it may or may not be that certain modifications would be needed for them to be enacted into English law. But there is nothing new about refreshing our understanding of justice by enacting certain rights into law.

Nor again are ideas of devolutionary or federal bodies as utterly unfamiliar to us as Dicey liked to pretend. From feudal times, through the century of the two parliaments and the brief life of Grattan's Parliament in Ireland, down to the separate legal and ecclesiastical governments of Scotland and the great white Parliament building on Stormont Hill, we have experience of a huge variety of chartered, independent bodies exercising a huge degree of self-government. Such parliaments may and have been abolished; charters may be revoked; appeals may be made to the High Court from all these subordinate bodies. But to concentrate on their ultimate subordination, to the exclusion of the vastness of their independence, is itself a kind of myopic legalism. The unitary orthodoxy is a poor description of the actual working of such bodies.

What I call, in an archaic phrase which might have appealed to Hallam or Dicey, 'the old spirit of our constitution' thus has in it a great deal more than the recognition of the law-making supremacy of Parliament. It has that certainly, but it also recognises, as Holt and Halsbury and Radcliffe and Scarman have also recognised in their various times, that, rightly understood, our Constitution is infused with several other shared assumptions.

The first assumption is that all parts of our government are subject to the rule of law and that the idea of law is logically and historically prior to the idea of parliamentary supremacy. It is nearly half a century since R. T. E. Latham pointed out: 'When the purported sovereign is anyone but a single actual person, the designation of him must include the statement of rules for the ascertainment of his will, and these rules, since their observance is a condition of the validity of his legislation, are Rules of Law logically prior to him.'[72] The latest edition of *Halsbury's Laws of England* still quotes the view of Bracton, who died in 1268, that the king was subject to God and the law, because it was the law that made him king; Dearlove and Saunders speak with a certain relish of this as 'challenging the orthodox doctrine'.[73] Yet it is the traditional view and one which, despite the assaults of positivist lawyers for nearly a century, is hard to dismiss. The fact that Parliament has no rival for law-making supremacy does not in any way render it exempt from the rule of law. In its conduct in relation to other organs of government and to private citizens, the House of Commons is bound to observe just the same kind of restraints as private citizens are bound to observe in their dealings with one another.

How is it to be punished if it oversteps the mark? The answer to this dilemma has not really changed since Bracton's day: 'the right to restrain an erring king, a king who should be God's vicar, but behaves as a devil's vicar (*minister diaboli*), is rather a right of revolution, a right to defy a faithless lord and make war upon him, than a right that can be enforced in form of law'.[74] The fact that the law had no means of punishing the king or of compelling him to make redress in no way undermined the principle that the king was under the law. Maitland emphasises: 'that the king is below the law is a doctrine which even a royal justice' (Bracton was an assize judge in Devon) 'may fearlessly proclaim. The theory that in every state there must be some man or definite body of men above the law, some "sovereign" without duties and without rights, would have been rejected.'[75] Nor was this because medieval England had a sense of law which was in some way defective. On the contrary, one recognises, even at this early date, several familiar features: the English pride in the distinctive character of English law – Bracton relies, as Dicey was to rely six centuries later, on inadequate information about Abroad for his assertion that only England was ruled by unwritten law and custom and not by *leges scriptae*, as benighted foreigners were.[76] At the same time, there is a certain uneasiness about what to call this body of rules; both Glanvill, half a century earlier still, and Bracton make some apology for describing these unwritten customs as *leges*;[77] they were well aware that laws, right (*ius*) and custom (*consuetudo*) were not the same thing and needed to be clearly distinguished, but they were also insistent that it was a mixture of all these things which constituted the law of England and that this mixture was England's glory. A century of legal positivism has tried to persuade us that all this stuff is obsolete and that today it is the sovereignty of Parliament which alone needs to be reckoned with. The evidence of our own eyes makes it clear that this is a delusion. For even the supposedly almighty House of Commons is clearly bound by rules of conduct which it would regard as unlawful to breach.

This is implicit in the most 'orthodox' statements about the law of the constitution, for example, in O. Hood Phillips's *Constitutional and Administrative Law*:

> The laws of the British Constitution comprise three kinds of rules: statute law, common law and custom (especially parliamentary custom). To these we must add constitutional conventions if we are to understand modern development and the manner in which the constitution works. The sources of the legal rules are the same as for private law, namely statutes, judicial precedents, customs and books of authority.[78]

The fact that Parliament, being the rule-making body, has the power to change any of these rules does not undermine the fact that it is itself bound by those rules until it chooses to change them – again following the procedures laid down by the rules.

The second assumption is that the rule of law fortifies the traditional and highly desirable separation of powers between legislature, executive and judiciary. Each power in the land – the Crown and its Ministers, the law-makers in Parliament, the judges – enjoys a separate and distinct authority under the law. And the separation and distinctness reinforce our liberty, because no power can go very far in oppressing us without running into the equally potent authority of some other power. If an officer of the Crown jails us without good cause, a judge will let us out again; if a Minister brings forward an outrageous tax demand or an unjust

Bill, the House will fling it out. The existence of separate and distinct sources of legal authority provides checks and balances which are absent in those systems where unrestrained political power is concentrated in a single body, whether it be in a king or a dictator, or in a democratically elected parliament. Such has been the theory since the constitutional struggles of the seventeenth century, and long before.

For a century now, there has been a determined effort to destroy or, failing that, to minimise and marginalise the belief that our Constitution is founded on the separation of powers. The omnipotence-of-Parliament theory demanded no less. Few, I think, have gone quite as far as Dicey's assertion that the necessity of maintaining the so-called 'separation of powers' was 'one of two leading ideas alien to the conception of modern Englishmen' – the other was the idea of the special rights and privileges of the government as against the private citizen – on which the *droit administratif* of France rested (as everyone now agrees, Dicey's understanding of *droit administratif* was at best hazy). He even, quite superfluously, included the French translation (*séparation des pouvoirs*) in brackets, as though to keep before the reader's eye the foreignness of the thing.

The conventional wisdom became that Montesquieu had misunderstood the mechanism of our Constitution. O. Hood Phillips speaks of Montesquieu's 'imperfect understanding of the eighteenth-century English Constitution'.[79] The Donoughmore Committee on Ministers' Powers (1932) – a key text, since it offers a rare exposition of what the Great and the Good thought the Constitution consisted of – echoed the conventional wisdom in stating that Montesquieu's theory 'is a very incomplete and to some extent a misleading account of that mechanism . . . It was not so much the separation of powers which was a characteristic feature of the English Constitution as the fact that the machinery both of local and of central government consisted of officials and bodies possessing a larger measure of autonomy.'[80] It was by these means, the Committee thought, that we enjoyed what Blackstone called 'the true excellence of the English government, that all the parts of it form a mutual check upon each other, and that in this distinct and separate existence of the judicial power in a peculiar body of men nominated indeed, but not removable at pleasure, by the Crown, consists one main preservative of the public liberty'.[81]

But the Donoughmore Committee's argument surely concedes as much as it defends. It is precisely the spirit of separateness and autonomy which nourished independence of judgment and impartiality among public officials.

Similarly, Jennings asserts that 'we must not assume that a separation of powers in itself is the foundation of liberty, or, to put it in another way, that tyranny cannot exist where there is separation of powers. . . . It is democracy and not merely the separation of powers that keeps Britain free.'[82] This seems both devious and sentimental. Democracy – by which he means the universal franchise – is not by itself guaranteed to protect minority rights. Jennings seemed unable to sense the imminence of 'totalitarian democracies', such as Nazi Germany, which might indeed express the will of the people but which would have no hesitation in extinguishing liberty, predominantly by snuffing out or subverting every independent institution, first and foremost parliament and the judiciary. All historical experience suggests that separation of powers is indispensable to liberty.

And if Montesquieu was right about that, may he not also have been more or less right about the nature of our Constitution? After all, Montesquieu was probably the greatest political analyst and observer the French have ever produced (Tocqueville and Raymond Aron being his only rivals). He might have misinterpreted a nuance or two, but could he really have mistaken such a central principle? An acute and impartial observer, then or now, would surely incline to agree with Leo Amery's assessment in *Thoughts on the Constitution*, 'Montesquieu was not, in fact, so wide of the mark as is sometimes thought when he made the division and equipoise of powers in our Constitution its chief characteristic and the secret of its success.'[83] Nevil Johnson uses almost the same words in *In Search of the Constitution*.[84] What Montesquieu was setting out to do was to contrast 'the English give and take between independent and coequal political forces and the independence of our judges – the natural and logical consequence of our conception of the reign of law – with the rigid centralization of all power in the French Monarchy'.[85] That comparison holds good today between all parliamentary democracies and all totalitarian states. The fact that there may be contact between and overlapping membership of the three arms of government is infinitely less important than their understanding of their separateness.

Alas, even the most careful descriptions, for example, in Wade and Phillips's *Constitutional Law*,[86] sometimes fail to distinguish the trees because of the tangling of the branches. To take the most trivial sort of example, the fact that the Lord Chancellor, the head of the judiciary, presides over the House of Lords is no more significant than the fact that the Vice-President presides over the US Senate; similarly, the situation of the Attorney-General as legal adviser to the government in both countries is a relatively minor connection. The fact that Ministers sit in Parliament (as the Act of Settlement had intended that they should not) catches the eye. This undoubtedly institutionalises ministerial intimacy with and, most of the time, ensures ministerial control over Parliament. Yet we must not exaggerate the degree of fusion. Only one in six MPs has any direct connection with the government; up to 50 per cent of the House's membership have been sent there to oppose the government with every fibre of their being; even the government's own backbench lobby fodder frequently has to be cajoled or menaced into supporting it. As seen from inside the bureaucracy, Parliament is a hostile, incomprehensible and alien place. This attitude soon comes to infect Ministers as well as officials. For an exhausted government traversing a morass (for example, the Labour government in 1978–9), the separation of powers is not a constitutional shibboleth but a painful reality experienced daily.

Moreover, it is clear that, in the famous Chapter VI of Book XI of *L'Esprit des lois*, Montesquieu is setting out not to give the reader an exhaustive description of our arrangements but rather to enunciate the general principles which actuate the system. When he says, 'There is again no liberty if the Judical Power is not separated from the Legislative Power and from the Executive Power,' it is clear enough that, in Madison's brilliant gloss, he did not mean that these departments ought to have no *partial agency* in, or no *control* over, the acts of each other. His meaning, as his own words import, and still more conclusively as illustrated by the example in his eye (i.e. England), can amount to no more than this, that where the *whole* power of one department is exercised by the same hands which possess the *whole* power in another department, the fundamental principles of a free constitution are subverted. (*The Federalist* No. XLVII)

Now Jennings does quote these very words, but seems unwilling or unable to understand them, because he goes on to brush them aside as a near-truism about the incompatibility of liberty and dictatorship. But they are crucial to the British Constitution no less than to the Constitution of the United States – where the powers also overlap, since the Senate has the right to confirm or overrule the President's nomination of Justices of the Supreme Court and members of his Cabinet, where the President may veto legislation passed by Congress, Congress may ultimately overrule the President's veto and the Supreme Court may declare unconstitutional laws passed by the Congress and by state legislatures.

The separation of powers and the rule of law are mutually supportive principles. Without the rule of law, power-hungry rulers will not respect the independence of the courts. And it is the independence of the courts (and of all quasi-judicial bodies whose decisions impinge upon the daily lives of the citizens) that nourishes the rule of law by enabling every public official to do justice according to law, and not according to the dictates of the party or the material interests of his relatives. This central principle, of responsible agency, animates the whole system. Not merely is the judge master in his own court, but also the advocates too are officers of the court and have a duty to obey both the letter and the spirit of its rules. The civil servant is not the servant of the political head of his department; it is true that his daily duties are to carry out the orders of this temporary pilot, but this is only part of his duty to execute the law – which, for him, includes not only the relevant statutes and administrative orders but also the obligation to be faithful, true and honest. See Queen Elizabeth I's 'mission statement' to Sir William Cecil, quoted by Sir Robert Armstrong,[87] or indeed the oath prescribed by Sir Robert Peel for his constables and still learnt by heart on joining the force.

These requirements may seem obvious, even banal; they are seldom much referred to in works on the Constitution. But they are, of course, fundamental – as we implicitly acknowledge in examining the shortcomings of other countries. An observer from Britain, when visiting Ruritania or Azania, will ask: Are the judges here independent? Are the bureaucrats honest and impartial? Is there an effective opposition to the government? All of these questions are different ways of enquiring after the separation of powers – a concept which, to say the least, is far from alien to us.

The third assumption is that checks and balances are vital to good government even or especially where their enforcement can only be a matter of self-restraint.

The fourth is that declarations of individual rights are by no means alien to our tradition and may be entrenched by Acts of Parliament.

The fifth is that devolved or even federal-style institutions are by no means unknown to us and that their ultimate subordination to Parliament is only in the last resort a restraint on their independence.

It would be silly to move from Dicey's claim that federalism is utterly unknown to our constitution to the opposite extreme of claiming that, in reality, traditionally our constitutional arrangements have been soaked in the federal spirit. But what does need to be said is that there are plenty of examples of parliamentary, legal and ecclesiastical power being devolved to bodies which have become accustomed to exercise *de facto* independence. Theoretically, their subordination to Parliament may be unbroken; but they act as if their powers derived not from the Westminster Parliament but from the customs and traditions of their own people. Thus we are accustomed to the operation of such quasi-independent institutions.

It must also be said that the historical context of the classical arguments for maintaining strict unitary constitutions derive from the early-modern period of weak central government. Historical experience there did seem to suggest that federations provided weak government. But Dicey's constant repetition of this assertion was already beginning to look old-fashioned in his day.

The position now is very different. It is federations which seem, on the whole, to enjoy a massive, even somnolent tranquillity – while unitary states seem to be blown about. And our greater fear is of the overweening power of the centralised state apparatus. Dicey tended to confuse weakness with deliberateness. It may be, on occasion, that federations are slower to respond to some new challenge than a unitary government; the need for the American President or German Chancellor to carry with him the component states (or, in the comparable case of a country where Proportional Representation produces an almost permanently hung parliament, the other parties in a coalition) may delay him considerably in mustering his forces; but delay is not always a bad thing, and there is certainly little evidence to suggest that, once committed, federations are any more vacillating or unreliable than unitary states. From the economic point of view, as opposed to the military or diplomatic, it is the consistency and stability which federations appear to offer that is particularly attractive.

The sixth and final assumption is that the Constitution is or ought to be more than an ever changing series of collections of custom and practice; that it would not be sustainable if, in practice, certain of the above principles had not been tacitly accepted as common ground throughout the otherwise tumultuous changes of the centuries. There exists such a thing as *the* Constitution.

3

THE PRESENT STATE

The monarchy and its servants

There is a bizarre truncation in almost all modern writings on the British Constitution. In setting out to describe a constitutional monarchy, perhaps the most remarkable and venerable of its sort and one which, at a not far distant time, coloured one-fifth of the globe pink, they jump straight to the government in general, or, most often, to the office of Prime Minister and the functions of the Cabinet in particular. The ways in which the monarch may play or has until recently played a part in the operations of these pieces of machinery are mentioned only in passing. Very frequently these mentions are couched in impatient or dismissive tones, as though the commentator was eager to shrug off obsolete impedimenta. Except – revealingly – in works of strict constitutional law, such as the section on constitutional law in *Halsbury's Laws of England* or Wade and Phillips's *Constitutional Law*, there is little attempt made to set the governmental institutions within their overarching monarchical framework or to examine whether or not this overarching framework might have some practical implications for such matters as the rule of law, the separation of powers, the authority of the government and its servants, the assent of the governed, and so on. The neglect of such an ancient and durable institution is surely remarkable.

Nor are we much better off when we turn to that handful of books which do attempt to examine the monarchy in any sustained manner. The dazzle seems to deter or derail sustained thought. In no time at all, even those observers who regard themselves as serious analysts are unmanned by the pageantry; the hand waves at the window of the coach, the band strikes up, the Lord Lieutenant steps forward, and the supposedly hard-headed constitutional theorist is on his knees or shaking his fist, according to taste (sometimes, remarkably, both at the same time).

Bagehot was perhaps the inventor of the sly drool, managing to conjure up the flash and glitter while at the same time flattering his readers that they at least were not to be taken in by it. But he was also a Victorian man of business writing for other men of business. And this presented a lurking problem never quite to be solved. The 'efficient secret' of the Constitution – that is, the omnipotence of Parliament – left the monarch herself functionless; the institution was a splendid, if somewhat gimcrack show, designed, quite successfully, to maintain the awe of the lower orders. It would not, of course, do to rely upon the personal qualities of the monarch; he or she was all too likely to be debauched or feeble-minded. Still, a long-reigning, sensible sort of king or queen might yet attain a degree of sagacity which it would be a pity to waste; idleness was, after all, a sin, and one could not wholly approve of an institution which condemned its First Person, who was to be the visible embodiment of the unity, history and greatness of the nation, to a life of enervating idleness. Bagehot, therefore, *invented a career* for British monarchs. They were to spend their time, if at all equipped for the task, in acquiring statecraft, in order that they might be able to exercise their rights, which were, as every schoolboy knows, 'the right to be consulted, the right to encourage, the right to warn'.

All royal biographers, all newspaper leader-writers and virtually all constitutional writers who have bothered to devote a page or two to the monarchy have followed Bagehot's formula, either tamely repeating it as gospel or rewriting it in their own words.

What is more, even now in the 1990s, the relations between the monarch and the Prime Minister of the day have, in the most peculiar way, become frozen in a pattern which is designed to permit the monarch to give the appearance of exercising those rights. The Tuesday evening audiences, in which the Prime Minister gives the Queen a digest of the political problems and events of the moment, have become obligatory, not to be cancelled except for the absence abroad of either party. There is also the Prime Minister's annual 'holiday' at Balmoral and the overnight 'dine and sleep' visits to Windsor; even these visits, which are, in fact, mostly a matter of picnics and party games, are sometimes mentioned as being part of an intimate 'working relationship'. Both Buckingham Palace and Number Ten Downing Street regard themselves as honour bound to depict these encounters as intellectually arduous and politically significant; 'woe betide the Prime Minister or Minister who is ill briefed; the Queen's huge experience of public affairs far outstrips that of any jumped-up politician; her memory is generally agreed to be formidable,' and so on.

But what sort of a working relationship is it? I do not mean, 'What are the tone and timbre of the meetings?' (they are often stiff and awkward, especially in the case of Mrs Thatcher, who regarded the overnight visits as largely a waste of time and the weekly audiences as not much better, although demanding her usual thorough preparation). What exactly is the sub-text which Bagehot has so successfully imprinted on our minds? Is not there something as fraudulent about it as the fraudulence which he diagnoses in the public pageantry? The Queen is indeed consulted, she may indeed utter encouraging words; on occasion, she may let fall, no doubt in carefully phrased and oblique terms, a warning, or at least a comparison with some previous political imbroglio of the kind Bagehot suggests:

> The king could say: 'Have you referred to the transactions which happened during such and such an administration, I think about fourteen years ago? They afford an instructive example of the bad results which are sure to attend the policy which you propose. You did not at that time take so prominent a part in public life as you now do, and it is possible you do not fully remember all the events.'[1]

But there is little evidence that the Prime Minister of the day, whatever his or her party allegiance, takes the slightest notice of the royal advice, except perhaps on matters directly affecting the Queen herself (for example, Mr Benn's unsuccessful battle royal as Postmaster-General to remove the Queen's head from the new designs for postage stamps[2]). The monarch is, by all the evidence of the twentieth century and most of the nineteenth too, in the position of a marriage guidance counsellor who must be visited in order to comply with some court ruling but whose words are totally unheeded by the unhappy couple.

Far from providing a substantial working role for the monarch, it is plain that these conversations are much more of a charade than the Trooping of the Colour or the Opening of Parliament (historical re-enactments which are as poetically purposeful as the celebration of Holy Communion). Why should Bagehot make so much of them, particularly as, in general, his man-of-the-worldliness would incline him to sweep away any such pretence? Is it the case perhaps that he is ready to concede what he knows perfectly well to be a futile set of rights, in order to ward off the threat of a more substantial and serious role which might be claimed for the monarch? In an extremely significant phrase, Bagehot says that 'it is during the continuance of a ministry, rather than at its creation, that the functions of the sovereign will mainly interest most persons, and that most people will think them to be of the gravest importance. I own I am myself of that opinion.'[3] Bagehot is thus keen to direct our attention to the day-to-day business of governing – precisely the sphere in which the monarch has little or no role to play. By contrast, he treats in somewhat peremptory fashion the extreme situations in which the Queen's role and responsibility are undoubted: a request for a dissolution of Parliament, or the choice of a new Prime Minister in case of death, illness or resignation, or a request to flood the House of Lords with new peers. One cannot help suspecting that he wishes to disguise the reality of the monarch's real role – the guardianship of the Constitution – by playing up her 'dignified' role of encouraging, warning and being consulted. And one can only further deduce that Bagehot does this to minimise any sense that the monarch retains some residual power to nibble at the sovereignty of Parliament and so to blight the political glory of his age.

Yet it is in these extreme situations that the Queen (or, for that matter, the Governor-General in a Dominion or the President in a republic) is clearly visible as the guardian of the Constitution. It is in such moments that her Coronation Oath – to govern according to law (the Oath harps obsessively on this duty, using the word 'law' or 'laws' half-a-dozen times) – is put to its most crucial test. As for many other public officials, the test is not simply one of courage and honesty, though it is certainly that; it is also a test of sagacity and discernment. Many intelligent men of goodwill might differ and did differ over whether George V should have agreed to create sufficient peers to pass the Parliament Bill of 1910; or whether he should have granted Ramsay MacDonald a dissolution in 1924; or whether he should have insisted on the formation of a National Government in 1931; or whether Queen Elizabeth II should have accepted Harold Macmillan's advice on the choice of his successor. Even if the rules in these matters were clearer than they are, situations will still occur in which the duty of the guardian of the Constitution – royal or non-royal, anointed or elected – remains deeply problematic. Sir John Kerr's dismissal of Mr Gough Whitlam in Australia is one such recent example; President Hillery's dilemma in 1982, after the collapse of the FitzGerald government, whether to call on Mr Haughey to form a government or to dissolve the Dail, is another; President Carstens' dilemma in 1982 – when he faced a governing party that had decided to engineer the dissolution of the Bundestag – was perhaps the most ticklish of the lot (see below p. 176–7). But nobody doubts in such situations that what the Queen or the President is trying to do would be correctly described as 'upholding the law'. The fact that unforeseen situations do not necessarily offer any pat rule of conduct does not mean that the search for the correct legal response is in any way non-legal. Nor is there anything arbitrary about the principles which will guide the head of state and her advisers in such circumstances – principles such as that the customs of the Constitution must be respected, that the Queen's government must be carried on, that the will of the electorate must not be thwarted, that the first necessity is to find a Prime Minister who can form a government that will command the support of a majority of the House of Commons. These are basic principles of constitutional law.

Nor is the difficulty dodged or solved by removing the power to dissolve from the royal prerogative and granting it to some other public official, such as the Speaker of the House of Commons (as recommended by Mr Frank Vibert of the IEA among others). For the Speaker, too, would come across situations in which the law was unclear or in which the various options all appeared to have their disadvantages. He would also work under the added embarrassment of being regarded as *parti pris*, having at one time been a colleague or an opponent of the principal actors. Kerr was a passionate opponent of Whitlam, Hillery an old comrade-in-arms of Haughey – hence the repercussions nine years later, when the attempt by Mr Brian Lenihan to be elected President after Mr Hillery's retirement was scuppered by allegations that he had telephoned Hillery on Haughey's behalf, pleading for Fianna Fail to be allowed to form a government rather than face an election – which, ironically, Fianna Fail was to win anyway.

And even if we were to discover and install some beautiful mechanical arrangements for dissolving Parliament and electing a fresh House of Commons – not as easy as it sounds in a system where the government must be sustained by a majority in the Commons and majorities may melt without warning; even then, the ultimate guardianship which rests with the head of state leaves potential questions at the extremes. Some duties do fall away as political life evolves; now that the Conservative Party – along with Labour and the Liberal Democrats – has elaborate machinery for electing its leader, the delicate consultations in which the Palace had to engage in order to discover which candidate was most likely to command the full support of his party do seem as remote as the 'enstoolment of an African chieftain', to which the whole business was once compared. But there is no guarantee that other equally taxing tasks will not emerge. Who, for example, would have thought that the unlikely figure of Sir John Kerr, as Governor-General, would have to consider whether or not to dismiss Mr Whitlam for what seemed to many (but not all) a violation of the Australian Constitution? Darker clouds than that have lowered over constitutional heads of state in almost every European country since the First World War. Who is to say that a British head of state would never have comparable dilemmas to face?

If he is presented with legislation which runs so contrary to justice that it is incompatible with his oath of office, what is his legal duty? Is he, for example, to approve the Acts of a quisling government installed by an invader? Is he to sign Acts legalising the deportation or murder of minorities? Is he to sign away his country's independence? And so on. The monarch's duty to uphold the law might present him or her with other questions too, less inescapably moral, more complex, yet not easily to be dodged. Mr Geoffrey Marshall enquires:

> can it be concluded that the power to refuse assent to legislation is now a dead letter? Under present constitutional arrangements, it may well be so. But . . . suppose, for example, that a Bill of Rights were to be introduced and protected against repeal by a special legislative procedure requiring a specified majority in one or both Houses. . . . If such provisions were introduced and subsequently disregarded by a government that believed them to be ineffective and did not wish to be bound by them, it might be that the Queen would have to consider whether such a government's advice to assent to legislation should be refused if the legislation had not been submitted to the previously prescribed procedure.[4]

It is fairly clear that, if such legislation failed to carry the Speaker's certificate, the monarch would be under no obligation to assent to it. But if a compliant Speaker had certificated important legislation – such as the repeal of a Bill of Rights – legislation which had not passed through the set of hoops in place at the time, then the Queen would have an extremely good case for saying that to give assent to such legislation would be contrary to her Coronation Oath and that she would not assent until the correct procedures had been followed. The fact that such contingencies may never come the way of any particular monarch does not mean that his guardianship is an empty thing; the guardian's profession is, as Bagehot said of bankers, 'a watchful rather than a busy trade'. But encouraging, warning and being consulted are not a monarch's real work; at best, they are preparation against the eventuality of real work.

The fact that the Queen is not an elected President and that Britain is not a written-constitution state does not really alter this fundamental role of guardianship, except to make it easier to misunderstand. And this misunderstanding is worth clearing up if we are to see the genuine questions which arise out of the way we are governed and which have been, rather incontinently, associated with the antiquity of the British monarchy and the veneration associated with it.

It is said, for example, that, because the British are subjects rather than citizens, they cannot fully enjoy the charter of individual rights and hence the sense of self-worth and independence that citizens of republics enjoy almost automatically. We breathe a stuffier air; our lack of enterprise is not in ourselves but in our constitutional arrangements. If we saw ourselves as citizens, we would enter into social contracts and sign up to charters of individual rights with a sense of entering into our destiny. Both our personal relationships and our economic efforts would be infused with a fresh sense of freedom if the monarchy loomed less large in our national life and our formal constitutional arrangements. Some members of this school of thought are explicitly republican; others merely want to see a diluted and recessive monarchy of the sort which they imagine operates in Scandinavia or the Low Countries.

The first difficulty with this argument is that, historically, 'free-born Englishmen', to use the refrain in E. P. Thompson's *The Making of the Working Class*, have seldom regarded the monarchy as an obstacle to the enjoyment of their immemorial rights. On the contrary, at varying times they have looked to the monarch to restore or enforce those rights which they fondly fancied had always been there; at other times, it is true, the monarchy was profoundly unpopular, and radical agitators, often covert or overt republicans, would be seen by many as the leaders who would give them back their rights. The point is that the traditional conception of these rights sees them as existing separately from the monarchy and indeed from other institutions, *including Parliament*; the

Englishman's rights formed part of the law which the sovereign was just as solemnly bound to uphold as anyone else.

Nor, as we have seen, does the English constitutional tradition recoil from spelling out these rights in statutes and charters which were intended as a permanent record and entrenchment of them: the Magna Carta of John, the Magna Carta of Edward I, the Petition of Right, the Bill of Rights, the Act of Settlement, and so on. No doubt any or all the clauses in these documents could be altered or improved on by subsequent legislation. The Act of Settlement's provisions excluding Ministers from Parliament were almost instantly overturned. But the intention of permanence was indisputably there.

Thus the monarchy has never until now been regarded as inhibiting the proclamation and entrenchment of individual rights. Nor, by the same token, does the sovereign's role in the dissolution of Parliaments in any way inhibit alterations in the rules for dissolution. The trend of legislation over recent centuries and the demands for further legislation have mostly been in the direction of automaticity – removing from monarchs or, more recently, from Prime Ministers, their discretionary powers over the summoning, non-summoning or dissolving of Parliament. Parliaments fixed for a certain period of years are not a novel demand, would in no way be unconstitutional and would no doubt be welcomed by the monarchy as largely, though not wholly, freeing it of an occasional delicate task in which it can rarely hope to satisfy all parties.

At this stage in the argument, all that needs to be made clear is that none of these proposed reforms in any way undermines or alters the position of the monarchy, which, for its part, offers no obstacle to any such reforms. And it is only Bagehot's wilful misunderstanding of the role of the monarchy and the reluctance of modern constitutional writers to examine that role which per-petuates the view that the modern monarchy presents any hindrance, except to those who are dead set on abolishing it altogether.

Rather than the monarchy throwing up a neglected problem to the constitutional reformer, it is only its neglect that presents the delusory aspect of a problem. As soon as it is even briefly considered, the monarchy is clearly revealed as no kind of threat to most plausible proposals for reform. Far from creating difficulties, say, for the entrenchment of a charter of individual rights, English and British sovereigns have been signing their assent to comparable charters for seven centuries. Nor does the monarchy present any sort of inhibition to installing more stable and predictable machinery for calling elections or for changing Parliaments or ministries. On the contrary, it is the present system which, on occasion, presents the monarch with tricky decisions, often without much in the way of precedent to guide him or her.

By the same token, the deferential-subject complaint seems equally threadbare. In times when the monarchy enjoyed substantial real political power, Englishmen, and later Britons, never regarded themselves – nor were they regarded by foreigners – as subservient and lacking in independence or assertiveness. Conservative and old-fashioned liberals might argue that, if their fellow citizens (not they themselves – this is one of those accusations that is seldom self-addressed) had become less independent and self-reliant in recent years, that was due to the excessive growth of the state in general and the welfare state in particular. But, leaving aside this argument, we can, I think, scarcely accuse the monarchy of having strengthened its hold on our deference in recent years. Popular attitudes – as chronicled by Tom Nairn in *The Enchanted Glass* (1988)[5] – are ambiguous, not to say two-faced: on the one hand, the slavish adulation of the tabloids presumably satisfies its customers; on the other, we see a harsh intrusiveness and a willingness not to mince words when a member of the royal family misbehaves. Deference does not seem quite the word to cover all this; it seems more like a hunger for enchantment in a disenchanted world, or at any rate like something which mere political reform is unlikely to be able to remedy.

Some political reformers seem to grasp at the failings of the monarchy as a scapegoat for their own dissatisfactions, without being able to define exactly what is wrong. A similar, allied scapegoat is the complaint that the British have no conception of the state. But, if the Crown is fully comprehended rather than relegated to a footnote about the modest remaining scope of the royal prerogative, then a reasonably clear notion of the British state emerges. Nor is the status of the servants of the Crown at all difficult to define. In *Whitehall*, Mr Peter Hennessy is rather inclined to mock as 'mere antiquarianism' the then Sir Robert Armstrong's remark that:

> I'm not sure that the underlying requirements of the civil servant have changed really in four hundred years. . . . When Queen Elizabeth I appointed Sir William Cecil to be her Secretary of State in 1558 she said: 'This judgement I have of you that you will not be corrupted by any manner of gift and you will be faithful to the State, and that without respect of my private will, you will give me the counsel you think best.' I think that summed it up pretty well. I think that is what we still expect of our Civil Service and I think that's what we still get out of it.[6]

But, on the whole, this does seem a perfectly adequate definition of what is required. Nor is there anything especially scandalous or puzzling about Sir Robert's statement in his note on the duties and responsibilities of officials that 'Civil servants are servants of the Crown. For all practical purposes, the Crown in this context means and is represented by the Government of the day. . . . The Civil Service as such has no constitutional personality or responsibility separate from the duly elected government of the day.'[7]

Civil servants are in the position of members of a ship's crew required to obey the orders of a pilot who has been seconded to them in order to negotiate the tricky shallows of which he is supposed to possess expert knowledge. They may have sailed these waters before themselves and so have their own ideas about the right course. But their duty is to carry out the instructions of the pilot, despite the fact that it is not he who employs, promotes or dismisses them and that his command is only a temporary one.

There are no doubt plenty of other real-world analogies to the situation of the civil servant. All that needs to be said here is that it is only by ignoring the monarchy as an insignificant cipher that any sort of mystery about the status of the Civil Service can be generated. As soon as we keep in our minds a reasonably clear image of the Crown, not only as a symbol of national tradition and continuity but also as the embodiment of the state, many so-called puzzles melt away.

In thinking about the Civil Service or the armed forces, one should never let slip from one's mind the image of the crown on epaulette or cap badge and the royal cipher on the black briefcase. These are insignia betokening a concrete reality and not mere sentimental memorabilia. The allegiance which is owed is a matter of the head as well as of the heart; and to understand the practical as well as the emotional implications of that allegiance is to dispel a great deal of the mystery which has surrounded modern discussion of the Civil Service. Less mystery has enveloped the military, where the hierarchy of allegiance, from commanding officer to regiment to Crown, is too unmissable, and the words of the Queen's Commission are too resonant to be drowned out by the din of modern bureaucracy. But in principle there is little different about the way the civilian members of the public service are recruited, managed and disciplined. Anyone who has seen the Civil Service from the inside cannot help noticing the genuine deference which the high-flying young Principal shows towards the Permanent Secretary of his Department who has the power over his recruitment, pay, discipline and promotion. By comparison, there is something mechanical about his effusive politeness towards his Minister, a mere bird of passage, a temporary pilot to be dropped at the whim of Prime Minister or electorate. If confronted with a question of conscience, it is his Permanent Secretary and not his Minister that he is expected to consult; if the matter needs to be taken higher, he or his Permanent Secretary will consult either the Head of the Home Civil Service or the Cabinet Secretary (sometimes the same person), not the Prime Minister, who may not even be informed about the whole business. For example, in the case of Clive Ponting, it was generally agreed that, rather than leaking or going public with what he considered to be the discreditable conduct of his Minister, Mr Michael Heseltine, he should have taken his anxieties to his Permanent Secretary and rested content with the advice given him by that dignitary.

Ever since the time of the Northcote–Trevelyan reforms in the middle of the last century, the young Principal in the Administrative class has faced much the same prospect: he is selected in his early twenties by arduous competitive examination, encouraged to think of himself as a Platonic guardian of the public weal, recruited to a department which is, so to speak, his regiment, from which he may be lent or seconded but rarely transferred and in which he may work until retirement. All of this was entirely intended by Sir Charles Trevelyan – the original of Sir Gregory Hardlines in Trollope's *The Three Clerks* ('We always call him Sir Gregory in the family,' Hannah Trevelyan told Trollope – an echo of the 1980s, when permanent secretaries endured being called Sir Humphrey by their more skittish Ministers and then themselves hurried home to catch *Yes Minister*). Trevelyan openly proclaimed the ambition of 'recruiting the flower of our youth to the aid of the public service' and did indeed succeed in recruiting them on the promise that they would be:

> an efficient body of permanent officers, occupying a position duly subordinate to that of the Ministers who are directly responsible to the Crown and to Parliament yet possessing sufficient independence, character, ability and experience to be able to advise, assist, and to some extent influence those who are from time to time set over them.[8]

From the start, their permanence, their brainpower and their detachment combined to separate them from the grubby pilots who clambered on board 'from time to time' to navigate the ship of state's passage through the treacherous waters. It was their duty to carry out the pilot's commands (and, unobtrusively, 'to some extent influence' him), but he had no power over them. He could and can at best politely enquire of the Head of the Civil Service whether it might be possible to transfer a Permanent Secretary with whom he has no rapport; over the hiring and firing of lesser officials, even his own private secretaries, he has little more influence. It is scarcely surprising that the average Minister takes only a spasmodic interest in the management of his Department so long as his immediate helpers provide him with enough effective ammunition to repel the assaults of the Opposition in Parliament – to most civil servants an uncongenial place, full of loudmouthed and frequently drunken ignoramuses who understand little and care less about the intricacies of administration.

We shall come to examine later the notorious problems which this separateness of the Queen's servants poses for efficient government. At this stage, what needs to be emphasised is the fact of the separateness. Ian Bancroft, Robert Armstrong's predecessor as Head of the Home Civil Service, asserted that 'the Service belongs neither to politicians nor to officials but to the Crown and to the nation'.[9] Peter Hennessy argues that there is a distinct difference of emphasis between this and Armstrong's interpretation of 'servants of the Crown'. Yet the two statements are surely answers to slightly different questions. Bancroft is pointing out that the Civil Service has continuing traditions and duties, both practical and ethical, which are independent of the commands of its political masters; Armstrong is answering the question whether, 'for all practical purposes', the Civil Service is a separate power in the Constitution, which it is not. The matter is put quite clearly in the Civil Service's own Code:

> Civil servants owe their allegiance to the Crown. In its executive capacity, the authority of the Crown is exercised through the Government of the day. Civil servants are therefore required to discharge loyally the duties assigned to them by the Government of the day, of whatever political persuasion.

Hennessy quotes this and calls it 'a ringing, high Victorian "Statement of Intent" '.[10] But it is the characteristic code of the civil service in any modern democracy. Such codes crystallise the moral obligations arising out of the civil servant's allegiance to Crown or state in almost every civilised nation. It is important to understand that these codes need not be imposed by Act of parliament; very often, as in Britain, they have been elaborated within the civil service over the years.

Hennessy, like most observers of the British Civil Service, is deeply impressed by its honesty: 'I have always found these anti-corruption statutes and rules utterly admirable and one of *the* greatest virtues of the British Civil Service.'[11] But the statutes, such as the Public Bodies Corrupt Practices Act and the Prevention of Corruption Acts, merely make it a little easier to prosecute wrongdoers who could have been prosecuted anyway since time immemorial for dishonesty under the common law. It is the code of behaviour which enforces such rigorously high standards and that code derives from common law tradition and draws its special rigour from the disciplinary powers which the heads of the Service exercise in the name of the Crown. The Civil Service is a self-recruiting, self-selecting, self-perpetuating, self-disciplining corps which regards loyalty to the Crown in its capacity as the embodiment of the nation as a great deal more than a mere shibboleth.

Having got this much straight – and many books on the Civil Service have little hope of doing so, since they virtually refuse to consider the implications of allegiance at all – we are then confronted by a peculiar and most unexpected puzzle. The role of the Civil Service and its relation to the monarchy have been well understood by civil servants for at least the past century, even if constitutional theorists and political journalists have not bothered to think about them much. Similarly, British monarchs and their close advisers, at least since the death of Queen Victoria, have had a clear understanding of what their duties are and what they are not; they have, on the whole, maintained an almost inhuman discretion and have intervened only on those occasions in which constitutional tradition expected them to intervene, such as a change of Prime Minister; nor have they objected when those occasions for intervention were whittled away, for example, by the tendency of modern political parties to introduce systems for electing their leaders.

Yet just at the very moment when this understanding seemed to have been thoroughly entrenched, so that no monarch would have dreamed of trying to interfere as Queen Victoria tried and few modern permanent secretaries would have tried to overdirect policy as Sir Robert Morant did at Education in Balfour's day, or as Hankey did in the Cabinet Office, we suddenly experience a remarkable change in the public posture and attitudes of the royal family.

Within the space of a single month or so (April–May 1990), we had the Princess Royal lamenting the shortage of services for the under-fives and urging central government and local authorities to match the level of facilities provided on the Continent. Before that, we had Prince Philip deriding the environmental ignorance of 'the cloistered precincts of the schools of monetary economists' and telling them to wake up to the need to switch to renewable sources of energy, to recycle waste and to control pollution, because 'things have changed since Adam Smith'.

Then came the Prince of Wales's warning about the plight of the poorer pensioners – 'there is a very real risk that the less fortunate will be left behind'. All elderly people, he said, must have the means to lead comfortable lives in affordable accommodation. In response to this, *The Times* suggested that the Prince should himself lead a civilian version of Dad's Army. And who, one imagines the Treasury asking wearily, is to pay for the civilian equivalent of their wooden rifles?

Any or all of these suggestions might have been highly desirable, but they all had implications for public expenditure. And if the total cost of implementing them all immediately were added together, the bill might not fall far short of the bills for the manifesto of some free-spending political party. There is certainly plenty of panache about the way royalty charges into any and every topic these days. What were once regarded as strict constitutional inhibitions on telling the government what to do are flung to the winds. Political sensibilities are cheerfully trampled on. As always when risks are taken, the quality of the outcome tends to be mixed. The Princess Royal sometimes grates, despite her tremendous work for Save the Children. Prince Philip has scored an exhilarating mixture of bull's-eyes and magpies. Prince Charles's speech in Hungary was one of the finest diatribes against communism heard in years.

But the really remarkable thing is that nobody – nobody at all, whether on the constitutionalist right or the socialist left – seems to have felt like uttering a peep of protest. The sort of royal opinion which only ten or twenty years ago would have had the media clucking about a constitutional crisis is now taken for granted as a natural element in public debate.

Since Prince Charles joined the revolt against the dreary brutalism of modern architecture with his notorious 'monstrous carbuncle' speech to the Royal Institute of British Architects (30 May 1984), members of the royal family must have delivered more spirited and incisive speeches on a greater variety of subjects than the two front benches in the House of Commons put together. The fact that the Queen herself has seldom if ever said anything controversial, certainly not in public, protects the formal impartiality of the monarchy. Nonetheless, it is the monarchy's authority which sheds its aura on the lightest utterance of 'a royal' and makes him or her a formidable opponent for a body of mere commoners.

What is remarkable is that the attention and argument that all these royal utterances have provoked has rarely invoked the constitutional role of the monarchy. That role tends to be brought into the argument only when the *politicians* are alleged to be interfering improperly – for example, in Mrs Thatcher's reported refusal to allow the Queen to pay a visit to the European Parliament. Would anyone have expected in 1945 that, nearly half a century later, the royal family would be playing a far more prominent part in public affairs than George V or George VI and their families would have dreamed of essaying? In retrospect, one is tempted to think, the age from the death of Queen Victoria to the mid-1980s may come to be seen as the age of reticent royalty, and historically the exception rather than the rule.

I do not think it is the royal advisers who have changed. Sir William Heseltine and Sir John Riddell (private secretaries to the Queen and Prince Charles respectively during most of the period under consideration) were as circumspect as Lord Adeane and Sir Alan Lascelles were in their day. It seems to be the rules of the game which have imperceptibly shifted. Why should this be so?

True, self-expression has become a general article of faith. Virtually everyone now seems to be in a position to answer back. There are no Silent Services any more. Lord Mackay has allowed judges to give interviews. Civil servants give copious and increasingly frank evidence in public to Select Committees. And the growing candour of civil servants in public does present something of a parallel to the growing candour of royal personages. Why should royal personages alone be excluded from the cult of personality?

But there is surely more to it than the understandable wish not to be a heavily censored figurehead all one's life. There now seems to be a positive expectation that the royal family will give a lead, not just by the example of their lives of service, but by their ideas and opinions.

The rights that Bagehot allowed the sovereign – to be consulted, to encourage, to warn – were, he took it for granted, to be exercised in private conversation with her Ministers. Under the new tacit dispensation, the same rights appear to be exercised in public, by the sovereign's family if not by herself, yet gilded and reinforced by the authority of the monarchy.

Is it possible that this leadership role has evolved, at least partly, as a result of the decline of the magic of Parliament, of a certain consequent loss of Parliament's authority and hence of a lessening of the awe and reverence it enjoys? What Jonathan Clark has called 'the Grand Whig Myth of the Mother of Parliaments' is certainly not quite what it was. In Scotland and Northern Ireland today, it is allegiance to the Crown rather than to the Westminster Parliament which is the dominant generator of loyalty to the Union. To many Scots and Ulstermen, our parliamentary arrangements seem remote, imperfect and neglectful of their interests.

Since Mr Major succeeded Mrs Thatcher, the Conservative Party has become noticeably less unpopular with Scottish voters, but after a decade of unalloyed power in the UK as a whole, it remains emphatically consigned to second or third place in Scotland and is still thought of as the English party. No such accusation could be levelled against Queen Elizabeth I of Scotland.

Obviously, developments at the European level seem unlikely to alter this relative decline of Parliament; it is less obvious but equally likely that they will improve the relative standing and liberty of action enjoyed by the British monarchy. Sceptics about the

Community adduce the protection of the monarchy as one of their arguments against surrender to federalism. Mrs Thatcher, for example, at one time asked for assurances that 'European union', whatever else it was to mean, would not mean endangering the British monarchy. But that is the least likely outcome. On the contrary, the more that day-to-day powers are spread between London, Brussels and local and regional authorities, the less inhibition there would be on the British (or any other) monarchy taking as energetic an interest in public affairs as King Juan Carlos already does in Spain. It was the jealous insistence on the exclusivity and omnicompetence of parliamentary sovereignty that silenced the British monarchy.

The roots of that insistence lay, I think, in the fragility of the parliamentary achievement, or at any rate in the perception of its fragility. It was only after centuries that the three kingdoms were welded into one – the fourth kingdom remained a thorny, bloody problem throughout the heyday of parliamentary omnipotence; it was only after a period of extreme anxiety, not to say near-panic, among the ruling classes that the industrial proletariat was absorbed into the political process. All this achievement seemed to rest upon the progressive twin enlargements – of the right to vote and of the powers of the elected House. Any rival tendency had to be suppressed, forcibly if need be, if the new form of parliamentary democracy was to endure; the Crown, the House of Lords, the judiciary – none of them was neutered without a struggle. Queen Victoria's diaries and letters reveal a non-stop guerrilla campaign against the removal of the powers – her indignation, bemusement and flagrant bias bearing no relation at all to Bagehot's sanitised sketch of the modern monarchy. The House of Lords fought every time: in 1832, in 1910 and even, it is often forgotten, in 1949. In earlier times, the judges, too, put up a decent fight. In Sir Ian Gilmour's words, 'Only at the onset of the collectivist era did the great judicial flight begin, the Courts leaving the field just when their presence was most necessary.'[12]

In the end, the need for parliamentary supremacy was accepted as the only plausible answer to the grumbling discontents of class and nation. But now a new era is upon us, in which the old dangers no longer seem so relevant and pressing.

We have long become accustomed to our troops serving under the supreme command of an American general. Now our interest rates skip at a nod from the chairman of the German Bundesbank; our beaches have to be cleaned up on the say-so of an Italian Euro-Commissioner. In such a world, it might seem an artificial anachronism to maintain a complete constitutional gag on our own royal family.

The old logic argued – as Mr Enoch Powell still argues – that our survival as a nation depended on Parliament being not merely the ultimate but the sole arbiter of our affairs.

This *concentration* of sovereignty is now less taken for granted. Even those who do not go as far as Lord Hailsham once went in denouncing the dangers of 'elective dictatorship' have become a little uneasy. There may be no consensus yet about how parliamentary sovereignty should be qualified or constrained, but the concept has lost its moral supremacy and no longer has the power to silence argument which it enjoyed until very recently. And it follows that, as soon as we recognise, however cautiously, that a wider distribution of power and influence is likely to strengthen rather than weaken democracy, it begins to appear unreasonable that the monarchy should be excluded from all day-to-day influence over the direction of our society. No doubt the more influence that princes and princesses attempt to exert, the sooner they will run up against the boundaries of propriety and the feeling that hereditary office-holders should not tell elected members what to do. But these are the problems of expansion, not of contraction. An outside observer would, I think, come to the conclusion that, on the evidence of the last decade, it is Parliament, not the monarchy, which needs to think the more urgently about the best means of securing a significant future for itself.

The Cabinet

If the monarchy and its servants have received scant attention from students of the Constitution in recent decades, the Prime Minister and the Cabinet have received too much. Indeed, Sir Ivor Jennings and Professor John Mackintosh wrote as if nothing else really mattered. Since the war, constitutional discussion has often been dominated by the question whether Cabinet government is gradually giving way to prime-ministerial or presidential government. Dick Crossman was prominent in this argument, bobbing up now on one side, now on the other, often depending on the treatment he had himself recently received from Attlee or Harold Wilson. More painstaking scholars have been diligent in collecting instances of occasions on which the Prime Minister has been frustrated or overruled by his or her Cabinet, as against other occasions on which the Prime Minister has bypassed or ridden roughshod over the views of Cabinet colleagues.

It is not surprising that what goes on behind the doors of the Cabinet Room should be so fascinating; it is, after all, the centre of power, its proceedings are secret and the rules by which it operates are a matter of evolving custom and can nowhere be consulted in unchallengeably authoritative form. As far as statute law goes, the Prime Minister and the Cabinet are mentioned only in what might be called 'housekeeping' statutes, to do with pension rights on retirement and the upkeep of Chequers. Neither the individual office nor the body is defined or established by law. This elusive, mysterious quality combines with the pungent, unmistakable fumes of real power to produce a heady mixture. It is the purpose of this chapter to calm the fevered senses and restore – by admittedly drastic means – some sense of proportion to our understanding of the roles of the Cabinet and the Prime Minister and their interplay at the heart of government.

The most drastic of the means here developed will be to allot neither subject any more space than has been allotted to the monarchy and will later on be given to other branches of the Constitution. This is not to suggest that these latter institutions are remotely to be compared with the Prime Minister and the Cabinet in terms of the power that they exert or ought to exert. It is rather to dispel the exaggerated mystery which naturally thickens around the Cabinet Room and, in dispelling the mystery, to reduce to relatively small dimensions the problematic or worrying aspects of the operations of the central executive. We shall have more to say and more to worry about when we come to consider the individual Ministry and more again on the subject of Parliament.

The simplest route – but one rarely taken – is to compare the operations of the British Prime Minister and Cabinet, first with those of Prime Ministers and Cabinets in other Western countries, and then, perhaps more tellingly, with the central executives of other bodies in this country – industrial and commercial corporations, professional and learned institutions, societies of all sorts, trade unions, and so on. This might seem an obvious first approach for anyone wishing to draw out the distinguishing features of the British Cabinet or indeed of Cabinets in Western democracies as a whole as compared with methods of organising the central executive in other centuries and systems. Yet even in works devoted to Comparative Government, such as S. E. Finer's work of that title, this is only done in passing; the modern political scientist seems absorbed with power to such an extent that the tussles between Parliament and executive or between the Prime Minister and his or her Cabinet tend to overshadow any attempt to isolate the characteristic features of the Cabinet system. Let us then make the attempt, in rough, summary form – the rougher and more summary the better if we are to make the point clearly.

First then, Cabinets meet *in private* – a less contentious and misleading phrase than 'secret'. Their proceedings are confidential. In modern times, a record is kept by a permanent official (Gladstone wrote his own minutes). These minutes may be published at a later date, usually much later (the present rule is thirty years later); or their main conclusions may be released at the end of the meeting; or one or more of the participants may choose to leak part of what went on. But it is a matter for the Cabinet and its members to decide what, if anything, may be published. No outsider has anything resembling a right to know.

Now there is nothing exceptional about this type of executive confidentiality; it is typical not only of all Western Cabinets, but of most of the executive committees of the other bodies mentioned above – governing bodies of corporations, colleges, trade unions and so on. There are very few such bodies which regard themselves as normally under an obligation to throw their proceedings open to the public or even to the rank and file of their membership. Such privacy is regarded as essential if the discussions are to be candid and unconstrained and if oneness of corporate personality is to be attained – an essential goal if the body's decisions are to carry authority and to be implemented effectively.

This privacy seems odd or questionable only if we compare or confuse such executive committees with deliberative and legislative assemblies, such as parliaments, in which open, public debate is of the essence. It is generally accepted that any attempt to open Cabinet debates to the public would merely result in serious decisions being further removed into inner secret cabals. This is not a theoretical danger. It actually happens in local authorities; if the full council and also its committees are held in public, then serious decisions are likely to be taken back into private meetings of the ruling party. Local councils are, in fact, an uneasy mixture of Cabinet and Parliament, the uneasiness of which is minimised only by the fact that so many of the decisions to be taken are relatively non-controversial or do not divide the parties.

Secondly, for similar reasons Cabinets and corporations all insist on *solidarity* – or collective responsibility as it is called in the case of the British Cabinet. Dissenting members must agree to be bound by the will of the majority and to defend the body's decisions, or at any rate not to be seen to oppose them in public too openly. Many types of corporation – for example, a large public company – will insist on loyalty to collective decisions even more fiercely than the Cabinet does. Constitutional historians are much interested in the rare instances in which an 'agreement to differ' has been allowed. Prime Ministers have twice in this century agreed to such public disagreement, both times in cases when the Cabinet might otherwise have broken up – over tariffs in the 1930s and over the Common Market in the 1970s – and for short periods only, after which the Cabinet would be and was expected to resume collective responsibility for the settled policy.

In 1932, after the general election of the preceding year had returned the National Government with its overwhelming majority, a Cabinet committee proposed a general tariff. Four members of the Cabinet disagreed and proposed to resign. The Prime Minister, Ramsay MacDonald, pleaded that their resignation would make his position 'embarrassing and humiliating'. After some wrangling, a 'modification of usual Ministerial practice' was announced, allowing dissenting Ministers on the subject of import duties to express their views by speech and vote. Neither House cared for this departure from normal solidarity, but it was rammed through by the Whips. However, the real lesson of this exception to the general rule comes through in the sequel: a few months later, the government pursued the general protectionist drift of its policy, not with a general tariff on all imports but with tariffs on imports from outside the Empire. The four free-trading Ministers then did resign, thus demonstrating that they could hold no permanent place in a Cabinet with a policy on a major issue which they so fiercely opposed. Neither Jennings nor Mackintosh[13] seems really to take the point that solidarity is not simply a tradition peculiar to the British Cabinet and therefore liable to equally peculiar exceptions but rather a quality intrinsic to an effective executive.

The second modern example of 'an agreement to differ', that of Harold Wilson's Cabinet in the run-up to the 1975 referendum on Britain's membership of the European Community, only re-inforces the point. The Cabinet and the Labour Party were in embarrassing disarray after the 'renegotiations' of the terms on which Britain had gone in. The referendum was a device to dispel the poison and settle the question, but, to do so effectively, the anti-Marketeers had to be given no pretext to claim that they had been muzzled and their case not properly put to the people. Thus Wilson gave the anti-Marketeers licence to speak their minds in the referendum campaign but not in parliamentary proceedings and official business.[14] This sometimes led to ludicrous episodes, such as the diehard anti-Marketeer Peter Shore's explanation that 'when I am speaking from the Dispatch Box of course I reflect the Government's policy as a whole – except when I am clearly reflecting my own policy'.[15] But here, too, the essential point is that the agreement to differ was extremely short-lived – between 20 March and 5 June, in fact. Wilson made it plain that Cabinet solidarity was re-established on 6 June, the moment that the result was declared[16] and policy settled. Once again, the exception proved the rule, namely that Cabinet solidarity, like Cabinet confidentiality, is not some sinister relic of the pre-democratic age; it is the *sine qua non* of an effective executive body.

The third characteristic feature of Cabinets is that the Prime Minister or chairman is *primus inter pares*. By virtue of his control over the organisation of the executive body, this somewhat misunderstood description is not outdated, as Crossman, Mackintosh and others have argued (perhaps the Latin gives it an antique veneer). A little thought will show that it was and still is a reasonably exact description of the relationship. The Prime Minister or chairman is a member of the board; he does not stand outside the board, nor does he employ his fellow members; like them, he is a servant of the Crown or the company or the college. He does not have the power formally to issue orders to his fellow members; their instructions or permissions are issued by the board as a whole.

Enormous powers are available to him but only if he has the will or the understanding or the support from his fellow members to use those powers effectively. Characteristically, those powers may include: control over the agenda of board meetings, distribution of portfolios, a dominant say in the recruitment and retirement of other board members, control over the establishment and membership of sub-committees and over the business allotted to them. These powers combined together add up to a tremendous leverage, but they are not of the same kind as the straightforward powers exercised by, say, the manager of a football club over his players or the editor of a newspaper over his staff. Even in cases where the decisions do, in fact, flow more or less directly from the will of the Prime Minister, they must be cloaked in collective decency. Thus the most naked example of prime-ministerial power – the reshuffle – is not only carried out in consultation with trusted senior colleagues, the Chief Whip, the Leader of the House, perhaps one or two others; it also has to be presented as 'a reconstruction of the government', that is to say, a collective exercise. The difficulty of sacking a single Minister – for example, in the case of Westland –

springs not simply from the political desirability of not appearing vindictive but also from the collective nature of the leadership body. Gladstone actually doubted whether a Prime Minister had any right to dismiss a Minister at all.

In one or two countries, such as the Netherlands, where coalition government is the rule rather than the exception, ministerial dismissals remain rare, since the government has been created only by a laboriously negotiated agreement between its constituent parties, and therefore the Prime Minister risks un-stitching the whole agreement by attempting to get rid of another Minister, even one of his own party, since the original allocation of portfolios has had to be acceptable to all parties.

The fourth characteristic feature is that there is no hard-and-fast rule about what decisions must be approved by Cabinet and what may be settled by individual Ministers singly or after consulting other Ministers relevant to the decision. Nor is there any hard-and-fast rule about the manner in which approval is sought. Nor is there any hard-and-fast rule about the organisation of sub-committees and the nature of the business which is brought before them.

One or two examples will demonstrate this point clearly enough. The examples we shall produce here should not be taken to establish their own pattern of custom as to what must go and what need not go to Cabinet and how far Cabinet Ministers or the Prime Minister may disregard or dispense with Cabinet approval. A different set of examples might suggest a different pattern. My point is simply that there is no pattern; the only limit on the behaviour of the Prime Minister and individual Ministers is *political tolerance*, that is, what the Cabinet as a whole will put up with. And even then, the consequences of overstretching that tolerance may be quite long delayed; it could be argued, for example, that Mrs Thatcher's eventual downfall was due to her habitual disregard of her Ministers' sensibilities, her reluctance to bring tricky issues before Cabinet or official Cabinet committees, and her habit of getting rid of Ministers who regularly opposed or at any rate did not enthusiastically support her policies.

Yet, against that, it should be pointed out that to survive in office for eleven and a half years represents a modern record; it was often argued in the 1960s and 1970s that the pressures on a modern Prime Minister were so exhausting that five or six years in power was the most that even the most robust leader could expect. Moreover, even if the rate of resignation or dismissal of Ministers under Mrs Thatcher was somewhat higher than under her immediate pre-decessors, it was the sheer length of her survival in office which was principally responsible for the large number of the disgraced and disappointed Conservative backbenchers. Anno Domini, pure and simple, was her principal opponent. In any case, it has been said of almost all long-surviving Prime Ministers in this century that they have degraded public life to an unprecedented extent – Asquith, Lloyd George, Baldwin, Macmillan, Wilson. In all ministries, there have been complaints of the Prime Minister's high-handed and underhand manipulation of Cabinet business on the lines set out in Mr Heseltine's resignation statement, in which he spoke of 'the emergence of what I consider to be the breakdown of constitutional government'.[17] His immediate complaint was that a ministerial meeting, scheduled for 13 December 1985, had been cancelled at Mrs Thatcher's behest because she feared that the meeting's conclusion might be sympathetic to Mr Heseltine's case.

Mr Hugo Young comments that 'in a system which allowed so much business to be conducted at the informal whim of the chief minister, one man's meeting could quite easily, and even honestly, become another woman's meeting-that-never-was'.[18] This ver-dict, while allowing, fairly enough, for the possibility of a genuine misunderstanding, implies that, under another, more rational system of government, no such misunderstanding could have arisen. One can only say that no such rational system seems as yet to have been invented, on this planet at least. The calling or non-calling of meetings, together with the inclusion or omission of items on the agenda, remains an important instrument of power (in my view, an indispensable weapon for the effective dispatch of business) for chief ministers, as for chief executives of all sorts. While it is in the nature of any board that its members must have the right and the duty to place important matters before the board, it is equally the chairman's right and duty so to arrange business that it is economically conducted and brought to effective conclusions. I am sorry to belabour such obvious points, but they must be clearly set down if we are to avoid the illusions of what might be called 'executive idealism' – the notion that the management of an enterprise can be governed by strict and unvarying rules of the sort indispensable for the scrutiny of legislation or the conduct of a court of law. The examples to which we shall now at last proceed will make this point, rather more vividly.

On 1 August 1914, Churchill, certain that Germany intended to attack France and to violate Belgian neutrality, asked the Cabinet to authorise full naval mobilisation. The Cabinet, still deeply divided on British intervention in Europe, refused and, when Grey asked for a decision as to whether Britain would eventually send an expeditionary force to France, decided firmly against that too. Nothing could be clearer.

After a solitary dinner at the Admiralty that night, Churchill was sitting down to a game of cards with F. E. Smith and Max Aitken when he received a message that Germany had declared war on Russia. He instantly went over to Number Ten to inform Asquith that, despite the Cabinet's earlier refusal, he wished to issue an immediate order for full naval mobilisation. Grey, Haldane and Crewe were already with the Prime Minister, that is, a senior quorum of the Cabinet; Churchill promised them that he would answer for the decision at Cabinet the following morning.

> The Prime Minister simply sat and looked at me and said no word. No doubt he felt himself bound by the morning's decision of the Cabinet. I certainly however sustained the impression that he would not put out a finger to stop me. I then walked back to the Admiralty across the Parade Ground and gave the order. Legal authority was not obtained until the Sunday. . . . However all the Reserves came up immediately with hardly one hundred exceptions, in spite of there being no Royal Proclamation. . . . The actual fact which is of interest for the future is that the mobilization was actually ordered against Cabinet decision and without legal authority.[19]

One might add that the decision was, in practical political terms, irrevocable; the Cabinet could not, without appalling humiliation, countermand it; nor could a policy of non-intervention have been coherently pursued, once the Fleet had been mobilised. So it could be argued that the single day-to-day decision which did most to bring Britain into the Great War was taken not merely in advance of but in defiance of Cabinet decision.

It is standard practice that the Cabinet does not decide on the Chancellor's Budget; it does not, strictly speaking, even debate its contents; it is simply informed of what is in the Budget a few days before the Chancellor addresses the House of Commons. The average period used to be four or five days; in 1933, it was twelve days and, in 1936, twenty-one days, in both cases because of the Easter recess. Sir Ivor Jennings takes very much on the chin this remarkable exclusion of the Cabinet from the most central element in economic management; the Budget statement, he says, 'occupies a peculiar position'.[20] More recently, the fear of Budget leaks has shortened the advance notice given to the Cabinet, to the barest minimum; Ministers are now told of the contents only on the morning of the Budget statement (after the Queen, who entertains the Chancellor to dinner the night before). The fear of the leak and of the consequent profiteering in the markets are only the convenient pretext. The prime reason is to prevent effective Cabinet intervention. Lord Kimberley claimed that the practice of laying Budget proposals before the Cabinet so late that there was practically no opportunity to discuss them began when Gladstone was Chancellor of the Exchequer under Palmerston. They were always quarrelling, and Gladstone kept his Budgets back to the last moment, in order to prevent Palmerston from getting the Cabinet to object to them.[21]

Modern Chancellors have to pay attention to the economic (usually highly politicised) instincts of their Prime Ministers; Harold Macmillan got rid of both Peter Thorneycroft and Selwyn Lloyd because their financial policies were too prudent and restrictive for his liking; Thorneycroft was overruled on a matter of public expenditure and was therefore forced into resignation – Macmillan's notorious 'little local difficulty'; Selwyn Lloyd was sacked in July 1962 – the equally notorious 'Night of the Long Knives' – on the grounds that he was tired and had lost his grip, but the underlying reason was his failure to respond to Macmillan's repeated urgings in favour of slacker budgetary policies. The modern Chancellor needs to pay little attention to the general economic views of other members of the Cabinet (although the Chief Secretary to the Treasury will be locked in constant negotiation with them on matters of public expenditure affecting their departments). The first that Mr Peter Walker, then Minister of Agriculture, heard of the abolition of exchange controls (one of the most important developments in Britain's economic policy since the war) was when he heard it on the radio.

The most dramatic recent example of the unimportance of the Cabinet in economic strategy was Sir Geoffrey Howe's 1981 Budget Statement which imposed an even more stringent squeeze on the economy at a time when unemployment was already at its highest level since the war. Jim Prior, like several other 'wets', was beside himself with anxiety and rage; 'I couldn't say anything bad enough about it'; he thought Howe's refusal to do anything for industry 'criminal folly', and so on. On the morning of the Budget Cabinet, having had an informal preview of the details, he had breakfast with Walker and Gilmour, but breakfast was as far as the rebellion went.[22] In Cabinet, Carrington, Pym and Whitelaw said they weren't terribly pleased, but all of them reasoned, like Prior, that they would do better to carry on fighting within, rather than 'sacrificing myself unnecessarily'. Resignation – in practice, the only weapon open on grounds of opposition to the Budget – is a rare thing; one could, in fact, say that the only recent example of resignation is one by the Chancellor himself, Peter Thorneycroft; the leaking of the Budget's contents has led to more resignations (J. H. Thomas in 1936, Dalton in 1947) than the actual nature of those contents. And it is this iron secrecy which ensures the impotence of the Cabinet in budgetary matters.

In early April 1986, President Reagan informed Mrs Thatcher that after another terrorist atrocity, this time in Berlin, he had decided to hit back against Libya. The attack would go ahead in any case, but its targeting would be more precise if F-111 bombers based in Britain could be deployed. As it happened, Mrs Thatcher was already on record as opposing a raid of this sort which, she thought, might produce 'much greater chaos' than terrorism itself: 'once you start to go across borders, then I do not see an end to it. I uphold international law very strongly.' Before acquiescing, therefore, she sought bolstering from Attorney-General Havers, who congenially agreed that a raid on Libya might be covered by Article 51 of the UN Charter, which permitted military action for the purpose of self-defence.[23] Mrs Thatcher then decided to approve British co-operation in concert with three senior Ministers, the Foreign Secretary Sir Geoffrey Howe, the Defence Secretary George Younger and Willie Whitelaw. None of them liked the idea – Howe and Younger had already publicly opposed retaliation of this sort – but they went along with Mrs Thatcher's passionate belief that the UK must be more than a fair-weather friend.[24] The Cabinet was not informed of Reagan's request until the actual night of the bombing; both the Overseas and Defence Committee and the full Cabinet were overwhelmingly hostile to unqualified support of the Americans; the general view of the Cabinet was that, if it was too late to refuse Reagan's request, Britain should distance itself from the Americans' position and should make it clear that any further request for use of the bases for such a purpose would be intolerable. Mrs Thatcher, in the first instance at any rate (later, two days after the raid, she was prepared to be more circumspect), refused to pay any attention to the Cabinet's views; not a single word could be said against the bombing, the Americans were right and their actions were both legal and legitimate. Thus even the modest, largely retrospective protest of the Cabinet was swept aside by the Prime Minister in what she saw as the wider long-term interests of the Western Alliance.

We have seen then that decisions which are delicate, embarrassing or challenging are often kept away from Cabinet, at least until they have crystallised and reached a stage when there is little or no possibility of countermanding them; such decisions may relate to foreign policy or to economic or, perhaps less often, to social policy. These decisions may effectively be taken by a small group of Ministers, whether meeting informally, as an *ad hoc* committee, or as a formal Cabinet committee; or they may be taken by the Prime Minister or by the Chancellor of the Exchequer acting alone, or by the two of them in consultation. The reasons for these practices are that cabinet is too large, too unwieldy; it can meet only once or twice a week for a couple of hours; its membership must to some extent reflect the broad coalition of views which makes up the governing party; even the most harmonious Cabinet is unlikely to be cohesive enough to operate as the thrusting leading edge of a difficult radical strategy.

But what about long-term strategy? It is often argued that, while Cabinets may have to be kept in the dark about this or that ticklish decision during a crisis, they are well suited to the more leisurely pace of strategic decision-making. J. Harvey and L. Bather, for example, in *The British Constitution and Politics,* adduce as the last and perhaps most significant function of the Cabinet that:

> *it formulates plans for the future*: since the state has a continuous existence, plans have to be laid now for anything up to fifty years ahead. Thus measures have to be taken to provide for future changes in the population before the end of the century, to develop atomic energy in co-ordination with other industries providing power, to plan new methods of defence, and to apply scientific advance to production.

True, they concede that 'it must be admitted that, to some extent, long-term planning is made more difficult by the Cabinet's being composed of frequently changing party politicians'. But, relatively undaunted, they carry on to the conclusion: 'Thus the Cabinet is the real policy-forming body in the British Constitution. It provides the dynamic impulses to progressive government or, as Professor H. Laski puts it, "the Cabinet pushes a stream of tendency through affairs". '[25]

Here at last is a heroic role for the Cabinet. Deprived of access to the exciting midnight-crisis decisions, it may at least see itself as the long-term pilot, the look-out commanding far horizons, the planner whose decisions will be felt by generations yet unborn.

Alas, here too expectations are doomed to be somewhat deflated. Let us content ourself with two important examples: the development of nuclear weapons, and the long-term planning of public expenditure. In neither sphere can the Cabinet be said to have had much of a look-in, nor to have distinguished itself when consulted.

Throughout the Second World War, Churchill excluded most members of his Cabinet from discussion about atomic weapons, or indeed from knowledge of their existence, and this tradition has continued little diminished to the present day. Attlee launched Britain's independent programme of atomic research without the knowledge of most of his Cabinet, let alone of Parliament and public. The Cabinet sub-committee GEN 75 approved the construction of an atomic pile to produce plutonium as early as December 1945. It was regarded as an 'of course' decision that Britain had to have a bomb, in Bevin's words, with 'a bloody Union Jack on top of it'. The formal decision to construct one was taken in another special committee, GEN 163 in January 1947. Why was it necessary to set up a second committee to cover much the same ground? Peter Hennessy[26] suggests that the answer can be found in the differing composition of the two committees. GEN 163 was GEN 75 minus Dalton, the Chancellor of the Exchequer, and Cripps, President of the Board of Trade. At a meeting of GEN 75 on 25 October 1946, both men had resisted, on the ground that the economy could not afford it, a proposal to spend £30 million or £40 million over four or five years to build a gaseous diffusion plant to produce uranium 235; they could have been expected, *a fortiori*, to resist a much more ambitious proposal to build a British bomb. Thus they had to be excluded if the larger project was to go through on the nod, as Attlee wished.

No mention of either project is to be found in the agenda of either the full Cabinet or its Defence Committee. Parliament was not informed until 12 May 1948 – and then only as a parenthesis in a low-key parliamentary answer ('all types of modern weapons, including atomic weapons, are being developed') and, as Hennessy points out, not for reasons of open government, but because excessive secrecy was delaying progress, since it was difficult for those engaged in various parts of the bomb project to know how urgent it was when the secret of the project's nature had been kept so successfully. Attlee himself said later of his Ministers that he thought 'some of them were not fit to be trusted with secrets of that kind'.

The next decision in the development of nuclear weapons policy – whether to proceed to the second generation of nuclear weapons with the manufacture of a British hydrogen bomb – was taken through the Cabinet procedure, with three meetings of the full Cabinet after exhaustive discussion in committee. But before jumping to the conclusion that we should therefore admire Churchill's constitutional propriety and deplore Attlee's impropriety, we should notice the differences: the country was now much better off, the scale of expenditure contemplated was proportionately much lighter and the likelihood of dissent on this question in a Conservative Cabinet was much less. Churchill knew he could afford to take the decision through Cabinet in a way that Attlee could not. Even so, the decision was not announced publicly until the Defence White Paper six months later in February 1953.

By contrast, in 1962 the cancellation of Skybolt and its replacement by Polaris had to be conducted largely in public because it involved protracted and difficult negotiations with the Americans. It was thus neither practicable nor desirable to keep the Cabinet out of it. Macmillan was punctilious in bearing reports across the Atlantic to his colleagues in the Cabinet Room. He had no alternative.

The next stage, the upgrading of the Polaris warhead system which was to become known as the Chevaline programme, seems to have had its seeds in research done at the Atomic Weapons Research Establishment at Aldermaston in the late 1960s into what could be done to compensate for the Wilson government's decision not to buy the Poseidon warhead. In 1973, the Conservative government authorised Aldermaston to move Chevaline into its development stage, but the most costly decision was to move on to actual production. That decision fell to the incoming Labour government after the first general election of 1974. It was taken by a group of five Ministers and was not communicated to the full Cabinet until six months later, after the second general election, in which Labour's manifesto had disowned 'any intention of moving towards a new generation of nuclear weapons'. Wilson tried to slip the Chevaline decision through Cabinet by describing it as 'certain improvements at a cost of £24 millions';[27] and, after a few mild protests from Michael Foot and Barbara Castle, the Cabinet swallowed it. The total cost eventually worked out at over £1000 million – a figure given to the Commons by Francis Pym in January 1980. Healey, who as Chancellor of the Exchequer had been one of the five taking the original decision, later repeatedly blamed himself for not investigating the project more seriously.[28]

When we come to the most recent major decision in the field – whether to buy Trident or to switch over to a lower-cost system based on cruise missiles – we find that the decision straddled the last years of the Callaghan government and the first year of the Thatcher government and that both governments treated the matter through the usual, highly secret group of four or five senior Ministers. In the case of Labour, this was undoubtedly prudent from the political point of view, since one of the four, David Owen, the Foreign Secretary, was fervently anti-Trident and pro-cruise, and any public hint of the disagreement would have left Labour even more vulnerable than usual to the perennial taunt that the party was weak-willed, muddled and divided on the defence issue. Within the Conservative government too, there was some discreet anxiety as to whether the country could afford to move on to the next and even more expensive generation of nuclear weapons systems – or even needed to. Authoritative figures, such as Lord Zuckerman and Lord Carver, were already saying it did not. If the Conservatives were to retain their superior authority on nuclear deterrent policy, an unbroken front was essential.

Thus it is clear from the whole post-war history of nuclear weapons policy that Prime Ministers have felt impelled to submit the issue to the full Cabinet, let alone to the public, only on the rare occasions when they felt that discussion would be totally harmless, usually because in essence the decision had already been taken. The idea that the Cabinet was the proper body 'to plan new methods of defence, and to apply scientific advance to production' would have provoked at best a grim and sceptical smile from any Prime Minister who has had to deal with the matter.

Let us turn to the civilian front and that central government task, the planning of public expenditure. It is true that, in recent years, it has become the practice towards the end of the session, in, say, mid-July, for the Chancellor of the Exchequer to submit to the Cabinet a paper on public expenditure for the next two or three years. But the purpose of this paper is not to provoke an exchange of views on the sort of totals that would be desirable or the proportion of GNP that ought to be consumed by the public sector. The purpose is to *tie down* Ministers in the spending departments to the Chancellor's preferred totals, so that, when detailed negotiations begin with the Chief Secretary in the early autumn, they do so within a framework already agreed by the Cabinet. Earlier Cabinets, especially Harold Wilson's, went through appalling ructions precisely because no such overall totals had been agreed in advance and so the battle between the free-spenders and the prudent-finance party could be fought anew in each department and over every item. These July Cabinets are a useful aid in the struggle to maintain consistent control over public expenditure, but they do not correspond to the Platonic idea of strategic Cabinet discussion.

There is, however, one recent (and catastrophic) example of such a discussion. On 9 September 1982, the Central Policy Review Staff submitted a paper to Cabinet in answer to a request (dating from before the summer recess) that it should spell out what would have to happen to the big spending programmes in a nil or low-growth economy if public spending was not to consume an ever increasing proportion of Gross Domestic Product.[29] In the case of higher economic growth, other, more encouraging scenarios were elaborated, but it was the suggested consequences of nil or low growth that took Ministers' breath away. They included an end to state funding of higher education; de-indexing of all social security payments; the replacement of the NHS by a system of private insurance; the freezing of the defence budget as a proportion of Gross Domestic Product. Now one or two of these proposals might, indeed, become necessary; the proposal for the defence

budget has, in effect, come to pass. But, presented as a programme, they were politically horrific, and Ministers more or less
refused to discuss them. Discussion, in fact, concentrated on how
such 'naive' proposals could ever have been brought before the
Cabinet (there were last-minute efforts to prevent this happening,
but the mills of Whitehall tend to grind remorselessly once they
have started grinding). The risk of leaks was appalling (and, to
show how genuine the risk was, the paper was leaked to *The
Economist* and reprinted a few days later); the proposals would have
to be killed for good and all; it would be fatal to give even the
appearance of having seriously considered them. This was, I think,
felt even by several Ministers who might have been friendly to one
or two of the proposals, if considered on their merits.

The only practical consequence of the whole sorry episode was
that, when the Prime Minister, after the 1983 general election,
decided to kill off the CPRS and to expand somewhat (from four
members to eight or nine) her own Policy Unit, her fellow
Ministers shed few tears. The CPRS, immured as it was within the
Cabinet Office and lacking a political head, seemed unable to
produce usable policy ideas, although it remained highly serviceable as a research unit on technical questions, such as the
appropriate pricing policies for gas or electricity. We shall discuss
the question of policy advice a little further in the next sections, on
the Prime Minister and the Department, but the relevant point here
is that the Cabinet did not *feel itself* equipped to discuss difficult,
long-term policy options; the fear of political embarrassment was
too overwhelming to run the risk of being seen to examine such
bleeding raw material. Implicitly, while continuing jealously to
think of itself as the supreme executive body, Cabinet recognises
that it is equipped only to approve dishes that are at least three-
quarters cooked; it is not itself the cook, and the Cabinet Room is
not the kitchen.

All this will be taken as obvious when applied, say, to the
running of a large company. It is axiomatic that business will be so
varied, so quick-moving, so unpredictable that to be bound by
unvarying rules and procedures would be not only disastrous but
virtually impossible. But students of Cabinet government tend to

be uninterested in workaday parallels. They are looking for the kind of hard-and-fast universal structure which befits the scrutiny and approval of legislation. They look, therefore, for the same precision and observance of procedural rules as we find, say, in the case of the House of Commons. Once again, the failure to distinguish between an executive body and a rule-making body bedevils understanding.

For years, constitutional analysts have been worrying away at Cabinet committees: first of all, attempting to discover their titles and membership, then trying to discover what business had been allotted to them and what had been allotted to other, *ad hoc* committees set up by the Prime Minister. Quite clearly, the model at the back of their minds was of a network of publicly established committees which, so to speak, had a right to all the business that fell within their subject areas.

Now no Prime Minister has ever acted in that fashion; it would be too cumbersome; some committees – H, the Home Affairs Committee, was always one – are notorious bottlenecks from which no useful decision can be expected (the reform of the dog-licensing system lay becalmed in H throughout most of the 1980s). Whatever the cause of its ineffectiveness – the personal qualities of the Home Secretaries of the period, the unwieldy nature of the membership, the unavoidable inclusion of the 'geographical departments', Scotland, Wales and Northern Ireland, so prominent on H – the fact remains that any radical or difficult reform would have little hope of getting through H. Any Prime Minister would therefore set up some fresh group to undertake the task; whether or not the group would be destined to become in turn an established Cabinet committee with a name of its own, whether it remained an *ad hoc* group, how long it would sit and who would sit on it – all these matters could not conceivably be reduced to any kind of hard-and-fast rule. Nor would it be reasonable to speak of more activist Prime Ministers, such as Lloyd George, Churchill or Mrs Thatcher, as 'undermining Cabinet government' because they preferred to set up their own groups of Ministers for specific projects.

But should not the existence of all these committees – large or small, formal or informal – be disclosed to the public? Does not open government require at least that we should be told when the government is looking into the possibility of privatising the electricity industry and which members of the government are doing the looking into? Modern authorities, for example, Rodney Brazier in *Constitutional Practice*,[30] wax indignant at the degree of secrecy and pooh-pooh the traditional defence offered by Sir Ivor Jennings and, most recently, in Lord Callaghan's minute of 1978, 'Disclosure of Cabinet Committees'. That minute argued that the status of a decision could be disputed if it was known to have been reached by a committee rather than by the full Cabinet; disclosure could reveal that sensitive matters were under discussion before government was ready to make an announcement; the lack of a committee on a certain subject – poverty, say – would open the government to accusations of sloth or indifference. To all these defences, Brazier and many other advocates of open government would merely retort that the public has a right to know. This is an alluring line of attack but, if closely examined, is a bit less robust than it sounds. Taken to its extreme, it would imply that the public has a right to know that Minister A initially subscribed to opinion α, but that was before he read the paper submitted by Minister B when he changed to opinion β. Further discussion in committee P shifted him decisively to opinion π, but a day's informal discussion at Chequers suggested that a compromise κ might prove more widely acceptable; further discussion in Cabinet (R) led to a compromise on timing ρ. If every stage of discussion is to be wholly transparent, government becomes a stuttering chaos.

Such transparency is not attainable in the real world. Ticklish decisions will be removed from the official machinery into genuinely secret and inaccessible conclave; this already happens, despite the supposed secrecy of Cabinet committees, since the risk of leaks is so great. There is much to be said for fuller, on-the-record briefings by official spokesmen, up to and including the Prime Minister's press secretary. But *some* degree of confidentiality must attach to the government's internal discussions, if substantive discussions are to take place in the committees in which they are supposed to take place. To introduce a personal impression here, I can only say that the problem of open government seems a great deal less real once one has had even a modicum of experience of life inside government. Details of most significant discussion in Cabinet and Cabinet committee appear to be made available to the press within forty-eight hours (if the Prime Minister of the day has asked for extra-special confidentiality, then the details may stay secret for as long as seventy-two hours). The exception is in cases where national security can plausibly be held to be at stake; then secrecy may continue to be upheld for as long as is necessary.

There are many other respects in which British government ought to be more open; both the United States and Scandinavian systems offer usable lessons. But I am less convinced than I used to be that secrecy is a *systematic* problem or that it is the principal underlying cause of the problems which do genuinely afflict us, such as the difficulty of imparting strategic direction to the executive and the failure of Parliament to scrutinise legislation effectively. At any rate, I doubt whether it is the secrecy of the proceedings of Cabinet and Cabinet committees which ought most to worry us.

How then are we to characterise the Cabinet system? What are we to make of the proposition that 'The UK is governed by Cabinet government'? The difficulty in answering the question lies not in identifying the reality but in describing it in terms which are recognisable to readers who have jogged along in the ruts of conventional political argument so long that they dislike the jolt of switching over to a fresh set of tracks. 'Cabinet government' is clearly not an exact, literal all-encompassing description of what we have; so many decisions are effectively taken by the Prime Minister and/or Foreign Secretary or Chancellor of the Exchequer, singly or severally; so many other decisions are taken by officials within Ministries, or by one 'lead Minister' in consultation with another Minister who has a proper but lesser interest in the subject. Most major decisions will be brought before Cabinet for approval, but in many cases, the Budget being the most notorious, approval is more or less formal, and, short of resignation, dissenting Ministers have little chance of making their dissent count.

Is 'Cabinet government' then a sham – the other possibility in our somewhat impoverished vocabulary? Certainly not. Every Minister, in framing his proposals, has to bear in mind what his colleagues will and will not tolerate. This is a matter not so much of constitutional propriety as of political prudence. True, in the case of the Budget or some major foreign policy decision, he knows he can ram it through; in the case of dog licences (or more recently dog slaughter), he may find the Cabinet blocking his path. But the Cabinet remains the crystallisation of the government as a collective entity. And, while it may often be a slothful, inattentive and forgetful body, it retains the power to leap into life any Thursday morning and assert its constitutional and actual rights.

But, it must be repeated, there is nothing very mysterious about a body of this sort, that is, one which lies doggo a good deal of the time, lets many decisions and proposals go past it on the nod, and only intermittently is stirred to action. This is how many of our analogue bodies operate, intervening to exert their legal responsibilities only intermittently and unpredictably; that may well be how the 'full board' explicitly interprets its duties, leaving the bulk of initiatives and decisions to departmental heads and executive committees, and asking only to be kept properly informed of the flow of business which requires its formal assent.

John Mackintosh summarised the role and limits of the Cabinet well enough in the early 1960s:

> the major task of the Cabinet is not to lead the party, to manage Parliament or to think out policy, but to co-ordinate administration, to ensure that legislative proposals are acceptable to the departments concerned, to keep the senior ministers in touch with all the various lines of activity and to give the work of the government a measure of unity.[31]

That is how it still is today, more or less. And there is nothing bizarre or futile about this manner of operation; it is a commonplace system. But we must not mistake the Cabinet for the engine-room. It is this misperception which has fostered such complacency about the central direction of British government since the war.

The Prime Minister

If the Cabinet is not the kitchen, is it then the Prime Minister who is the cook? And is it the Study upstairs at Number Ten which is the real centre of government? This is certainly the modern belief, intimated and suspected ever since the turn of the century (we have already seen Dicey, Morley and Asquith describe the potential of the office in just those terms), but only since the last war systematically advanced as the guiding principle. Two world wars and the militarisation of government are probably responsible for engraving this image of government upon our minds. It was, after all, first Lloyd George and then Churchill who made us think of Number Ten as the unsleeping nerve centre of the body politic; the Cabinet Office was essentially a creation of the First War, although its permanence was confirmed only later; the Second War dictated a more pervasive command economy, more pervasive, we were later to hear, than had been thought necessary in Nazi Germany. Since the war, both the mass media and academic students of politics have increasingly personalised the government of the day and come to see the Prime Minister not only as the embodiment of the administration but also as its director in the strong sense of that term, enjoying both the prominence and the autocratic powers comparable with those of a film director, newspaper editor or football manager and, like them, subject only to dismissal at the hands of a faceless body of managers.

This view is most clearly put by John Mackintosh in that influential work, *The British Cabinet*:

> While British government in the latter half of the nineteenth century can be described simply as Cabinet government, such a description would be misleading today. Now the country is governed by the Prime Minister who leads, co-ordinates and maintains a series of ministers all of whom are advised and backed by the Civil Service.[32]

Mackintosh points out that 'This is not Presidential Government because the Premier can, in exceptional circumstances, be removed and he will collapse if deserted by all his colleagues or by his party.'[33] The fact that the Prime Minister has not been directly elected by the people is naturally of the greatest importance; he needs to conserve the support of his ministers and his backbenchers if he is to govern effectively or at all; the President of the US and the President of France can govern for long periods without the support of Congress or the National Assembly by virtue of their direct election.

This view is enthusiastically backed by R. H. S. Crossman, both in his introduction to Bagehot's *English Constitution*[34] and in his Godkin Lectures of April 1970, as he was just coming to the end of six years in the Cabinet.

> To point out instances of Prime Ministerial impotence or voluntary self-limitation, therefore, does not affect my contention that the powers a modern Prime Minister can legitimately exert without challenge by Cabinet colleagues are vastly more extensive in the area they cover and intensive in the centralisation of decision-taking they involve than those exerted by a Prime Minister in the time of Bagehot, or indeed up to 1914.[35]

This picture is somewhat confused by his statement in the Bagehot introduction that, even in Bagehot's time, it was a misnomer to describe the Prime Minister as *primus inter pares*; even before 1867, the Premier enjoyed 'near-Presidential powers'.[36] After all, had not Bagehot himself claimed that 'we have in Britain an elective first magistrate as truly as the Americans have an elective first magistrate'? If then a mid-Victorian Prime Minister was, let us say, 90 per cent of a President, how much more presidential can a modern Prime Minister be, seeing that, as both Crossman and Mackintosh rightly concede, he can never be 100 per cent presidential since he – and, as we now know, she – can still be ejected by the Cabinet and/or the Parliamentary Party? To say, as Crossman does, that 'as the machinery of government increases in size, the man at the centre of the government must anyway become more powerful'[37] seems to confuse the *proportion* of power held by the Prime Minister (as opposed to that held by Cabinet, Parliament and bureaucracy) with the total *quantum* of power over the citizen held by government as a whole.

At all events, although it may sometimes be hard to discern exactly what they mean, Mackintosh, Crossman and many other modern commentators on the Prime Minister's office, both academic and popular, do all tend to give the impression that primeministerial power these days operates much more smoothly, directly and habitually upon the government machine than it used to. Having, as it were, seen through the pretensions of Cabinet government, the modern fashion is to swallow more or less whole the alternative theory of prime-ministerial government.

The natural deduction from this – a deduction now and then deduced – is that failures of British government since the war must be, in large measure, due to the personal inadequacies of successive Prime Ministers. If it is the case that the system permits their will to flow smoothly down the usual channels to issue in edicts and Acts in the form in which he or she first conceived them, then indeed there would be no other possible deduction, no snag, grit or bottleneck in the system which could be blamed, no alternative scapegoat.

But modern British government is not like that, and to accept this simple personification of the system is not only to fall into a sentimental trap but grossly to misread the realities and hence to underestimate the difficulties of imparting a coherent and sustained dynamic to government policy.

Unfortunately, modern discussions of the Premiership tend to be somewhat sketchy in describing how the office actually operates, what staff are at its disposal, how its commands are issued and what means are available for enforcing its will. Historians of, say, the reign of Louis XIV or the command of Field-Marshal Haig would be likely to devote far more attention to such matters, recognising that here lies the key to effectiveness of monarch or commander.

What follows is no doubt also sketchy, but it has at least the merit of placing the nuts and bolts at the forefront of the discussion of the office.

First then, the Prime Minister has a tiny staff, considerably less than the staff at the disposal of the mayor of a German city. Harold Macmillan claimed that when he entered Number Ten he had a staff of only six persons.[38] Crossman discovered that in Wilson's time the Number Ten staff comprised sixty-four including all secretaries and typists, whereas the White House staff in 1970 numbered 1292. To use a somewhat different standard of counting, *Vacher's Parliamentary Companion* of February 1990 lists twenty-seven staff in Mrs Thatcher's office. Of these, nine were members of her Policy Unit (a relatively recent innovation, dating from 1974). Several others were not relevant to the central conduct of government business – the secretary for honours and appointments, for instance, and Mrs Thatcher's constituency secretary.

At this point in the discussion, it is frequently argued that the size of the Prime Minister's personal staff is a misleading indicator. Ever since the establishment of the Cabinet Office in the middle of the First World War, Prime Ministers have been able to call on the services of a much larger and more high-ranking corps of advisers sitting at their desks only the thickness of a wall away – namely, the Cabinet Office. In this warren of offices and meeting-rooms work an impressive number of deputy secretaries and under-secretaries – the pick of their departments – under the direction of the Cabinet Secretary. Highly specialised expertise is on tap here: the government's chief scientific adviser, the grand panjandrums of the intelligence community who service the Joint Intelligence Committee, and in its day (1970–83) the Central Policy Review Staff, at its peak almost equal in size to the entire complement of the Prime Minister's personal staff, and recruiting inventive and energetic minds, not only from the Civil Service, but from industry, the City and academe.

All this, alas, is of little practical use to the Prime Minister. For the green baize door between the Cabinet Office and Number Ten is locked. Literally locked; to pass from one to the other, a key must be borrowed from the Prime Minister's private office or from the Cabinet Secretary's office. The practical reason for this is security, but the symbolism is not lost on those who venture across the great divide. For in no other part of the Civil Service is there a more glacial determination to preserve the Service's independence and lack of political commitment. While private secretaries, and indeed more senior officials within a department, may sometimes commit themselves whole-heartedly to their Minister's cause, the briefs circulated to members of Cabinet and the separate 'handling brief' provided for the Prime Minister exhale a studied neutrality; these briefs rehearse, in bland and unspecific form (partly, it must be said, for fear of leaks), the advantages and disadvantages of various courses of action. But the pros and cons will be listed without nuance, and, more damagingly, with little or no hard argument or information. Nothing is more remarkable to outsiders than the uninformativeness of a Cabinet brief: statistics will be skimpy, if present at all; comparisons with the experience of other countries or of earlier administrations conspicuous by their absence. The convention that one administration may not consult the private papers of earlier administrations naturally predisposes government towards the repetition of error.

Many of these shortcomings are inherent in the construction of the Cabinet Office. Its business is to serve the whole of Cabinet and not to weight its briefing in support of one faction rather than another. Moreover, although members of the Cabinet Office will consult the relevant officials in the relevant department (including members of the Prime Minister's own office), they may well have little experience of or feel for the subject under discussion; a man seconded from the Treasury may well be assigned to do a briefing on some unavoidably technical proposal for the reform of the secondary examination system. The cult of the generalist reaches its apogee in the Cabinet Office and leaves the average member of Cabinet woefully underbriefed in all subjects but his own department's. It is partly for this reason that, in many crucial Cabinet debates, significant contributions will come only from the responsible Minister and his predecessor, who still retains a working recollection of the issues. Occasionally, another Minister who served as a junior Minister in the department will chip in on the basis of what he remembers from a year or so back. But, in general, the quality of information provided by the system is poor – and this includes the information provided to the Prime Minister. In recent years, the Policy Unit has been able to offer a rough-and-ready service, but neither the quality nor the number of its staff has ensured the sort of standard that we would expect to be available to the chairman of a large organisation. In theory, there may appear to be no reason why the material provided by the Cabinet Office should not be at the same time rich in information and argument and utterly drained of partiality. But in practice, the neutrality and the systematic avoidance of the appearance of bias tend to prevent the Cabinet Office's work from providing the concrete and specific material which would underpin sensible and coherent decision-making. Senior civil servants have always been loath to accept this. Almost to a man, they deplore Mrs Thatcher's decision to abolish the CPRS after the 1983 election; Sir Burke Trend called it 'a disastrous mistake'.[39] Permanent secretaries can point to the calamitous results of pursuing the poll tax in defiance of all official advice. But that calamity was pursued in defiance of all political advice too; the question to be addressed by supporters of the CPRS and the Cabinet Office in the forms in which they evolved is a rather different one: whether the present rigid dichotomy between 'policy' and 'administration' really provides the quality of advice that both the Prime Minister and the Cabinet might reasonably expect; or, to put it another way, whether the locking of the green baize door is not an absurdity.

Having then recognised the imperfections of the advice available to Prime Ministers and the crippling smallness of their staff, we must now examine how the Prime Minister's will is conveyed to the furthest corners of Whitehall. The most common form of communication is from one of the private secretaries to the private secretary of the relevant Minister. The letter will take the form:

Dear George [all civil servants of the same rank are assumed to be on Christian-name terms, regardless of whether they have actually met], The Prime Minister has seen your minute of 21 July. She [we will assume that Mrs Thatcher is still in office, since hers is the fashioning of it which is still most familiar to us] is still anxious that the widget industry should be privatised within the lifetime of this Parliament. She believes that a direct sale rather than a flotation might be practicable and would be grateful if your Secretary of State would consider this possibility.

Yours ever, Terence

I choose this imaginary instance in order to bring out several points. First, the characteristic method of communication between Prime Minister and Minister is *indirect*, in order that the Prime Minister should appear not to be giving orders to a fellow Minister but to be consulting and conversing with him; secondly, the Prime Minister has few resources of his/her own (until Harold Wilson's invention of the Policy Unit, virtually none) and must therefore rely upon the supposed expertise of the Secretary of State's department. Thirdly, when and if a proposal for the privatisation of widgets is to be brought forward to go through the hoops of collective discussion remains a matter for the Secretary of State; once he has produced a paper, which he may informally consider at a meeting with, say, the Prime Minister and the Chancellor of the Exchequer, that paper will go to the relevant Cabinet committee. In this case, it might be a Nationalised Industry sub-committee of the Economic committee, E (NI) – probably under the chairmanship of the Chancellor. If approved, it will then go to Cabinet, and then into the Legislation committee, L, to find a place in the timetable for the government's legislative programme in the following session. But not merely is the form of the proposals – here, the method of sale, the proposed structure of the industry after privatisation and the proposed timing of the sale – entirely a matter for the Minister, so also is the decision whether any proposal at all should be brought forward.

This is not merely a theoretical possibility. While Mr Peter Walker was Secretary of State for Energy, for example, there could be no question of denationalising the electricity industry, and it remained inevitable that, whatever the Prime Minister and other senior members of the Cabinet might think, the gas industry could be denationalised only as a monopolistic single company, because of the influence of its then chairman, Sir Denis Rooke, over Mr Walker. Mrs Thatcher could not by herself compel the Secretary of State to follow her own preferences; nor did she consider mobilising the will of the Cabinet to coerce him into doing so; indeed, it is not at all clear that the Cabinet would have been willing to force a Minister into pursuing a policy to which he was so opposed. Even supposedly more compliant Ministers successfully resisted Prime Minister's requests: Mr Tom King was reluctant to privatise the water industry; Mr Norman Tebbit initially resisted several proposals for tightening trade union law; Mr Mark Carlisle showed little or no interest in reforming the structure of state education. These examples – and many more could be produced – are taken from a period popularly thought of as one of prime ministerial dominance over a compliant Cabinet.

What other methods, apart from the routine correspondence between private secretaries, are available to a Prime Minister wishing to get her way? (Again, I use the female pronoun, because the Thatcher example makes the point more strongly.) There is, most obviously, the face-to-face meeting. The Prime Minister may summon a slothful or stubborn Minister and, perhaps fortified by the presence of an ally – often the Chancellor of the Exchequer –may try to browbeat the Minister into doing her will. A record will be made of the meeting by the private secretary in attendance and circulated to the parties as a reminder of what was agreed and as guidance to the department which has to implement the conclusions. But, in practice, these discussions do not have the one-sidedness of the headmaster's study or the chairman's office. All these politicians have, after all, clambered up the ladder of preferment together; they are no respecters of one another's persons. It is remarkable how frequently 'having Tom in' fails to produce the outcome desired by the Prime Minister. Where a stand-off or draw is possible, given the nature of the topic, then that is what frequently results. For example, Mrs Thatcher was notoriously eager every year to increase the ceiling for mortgage tax relief in line with inflation; the Chancellor of the Exchequer was equally keen to lower the ceiling, in order to remove this inequitable subsidy, which was widely thought to be part of the cause of the ballooning inflation in house prices. In practice, there was one modest increase in the upper limit, from £25,000 to £30,000, in 1983, but thereafter the level stayed unchanged year after year, its benefit progressively eroded by inflation, because neither side would give in.

Another method by which Prime Ministers try to get their way is to summon a group of Ministers for a day's conference, most often at Chequers but occasionally at Downing Street, to consider an area of policy in its broadest aspects – government support for agriculture or the future of the Health Service, to take two actual examples. These conferences, known to Mrs Thatcher by the misleadingly innocuous title of 'seminars' (a term also used in the Wilson–Callaghan years to describe the top-secret committee on monetary policy),[40] might involve the relevant permanent secretaries, plus members of the Downing Street Policy Unit and possibly one or two others who might seem to have some relevant knowledge; but the principal purpose would be to attempt to inject the Minister with a modicum both of fresh information and of new ideas, in order that he might return to his department infused with renewed zeal for reform. Occasionally, the cast assembled would be larger, and the agenda would cover several departments; on several occasions, more than a dozen Ministers would assemble at Chequers to discuss a long shopping list of measures 'to remove the shackles on enterprise'. These might include anything from proposals to lower the cost of development land to measures to abolish the statutory control of wages in certain trades. The purpose was not so much to explore the ramifications of these issues (many of them had already been discussed *ad infinitum*, both inside and outside government) as to mobilise the government's collective will in the direction of reform, so that the department responsible might begin to feel that its intransigence was no longer sustainable. But once again, if the Minister responsible was opposed in principle to the proposal, no further progress could be made on it. To return to the example of Mr Peter Walker, so long as he was Secretary of State for Agriculture, 'production at all costs' would remain the strategy. Any prospect of reducing the huge cost of government support for agriculture would have to await the arrival of a more compliant Minister in the shape of Mr Michael Jopling.

Nor is this phenomenon confined to Mrs Thatcher's

Premiership (especially her early years in office, when she was outnumbered in Cabinet by her opponents). Equally forceful Prime Ministers have found themselves baulked on important issues by Ministers whom the outside world regarded as dim or subservient yes-men. For example, Harold Macmillan was driven to distraction by Selwyn Lloyd's refusal (admirable refusal, as it happens) to adopt more expansionist policies at the Treasury; he managed to change the policy only by changing the Minister and installing the more compliant and expansionist Maudling. Eden was ultimately forced to abort the Suez expedition under pressure of the warnings of dire economic consequences from Macmillan, then the Chancellor of the Exchequer. With hindsight, these warnings about the impending collapse of sterling seem neither plausible nor innocent, but Eden had no means of contesting them – no expert economic advisers to counterbalance the Treasury, no economic knowledge of his own, no other Minister to bring in on his side – and tamely had to give way.

As a rule, in matters of war and peace, the Prime Minister's will encounters fewer obstacles or, at any rate, few obstacles that count. In the run-up to the Falklands War, the Foreign Office and Francis Pym, the new Foreign Secretary appointed after Lord Carrington's resignation, were persistently sceptical of the wisdom of going to war – as was a considerable part of the Cabinet Office. Their hesitations were swept away by the Prime Minister with the galeforce wind of public indignation filling her sails. Neither Chamberlain nor Churchill, in their different ways, seem to have encountered much difficulty in remoulding diplomatic and military strategy to their liking.

But in social and economic policy even the most dominant Prime Ministers who have already remade the Cabinet to their liking may continue to be baulked in the pursuit of their dearest objects. Mrs Thatcher's campaign to find a substitute for the rates took virtually all her decade in office, exhausted successive Environment Secretaries, and proved ultimately catastrophic for her personally, not to mention leaving local government structure and finance in a state of total chaos. The most dominant peacetime Prime Minister of the century did prove ultimately that the Prime

Minister's will can be made to prevail over that of her Ministers, if he or she cares enough, but the cost was so prohibitive that, for some time to come, it seems likely that the opposite lesson will be drawn from the poll tax fiasco: namely, that the Prime Minister is unwise to push too far.

But most modern Prime Ministers have succumbed to the dangers of not pushing hard enough or long enough, because of the extreme difficulty and unpleasantness of imposing the will of Downing Street upon a recalcitrant department or departments. Sometimes, it has been the case that the departmental Minister has been willing enough to pursue reform, but other Ministers or external vested interests have stopped the reform dead in its tracks. Mrs Barbara Castle was eager to produce her White Paper on trade union reform, *In Place of Strife*; it was the trade unions and their ministerial spokesmen, led by the Home Secretary, Jim Callaghan, who forced Mrs Castle and Harold Wilson to make their humiliating climb-down in June 1969. But, more often, the best ideas of mice, men and policy units have foundered on the scepticism of the relevant ministry.

The most recent *locus classicus* here is the passage in *Prime Minister*, Bernard Donoughue's memoir of the Wilson–Callaghan government, in which he goes through the agenda of reform suggested by the Prime Minister's Policy Unit, an agenda endorsed by the Prime Minister and undoubtedly reflecting the tenor of public anxiety and aspiration at that time, and shows how each proposal received a dull or negative response from the relevant Minister, supported by the conventional wisdom of his department. When it was suggested that Labour should respond to the popular demand among council tenants for the right to buy their own homes, Harold Wilson 'welcomed the suggestions enthusiastically'.[41] A Cabinet committee (MISC 127) asked officials to draft specific policies, but the responsible Minister, Anthony Crosland, and his advisers (although not most of his regular officials) were particularly disappointing in their reactions. There was an equally dull departmental reaction to Callaghan's Ruskin College speech in October 1976, made in response to the growing public anxiety about the poor standards in state schools. Shirley

Williams was 'unhappy that the Prime Minister had trespassed into her ministerial territory'; when the Prime Minister asked for a follow-up Green Paper, 'officials made it clear they were not enthusiastic'; the draft they produced was dim and complacent, but, despite the protests it provoked from Downing Street, it survived to be published more or less unchanged. Donoughue tells us that efforts to shake up broadcasting, engineering and legal services dribbled into the departmental sands in much the same way. Many of the ideas later resurfaced during the Thatcher years (as they would have done, whoever had succeeded Mr Callaghan as Prime Minister) and were carried through, more or less effectively, to some kind of conclusion, but only after remorseless nagging and repeated reshuffles.

The Prime Minister's powers are well known: to hire, fire and reshuffle Ministers; to summon or not to summon Cabinets and Cabinet committees; to control their agenda, to sum up their conclusions and to oversee the writing of the minutes; and to choose the date of the general election. These are formidable powers which, carefully husbanded and judiciously deployed, may enable a Prime Minister to survive in reasonably good order. But to drive through a coherent and sustained strategy requires a good deal more in the way of inexhaustible energy and unbreakable willpower. For the system resists coherence and co-ordination, deflects energies and fragments the will.

In normal times, and with a normal Prime Minister, we do not have prime-ministerial government. What we have is what might be called 'a loose-baronial monarchy' or neo-feudalism.

To recall Jolliffe's description of the England of Henry II: 'Far from being a single community at the disposal of the king's agents, the county was a patchwork of administrations, some where the king had all, some where a greater or less degree of privileged right prevailed, and much of which it could be said, *ibi domino Regi nihil accrescit* – "here the lord king has nothing".' The granting of tenures, the summoning of parliaments – all that was certainly the king's right – but to fail to understand the loose-knit, unco-ordinated, unpatterned nature of the system is to fail to appreciate how slippery and unpredictable and fluctuating a thing his power was. We must not be deceived by the public-relations panoply of modern Prime Ministers into mistaking their power for anything more solid or systematic.

The Minister and his department

That people may have a fairly shrewd idea of how they are governed is not a conception which either political scientists or political journalists are happy to entertain. It is the occupation of both trades to reveal what has allegedly been kept hidden and to dispel what they maintain are popular illusions. Both newspapers and academic journals are full of 'unmasking work'; both concentrate in particular upon the most glamorous part of intra-governmental dealings, those between Prime Ministers and their senior Ministers. Both popular and academic works, like the memoirs of politicians, tend to heighten the unreal exaggerations of the competing myths of 'Cabinet government' and 'prime-ministerial government'. We are happy to swallow these exaggerations as entertaining, if a little overspiced, versions of the political process. But it took a mere television series to provoke a genuine shock of recognition from governors and governed alike. Translated into a variety of languages and cultures, *Yes Minister* continues to produce that same shock, that same instantaneous understanding among utterly non-political viewers that 'Yes, this is what it must be like.'

To call the series 'a satire on bureaucracy' is to imply the possibility of non-bureaucratic or less bureaucratic systems of governmental power and leave the impression that there is something avoidable or transient about the comedy of the conflict between permanent officials and their political masters. But there seems, on the contrary, to be something universal and inevitable about this conflict. At any rate, *Yes Minister* certainly provides a convenient starting-point for an outline of the British ministerial department, with its local peculiarities and its systematic similarities to government departments in other systems.

Let us begin by identifying the three main sources of the department's power. The first is its *continuity*. As Crossman put it,

'The greatest danger for a radical Minister is to get too much going in his department. Because, you see, departments are resistant. departments know that they last and you don't.'[42] A little delay, a modicum of obfuscation, a plea for more time to complete the research or the consultation or the drafting, and there is a good chance that the over-demanding Minister and/or his headstrong government will be gone, and the department will be able to breathe a sigh of relief and reflect that its delaying tactics were wholly justified in the interests of the smooth continuities of good government. The Civil Service is not ashamed of regarding itself as the unofficial brake in a constitutional system which has become so deficient in effective checks and balances. The experience of the Thatcher government suggests very strongly that a party needs to win a couple of elections in a row, or at least a landslide victory, for permanent officials to regard the new government as matching their own permanence and representing a sea change in the political life of the country.

This continuity reflects itself not only in the uninterrupted existence of the department (although one or two of its functions may now and then be redistributed, to the glee of the gaining department and the chagrin of the loser), but in its staff. Efforts have been made at intervals to permit the introduction of fresh blood and to circulate the old blood more vigorously; in 1919, Sir Warren Fisher introduced a unified career structure for the whole service, in order to prevent fresh young brains congealing in the same department all their lives; in the 1960s, the Fulton Committee vainly recommended the introduction of highly qualified specialists at various levels and ages to undermine 'the cult of the generalist' – the first-rate high-flier who can put his mind to anything but is never asked to do so for very long in case his flight-path should be impeded. Nothing much has come of these admirable initiatives. Take three typical departments – Energy, Education, Transport. During the 1980s, the senior officials (permanent secretary, deputy secretary and under-secretary) at all three had spent virtually their entire careers in the Civil Service and many had spent the last ten or twenty years in their current department. The nearest thing to an exception was Mr Philip

Halsey in the DES, who had been headmaster of Hampstead School before coming to the department twenty years earlier; though more emollient in manner than the other leading representative of continuity in that department, Mr W. O. Ulrich, he was no less sceptical of any departure from the conventional educational wisdom of the time. Quite a few of the officials had gained relevant experience in the contiguous field of Housing and Local Government; they were also likely to have spent a year or two in the central machinery, either at the Cabinet Office or as a private secretary in Number Ten Downing Street. Indeed, for a permanent secretary never to have been seconded to another department – as with Sir Peter Lazarus at the Department of Transport – was quite a rarity. It was more often the case that a new permanent secretary would come from the Treasury or the Cabinet Office, such as Sir John Caines and his predecessor Sir David Hancock at the DES, Sir Alan Bailey at Transport, Sir Peter Gregson at the DTI. A rare exception is Sir Alan's successor, Mr Patrick Brown, who started his career with Carreras, the tobacco manufacturer, and Urwick Orr, the management consultants, before joining the Civil Service in his early thirties; after helping to sell off the National Freight Corporation, the buses and the ports and preparing much of the Property Services Agency for a similar destiny, he was appointed Permanent Secretary to the Ministry of Transport in June 1991 – in my view, more or less the ideal flight path for a senior civil servant. These senior appointments, in modern times being handpicked by the Cabinet Secretary in consultation with the Prime Minister (formerly the Minister might select his own senior men), are often alleged, quite wrongly, to be an important element in the growth of prime-ministerial power. Crossman, for example, says in his introduction to Bagehot that:

> the centralisation of authority, both for appointments and for policy decisions, under a single head of the civil service . . . responsible to Downing Street has brought with it an immense accretion of power to the Prime Minister. He is now the apex not only of a highly centralised political machine, but also of an equally centralised and vastly more powerful administrative

machine. In both these machines, loyalty has become the supreme virtue, and independence of thought a dangerous adventure. The post-war epoch has seen the final transformation of Cabinet government into Prime Ministerial government.[43]

This is a grotesquely melodramatic picture, at least as far as the administrative side goes. In so far as these selections from the central machine have been chosen for their malleable, biddable qualities, they will instantly put those qualities at the service of their new departments; in no time, they tend to be absorbed and coloured by the departmental culture. After all, their whole training has taught them to be likeable, 'helpful' (the great Civil Service word of approval), sensitive to atmosphere and, above all, responsive to immediate authority.

And – we come now to our second source of the department's power – it must always be remembered that it is the department which has the *authority*. When the Minister rises in the Commons to announce that 'I have decided that in future, etc. etc.', there may be something risible about the pretence that he has personally, after much mulling, decided to do this rather than that. He may, as often as not, be unreflectively rubberstamping the recommendation put before him by his civil servants; as often as not, he may be right to do so. Crossman was correct in urging the incoming Ministers to concentrate on two or three important lines of policy, rather than trying to set off on a dozen things at once; a human being has only so much energy, and the day has only twenty-four hours. But, from the point of view of the Civil Service, what matters is that it is the Minister who has the legal authority. As the lawyers would say, the law knows nothing of the Prime Minister or of the Cabinet; as we have seen, there are a few glancing references in statute to Cabinet Ministers' pensions and the Prime Minister's occupancy of Chequers, but that is all. It is the Secretary of State who is the power in the land. Cabinets and Prime Ministers can only encourage or discourage him in his course; they cannot instruct. This may sound like a formal distinction. It is, in practice, a very real one when a department wants to dig its heels in. If a department persists in asserting that the wishes of a Prime Minister or a Cabinet committee are impractical or ill advised, there is not much that the Prime Minister or the Cabinet committee can do about it, short of dismissing the unhelpful Minister, a step which may well be taken if the Prime Minister attaches high priority to the policy thus frustrated but which cannot be taken, without exhibiting damaging governmental disarray, until the next reshuffle.

The department enjoys this considerable scope for resistance to the wishes of the central leadership because of its third great advantage – *staff*. The huge gap between the numbers employed by the central machine and those employed by the department offers proportionate advantages in argument. The department simply knows more than the Cabinet Office or the Prime Minister, even when the latter is, or was, backed up by the Central Policy Review Staff or the Number Ten Policy Unit. Much of the detailed information deployed in the argument must perforce come from the department. It may well be the case (it usually is the case) that the department is woefully under-informed; typically, it lacks the kind of comparative material which alone may make it possible to judge standards of performance: between the UK and France, let us say, or between state schools and private schools. Or the information will be collected on an inert or negative basis which is near valueless for building up a picture of the real world; for years, the Ministry of Labour and the Department of Employment had only the most minimal information on the jobs market, concentrating their statistical efforts on *un*employment, a residual indicator which has often proved a highly misleading policy guide.

But, at all events, the department has and always has had the weight of manpower. In Trollope's *The Three Clerks*, that matchless picture of the Civil Service at the moment when the Northcote–Trevelyan reforms were being introduced, it is the measure of Sir Gregory Hardlines's budding glory – he is appointed Chief Commissioner of the Board of Civil Service Examination with a salary of £2000 a year – that 'he was to be a great man, to have an office of his own, and to reign over assistant commissioners and subject secretaries'.[44]

In the modern era, Professor James Buchanan has pointed out that, once we begin to look at bureaucracy in terms of:

the constraints and opportunities faced by individual decision-makers . . . we can, of course, predict that individual bureaucrats will seek to expand the size of their bureaux since, almost universally in modern Western societies, the salaries and perquisites of office are related directly to the sizes of budgets administered and controlled. The built-in motive force for expansion, the dynamics of modern governmental bureaucracy in the small and in the large, was apparent to all who cared to think.[45]

Bureaucrats cannot help becoming 'rent-seekers' (Gordon Tullock's term) in just the same way that entrepreneurs cannot help becoming profit-seekers. It is their occupational deformation to regard the size, financial resources and morale of their department as intimately connected with the public good. This phenomenon is so familiar to us in all the other institutions in which we have our daily being that we take it for granted that it must apply to the public service too; it is only the political reformer to whom these things come as a surprise, because he has never considered precisely how the governmental enterprise for which he has been so enthusiastically campaigning would operate in concrete reality: how it would maintain its authority, its access to public finance, its area of operations, and hence how its staff would be motivated and what would be their priorities. All this has now been spelled out in the work of Tullock and Buchanan and dignified by the title of the 'Economics of Politics'. To the ordinary layman, it all sounds much like the familiar old way of the world.

Contrary to Professor Buchanan's nice-minded critics, there is no inconsistency between this analysis and our earlier remarks about the dedication and loyalty that civil servants may offer to the Crown. The two phenomena coexist. The civil servant values the services he offers at a high price and is inclined to think that the Crown would be still better serviced if he and his colleagues were better supported – by research facilities and equipment, by incentive payments and by more assistants. Conversely, it is inordinately difficult for him to conceive that his particular project or section ought, in the interests of the nation, to be discontinued, let alone that the nation would be better off if his department were to be wound up. Yet if we take the present moment (the autumn of 1991), there is a decent case for winding up several entire departments which now occupy the attention of a Cabinet Minister – Energy, Agriculture and Employment all being candidates.

Yet how are these possibilities to be coldly and impartially evaluated? How can we ensure that they are proposed at all? In a well-known leading article (15 February 1977), *The Times* asserted: 'The constitutional position is both crystal clear and entirely sufficient. Officials propose. Ministers dispose. Officials execute.' To start with, I am not sure that 'constitutional' is entirely the right word here. Most of what is involved relates solely to the organisation of the executive arm of government, which cannot, strictly speaking, be described as a constitutional matter. But the real difficulty comes from the word 'propose'.

Are civil servants, however senior and experienced, really equipped to propose or even to set out alternative proposals? Are they, *a fortiori*, equipped to have the monopoly on such proposing? After all, when under fire in front of Select Committees, senior officials are reluctant to accept any responsibility for policy, and even more reluctant if the policy in question can be described as 'political'. Yet the whole business of proposing is itself part of making policy; the intellectual framework in which the proposals are brought forward, the nuancing of the pros and cons, not to speak of the timing, can scarcely be neutral matters. When civil servants are accused of straying into the making of policy rather than restricting themselves to implementation, they will indignantly deny the charge; but it is impossible for them not to stray the moment they begin to formulate options. The question is not whether they should somehow be kept back out of the policy arena – a virtual impossibility in view of their place at the heart of the action – but rather whether others should be allowed in to challenge their formulations and whether they themselves should be equipped with more varied qualifications and a wider experience of the world.

The idea of seriously curbing or compartmenting the powers of the bureaucracy is an idle fantasy – a genteel version of Marx's angry dream of a state that would wither away; a modern state and the modern citizen (well, any state and any citizen) require honest, precise, steady and predictable administration, in other words, a bureaucracy. The challenge is not to pretend that we can dispense with these virtues but to see if we can make the bureaucracy also responsive, adaptable and reasonably far-sighted. Can we impart to the departmental machines all the enormous virtues of Sir Gregory Hardlines – his integrity, his fidelity, his energy – without at the same time groaning under the rigidity of his colleague, Mr Fidus Neverbend? Is there any middle path between the wholesale upheaval which takes place in most US government departments on the election of a new American President (with its importation of a contingent of placemen, who contain more than their fair share of arrogant and ignorant friends of the new administration) and the frigid virtue of the Whitehall system which does its damnedest to reduce to a minimum the number of irregulars imported by incoming Ministers and to keep those special advisers as far away from the levers of power as possible? Can we avoid the corrupt excesses of the American 'spoils system' without being confined to the sterile and fossilised tendencies of the Whitehall tradition?

The most straightforward route is obviously to introduce something on the lines of the French ministerial *cabinet*; this is the route approved by the House of Commons Treasury and Civil Service Select Committee and the Royal Institute of Public Administration.[46] A more detailed proposal was worked out at a series of seminars at the Institute of Directors in 1986 by the Reskilling Government Group under the leadership of Sir John Hoskyns. Ministers with departments to run would, in the first instance, be equipped with 'an enhanced private office', containing six to eight outsiders with a variety of experience and expertise. The Hoskyns group envisaged that the *cabinet* (or *Minister's policy unit*, as the Treasury and Civil Service Select Committee preferred to call it, to avoid the frenchified timbre) would consist of a head at deputy-secretary level, two outside experts, two outside 'politicos', two 'rough diamonds' (to challenge conventional thinking) and one insider (career civil servant), to be appointed at ranks ranging from under-secretary to principal. The total salary cost (at 1986 levels) of twenty such *cabinets* would have been £3½ million.

There is no question of any constitutional precedent being breached here. Decades before Harold Wilson and Margaret Thatcher set up their policy units, Lloyd George had had his Prime Minister's Secretariat, Churchill his Statistical Section (which covered a multitude of irregulars) and Attlee his Central Economic Planning Staff.

Even the Hoskyns agenda may seem a little over-elaborate. It might be possible to impart a strategic energy to the direction of the department – or at least to the crucial aspects of the department's operations – with rather less risk to the British Ministry's genuine virtues: honesty, impartiality and consistency of administration. We may accept from Crossman's analysis the point that, in any given department, there are only two or three major lines of policy which a Minister can effectively pursue in an unorthodox or unfamiliar direction. To achieve this, he will not need to saturate the upper reaches of the department with his own nominees from outside; that would look like jobbery, and, in quite a few cases, corrupt, incompetent or half-crazy people would undoubtedly be appointed. What then is the minimal number of outsiders that a Minister would need to bring the department round to play the desired constructive part in the Government's overall purpose?

My guess is that, in the central direction of his department, the Minister needs a critical mass of no more than four to six advisers from outside; one at least should enjoy the senior rank of deputy secretary or under-secretary, to prevent the incomers being written off as a corps of office boys. In addition, the Minister might also need two or three outside experts seconded in, at assistant-secretary level, on temporary assignments, to deal with specific aspects of the new policy which the existing officials would find baffling or repugnant.

This is much more important than it may sound. It is not enough for the outsiders to form a significant cluster in the Minister's office. When contemplating a radical departure from the accepted wisdom, he must be able to *reach down* some way into the department, in order to get the new approach converted into detailed and usable proposals. Otherwise, he will be baulked by a succession of nitpicking objections, to which he himself lacks the resources to provide convincing answers. Where the objections are genuine, he needs advisers in the drafting process who will use their ingenuity to find sensible ways round them. Any Civil Service has to operate on precedent; predictable administration would otherwise become impossible; individuals and corporate bodies would become subject to arbitrary whim. But the defect of this virtue is that the department tends to become not only hostile to but incapable of grasping the essentials of any new way of doing things. The DES, for example, was, for a period of years, not only suspicious of but appeared quite baffled by the concept of state schools 'opting out' of local authority control with a view to improving their academic and managerial standards. They had no experience of how to pluralise the system, since all their efforts had been directed, within the DES's somewhat neutered potency, towards co-ordinating and collectivising it.

Similarly, denationalisation was in most departments regarded as impracticable; it was said to be impossible at this stage in history to 'unscramble the omelette'. Lack of expertise – and hence of self-confidence – led not only to delay but to huge expense, until a new corpus of experience in privatisation had been built up. If ministers had imported one or two experts on flotation techniques, some of the enormous fees paid to merchant banks might well have been saved. Innovation has proved appallingly costly; it is hard to say whether the transitional expenses of denationalisation were more or less of a strain on the public purse than the terms of compensation for nationalisation which left so many former owners of coalfields chuckling all the way to the bank.

The concept of 'special advisers' drafted in from outside by Ministers with the approval of the Prime Minister, enjoying Civil Service pay and conditions and with full access to secret papers, has had nearly two decades to become accepted; it would be only a further modest step to give Ministers a 'right to nominate' up to eight special officials with a limitation on the ranks to which they might be appointed – no more then one deputy secretary, no more than two under-secretaries or three assistant secretaries, say. Many more temporary appointments of this sort used to be made in wartime; it is the post-war fossilisation of Civil Service practice that has made such a damaging contribution to the arthritic and amateurish performance of British government.

What needs to be stressed about these or any other comparable proposals is that their *constitutional* implications are negligible. We are simply talking about modest changes in the organisation of the executive. To revert to our earlier metaphor, we are tinkering with the engine; we are not attempting to redesign the architecture. If such tinkering has a place in a book about the Constitution, it is only because the misunderstanding of our Constitution is so pervasive that it seems obligatory to offer, if only in passing, one or two answers to the impatient questioner who wants to know how we propose to make the government work better and imagines that this is the same thing as talking about the Constitution. Having offered these asides (which are in truth irrelevant to our main purpose), we must re-emphasise the central point here: that the department, representing such continuity of existence, and such an accumulation of legal authority, public funds and public employees, remains and is likely to go on remaining a formidable centre of power in the British system, whatever the fashionable notions may be about the relative ups and downs of 'Cabinet government' and 'prime-ministerial government'. The loose-baronial nature of the system is not something accidental or fleeting; it is inherent. This is the reality of day-to-day executive power, to which would-be reformers of government machinery must pay serious attention. Constitutional architects must look elsewhere.

Parliament

'Britain is a parliamentary democracy.' The claim seems at once so simple and so resonant as to need no further embellishment or explanation. We carry it around as an inherited piece of luggage which we are not required to unpack. If one or two awkward characters raise objections, it is not usually to the first half of the phrase. 'I slightly bridle', Mr Enoch Powell once remarked, 'when the word "democracy" is applied to the United Kingdom. Instead of that, I say, "We are a Parliamentary nation." '[47] From different political standpoints, Mr Tony Benn and the signers of Charter 88 would agree that the United Kingdom is at present only imperfectly a democracy but would add that our most strenuous efforts should be directed towards making it perfectly so. None of these parties would, however, bridle at the designation 'parliamentary'. That, all agree, is at once the distinguishing feature and the chief glory of our polity.

Yet this claim in its present form seems to be relatively recent and not much found before the Great Reform Bill. The phrase 'parliamentary government', according to the Oxford English Dictionary, dates back only to the age of Disraeli and Bagehot. 'Parliamentarian' and 'Parliamentarianism', as applied to a system of government, appear to be no older than the 1880s. Earlier references appear to relate mostly to specific acts and usages of specific parliaments – the Civil War, the Parliament of Paris, 'parliamentary trains' – or, allusively, to the manners of Parliament, in the use of 'parliamentary' as an epithet denoting deliberateness, civility, formality or rhetorical trickery: 'parliamentary pace', 'parliamentary language' and so on. Before Dicey, in the age of Hallam and certainly in the age of Burke, it seems to have been more common to pride ourselves upon the glories of our Constitution without singling out its parliamentary part. Burke argues that 'the revolution [of 1688] was made to preserve our *ancient* indispensable laws and liberties, and that *ancient* constitution of government which is our only security for law and liberty'.[48] Our liberties were to be regarded as an entailed inheritance. 'By this means our constitution preserves an unity in so great a diversity of its parts. We have an inheritable crown; an inheritable peerage; and a house of commons and a people inheriting privileges, franchises, and liberties from a long line of ancestors.'[49] Obviously, there is more than a touch of romance about this picture. Even in Burke's day, the realities of power were not so picturesquely balanced. But the principle of *constitutional diversity* was seriously, passionately held; that is the guiding principle of this, one of the two greatest political treatises in our language

(*Leviathan* being the other); of parliamentary monotheism there is not a whisper.

Earlier authorities than Burke were fully aware of the tremendous power of Parliament. Blackstone said 'true it is, that what the Parliament doth, no authority upon earth can undo' and quotes Coke: 'the power and jurisdiction of Parliament . . . is so transcendent and absolute, that it cannot be confined, either for causes or persons, within any bounds'. Dicey in turn quotes this famous passage but without noting that Blackstone's whole purpose is to hammer home a *warning*. Blackstone emphasises that 'some have not scrupled to call its power, by a figure rather too bold, the omnipotence of parliament', only in order to go on to argue how important it is that MPs should be:

> eminent for their probity, their fortitude and their knowledge; for it was a known apophthegm of the great lord treasurer Burleigh 'that England could never be ruined but by Parliament': and as Sir Matthew Hale observes, this being the higher and greatest court over which none other can have jurisdiction in the kingdom, if by any means a misgovernment should any way fall upon it, the subjects of this kingdom are left without all manner of remedy. To the same purpose the President Montesquieu, though I trust too hastily, presages: that as Rome, Sparta and Carthage have lost their liberty and perished, so the Constitution of England will in time lose its liberty, will perish: it will perish whence the legislative power shall become more corrupt than the executive.[50]

Dicey's quoting of this crucial passage seems almost comically blind; he rehearses a long and distinguished tradition of fearing overmighty Parliaments and then passes on, pretending that the authorities he quotes lend enthusiastic and unequivocal support to his belief in the omnipotence of Parliament.

Over the succeeding century, the notion that our system is or ought to be parliamentary, in the sense of being solely and exclusively parliamentary and nothing-but-parliamentary, has gained ground by leaps and bounds. The immediate difficulty about this notion is that it fits so ill with the existing realities of government. We are therefore adjured to look back to a golden age of parliamentary democracy, located, I think, somewhere in the nineteenth century (but where precisely? – surely not before the coming of universal franchise for at least one sex). In that age, otherwise unmodern in its arrangements, Parliament, we are led to believe, exercised real power over the executive. Alternatively, it is sometimes argued that, while nineteenth-century parliamentary democracy was imperfect, it was proceeding towards genuinely popular democracy when the ever resourceful ruling class managed to frustrate the process. But both the fact and the date of this frustrating are rather hard to establish. To an outside observer, it might seem that the extension of power to the organised working class or classes had gone hand in hand with the decline of Parliament rather than been frustrated by that decline.

Despite these historiographical snags, the belief that the parliamentary essence of our system could be perfected or retrieved continues to flourish. Charter 88 wants its 'new constitution settlement', among other things, to 'place the executive under the power of a democratically renewed parliament and all agencies of the state under the rule of law'. These are offered as two legs of the same pair of trousers; and yet one can well imagine 'a democratically renewed parliament' which, with the executive placed under its power, might act in a terrifyingly arbitrary and lawless fashion, arresting people it disapproved of, silencing minorities, seizing property on trumped-up excuses.

Again, Mr Benn's Commonwealth of Britain Bill, presented to Parliament in May 1991, purports to gather considerably more power into the hands of 'a democratically renewed parliament': his House of Commons would elect the Prime Minister and approve or disapprove the Prime Minister's choice of Ministers; together with his House of the People, a second chamber elected regionally and proportionally, it would elect a President who would exercise the powers now exercised under Crown prerogative; the House of Commons would also have the right to veto nominations to the High Court which would be made by the President.[51] Other blueprints for constitutional change go further on this latter point, suggesting that the judges should be either directly elected or elected by Parliament.

Common to all these blueprints, then, is the belief that our system does not at present fulfil the parliamentarianism which ought to be its quintessence. Far from pausing to examine what a parliament most appropriately can do and what it cannot and how far our present Parliament fulfils its proper role, there is an almost manic insistence that any accretion of power to Parliament, however delivered, is bound to be an improvement – a genteel version, in short, of 'all power to the soviets'. To draw attention to this kind of parliamentary monotheism is in no way to underestimate the central and leading role of Parliament, nor to brush aside the serious weaknesses of present parliamentary practice. But we shall make little progress if we try to refuse to pay full attention to the qualities of proportion, balance and separation which characterise any usable constitutional architecture.

What do Parliaments do best? What do they do badly? What are they utterly unfit to do at all? The answers to these question are not all that difficult to find. Possible functions for a parliament may be divided into three families: first, remonstration, endorsement, debate and redress of grievances; second, scrutiny of legislation; third, control of the executive. Each family is a sprawling brood liable to overlap and overspill. Some executive actions, such as Orders in Council, or clauses in a Finance Bill, may partake of the character of legislation; legislation may in turn be a response (sometimes an instant response) to parliamentary remonstrations; and what MPs are remonstrating about will very often be some unpalatable action by the executive. But the threefold division does give us a rough guide to help us make sense of what we see and hear and read of the proceedings of Parliament. An MP protesting about the lack of safety on trawlers or the lack of books in primary schools is remonstrating; sitting in committee on the Dock Labour Bill, he is scrutinising; asking questions about the cost of the Trident programme, either in Select Committee or during Defence questions, he is attempting to control the executive.

Rather than attempting to arrive at a single answer as to whether Parliament is prospering or declining, we will find it much simpler if we tackle these three aspects of an MP's work separately. Then it becomes clear, I think, that, as a remonstrator, the modern MP equals if not surpasses any of his predecessors; backed by the inflammatory power of the modern media, strengthened by the ammunition provided by the new array of Select Committees (now covering virtually the whole range of departmental activities), he has a variety of opportunities to ventilate the grievances of his constituents and those of other people and interests; he can put an oral question, hand in a written one, demand an adjournment debate, weave the rehearsal of the grievance into his speech (although there he is competing with 600 other MPs to catch the Speaker's eye); he can buttonhole the Minister in the lobby, or write to him at the ministry, or suborn one of the Minister's quiverful of junior Ministers or his parliamentary private secretary. Meanwhile, back at the ministry, the civil servants know that to deal promptly and helpfully with any problem arising out of Parliament is the shortest way to the Minister's heart; if they keep him out of Commons scrapes, he will be all the readier to listen to their advice on policy. Thus what might be called 'the machinery of remonstration' is pretty well greased these days, and this is not to be undervalued. Remonstration was, after all, one of Parliament's earliest functions; it is one that continues to give life and spirit to the Commons of today, and it constitutes a useful avenue of justice to supplement the regular courts and tribunals. Moreover, MPs as a body and their relevant committees, such as the Procedure Committee, are always alert to ways and means of improving the system, of reactivating devices that have gone dead or been neutralised or swallowed up by the executive, such as the allocation of debating time to private members and the right to demand an emergency debate under a certain Standing Order of the House. Backbenchers are, rightly, never satisfied, but, by all historical and comparative standards, their opportunities to ventilate and, with luck, to remedy their constituents' grievances are far from dusty. If Parliament has declined, it is not in this respect.

When we turn to the scrutiny of legislation, the picture is quite different and a good deal more discouraging; judged by an ideal standard, rather than the standard of past parliaments, it is dismal. The principle that the government of the day has the right to use its majority to get its business through has made a mockery of all the subtle machinery of the Committee and Report stages of Bills. Only a somewhat shamefaced conspiracy between the two front benches and the parliamentary press lobby prevents the scandalous spectacle of Committee proceedings being more fully brought home to us: the Ministers wearily reading out their briefs, the Opposition spokesmen trotting out the same old amendments purely for the purposes of party rhetoric and without any serious hope of improving the Bill, the government backbenchers – pressed men present merely to make up the government's majority – reading the newspapers or answering their letters; it requires only a few top hats, brocade waistcoats and cigars to complete a tableau of almost Regency sloth. Occasionally, the government Whips do make a mistake and nominate to a committee a couple of unreliable backbenchers who, out of boredom, spite or, now and then, a genuine desire to improve the Bill, vote with the Opposition to pass an unwelcome amendment; however, nine times out of ten, the government will insist on the amendment being reversed at Report stage.

Nor, except on uncontroversial matters, do amendments passed by the House of Lords suffer a happier fate, no matter how exhaustive and expert the debate in the Upper House may have been. Once again, the government will steamroller the Bill back into its original shape. Even when acting within the constraints of the 1911 and 1949 Parliament Acts and the 'Salisbury Rules' (the convention by which the Upper House restrains itself from wrecking Bills on which the country has, by implication, given its verdict at a previous general election), the Lords now know that the Commons will automatically overturn its verdict. The War Crimes Bill of 1990 was not a money Bill, nor had the question come up at the preceding general election, and yet the Commons was outraged by the Lords' rejection of the Bill, and Mrs Thatcher did not hesitate to reintroduce it; nor did Mr Major, when he became Prime Minister, despite the fact that he himself had originally voted against the Bill. No incident could more clearly demonstrate the Commons' view of the unchallengeability of its wisdom.

Oppositions may use the weapon of delay, either for purposes of party advantage or because they genuinely believe the Bill is a bad Bill. But here too the government has become increasingly impatient of opposition. The *comble* in this particular erosion of tolerance was the decision of the Major government to impose a 'guillotine' (the timetable motion which curtails the otherwise open-ended debate on a Bill by allocating a fixed number of days during which discussion on each stage of the Bill must be completed) on discussion of the Dangerous Dogs Bills; in fact, they forced the Commons to take all the stages on a single evening, 10 June 1991. This was despite the fact that the measure was by no means a simple one, was hastily conceived as second thoughts, after equally hasty first thoughts (that all dangerous dogs should be slaughtered), and expert opinion on the question was sharply divided.

In the course of the guillotine debate on the dogs Bill, Mr Richard Shepherd, the independent-minded Conservative MP for Aldridge-Brownhills, pointed out the startling increase in the use of the guillotine by recent governments, as follows:

1945–50	3
1950–60	10
1960–70	13
1970–4	8
1974–9	21
1979–83	30
1983–7	10
1987–90	28

While Mrs Thatcher is clearly the principal villain of the piece, there is, equally clearly, a general tendency for governments to resort more often and more quickly to the guillotine. Mr Shepherd went on to point out that the early months of the Major government scarcely suggested any return to restraint; on the contrary, the government was now guillotining Bills with which the whole House was more or less in agreement – such as the Bill to undo the effects of the poll tax and the Bill to muzzle dangerous dogs.

It is sometimes said that there is a vestigial safeguard in the existence of the custom that the government does not guillotine Bills 'of a constitutional character'. This custom seems one recently more honoured in the breach than the observance: the Callaghan government attempted, unsuccessfully, to guillotine the debate on the Scotland and Wales Bill 1976 (the only occasion since the war when a guillotine motion was lost) and, undeterred and un-ashamed, tried again with the similar Bill the following year and had better luck. Other Bills of an important rule-making or constitutional character which have been guillotined in recent years include the British Nationality Bill of 1981 and the Local Government Bill of 1985 (which abolished the GLC and the six metropolitan counties) and, most spectacularly, the Bill which passed into our law the Single European Act of 1986 as the European Communities (Amendment) Act 1986.

Something comparable is to be observed when we look briefly at the record of the Commons in exercising effective control over the non-legislative actions of the executive. Characteristically, the response of the Commons, whether on domestic or foreign policy, will be one of *retrospective* endorsement, whether the endorsement be heartfelt or whipped. This may come as a shock to those who have unrealistic expectations of what a Parliament, that is to say, a large, unwieldy, heterogeneous debating chamber, can achieve in the face of a coherent government with a comfortable majority, but it is scarcely a novelty. From the beginning, the House (later Houses) of Parliament has, above all, been the place where the monarch sought endorsement for his actions, not the place where he conceived those actions or took counsel as to what form they should take. Modern critics who complain, for example, that the Select Committee on Nationalised Industries used to uncover waste and mismanagement only months, if not years after the event, have, I think, in their minds a model of prompt scrutiny which would be extremely difficult to carry into practice, certainly in fast-moving situations in which an uninterrupted flow of decisions is required of the government, as of any executive. In cases where the decisions are more of a long-term, prospective nature, a parliamentary committee can sometimes exercise its influence before the decision is set in concrete: on questions of long-term public investment, for example, or of government policy towards Eastern Europe. It may well be that pressure from the Commons will form an important part of the public pressures which have impelled the government to permit more investment in British Rail and the London Underground and to offer more help to the new democracies of Eastern Europe.

There have been occasions on which the Commons has, by luck more than calculation, happened to intervene at a decisive moment. On the Falklands, for instance, it was the savaging of the Foreign Office Minister, Mr Nicholas Ridley, by the 'Falkland Islands Lobby' on the back benches which deterred the British government from pursuing the idea of a leaseback solution to the dispute with Argentina over the sovereignty of the islands. Then later, it was the bellicose indignation with which the Commons received the news of the Argentine invasion which helped to cause the sending of the task force. More significantly, the defection of so many Conservative MPs in the vote of 8 May 1940 on the Norwegian fiasco did tip the balance and bring about the resignation of Chamberlain and the accession of Churchill.

But these are rare exceptions in which MPs, with the wind of public opinion filling their sails, have had the chance to intervene at a decisive moment. They are not typical of the usual place of Parliament in the scheme of British decision-making, which is retrospective and compliant.

Indeed, the very exceptions indirectly reinforce the central point, that the government can pray in aid for all its actions, however high-handed they may appear to constitutional theorists, the driving imperative of the people's mandate. The people have spoken (though it may be three or four years since they spoke), and their will must not be frustrated; this is the meaning of Dicey's inelegant formulation that, while Parliament is the 'legal sovereign', the people are the 'political sovereign'. Indeed, as we have seen, when it came to Home Rule, Dicey wanted to give the 'political sovereign' an opportunity to declare its will more directly and emphatically than it had at a general election, by the government holding a referendum. The pervasive discipline of the party machine is justified on the grounds that, only by such discipline, can the will of the people be reliably and thoroughly carried through. As Crossman put it, the Labour Party saw itself as the 'battering ram' of social change; individual deviation was a forbidden luxury for a people's delegate, and he must not fall into the self-indulgence of regarding himself as a representative in the sense that Burke so described himself to the electors of Bristol. From the point of view of the Labour movement, shipshape most certainly did not mean Bristol-fashion.

Before the war, this Labour theory was put still more brutishly by several of its leading figures who later became such painfully respectable exponents of parliamentary democracy. In 1933, in *Problems of a Socialist Government*, Sir Stafford Cripps and his co-authors advanced the view that 'the Party' should appoint the Minister, subject to 'the right at any time to substitute a fresh Minister in the place of any it desires to recall'. An Emergency Powers Bill would be passed through all its stages on the first day of the session, followed by an annual Planning and Finance Bill, which would 'take the place of the King's speech, the Budget, financial resolutions and the second reading debate on most of the important measures of the year. . . . It is idle once Parliament has decided upon a certain course of action, to discuss its wisdom again and again.'[52] Attlee believed that Labour MPs, liberated from attendance at superfluous debates, would be fully occupied seeing to it that 'the will of the Central Government is obeyed', because 'we have to take the strong points of the Russian system and apply them to this country'. The executive was only, after all, in Laski's words, a 'Committee of the Legislature'.

Far from these ideas being sinister and foreign in their origin, they had a homely ancestor in Bagehot's view that the Cabinet was in substance only 'a committee of the party majority', which had delegated to it, for greater convenience, the day-to-day exercise of the power which had been entrusted to it by the electorate. The Cripps–Attlee–Laski reading was merely the logical culmination of the denial of the separation of powers. In a unitary state of this kind, the general will must flow unimpeded through both the legislature and the executive, unchecked, unbalanced, unchallenged.

The theory that drives on this disregard of the spirit of parliamentary procedures appears to be a kind of vulgar - Rousseauism. What matters is to ascertain the General Will and then to implement it with no ifs and buts (Rousseau himself was considerably more hesitant and qualified, and the constitutional advice he gave to Poland and Corsica rather more hedged and measured). This vulgar Rousseauism brings us directly to a plain contradiction, though one which constitutional reformers, certainly those of Mr Benn's colour, are somewhat reluctant to confront. The more democratic (in the vulgar-Rousseauist sense) that you make Parliament, the more unhesitantly and unqualifiedly its votes and arrangement of business give effect to the will of the people, whether declared by implication at a general election or directly through a referendum, the less, inevitably, Parliament can be 'parliamentary', in its first general, early-nineteenth-century sense of 'slow', 'deliberate', 'courteous', 'attentive to the wording of commas and sub-clauses' (to the point of pedantry). The whole endless parliamentary process of refraction, revision, consultation can, in this perspective, be seen only as an elitist impediment. If by 'democracy' you mean the instantaneous, immediate, hot-and-strong breath of public opinion – which is what people often do mean – then parliamentary democracy is an oxymoron, a contradiction in terms.

But if the intention is to deliver to the electorate steady, thoughtful and consistent government, which pays careful attention not only to the will of the majority but also to the aspirations, fears and interests of minorities, then the more parliamentary – the more indirect, refracted and laborious – the system becomes, the more it is likely to fulfil its function. And here, inevitably, one bumps into an unsought but unmistakable distinction between the voters as political agents – that is, having the right to issue commands – and political patients – entitled to expect their complaints to be attended to by trained experts. One may call parliamentary government 'democratic' in the sense that its procedures maximise those satisfactions which politics can supply for as many people as possible; but, if it does so, it satisfies people very largely as consumers of government rather than as its producers; it is outcomes rather than inputs which are maximised; political participation will be accorded a lower priority than getting government off people's backs, happiness put before power as the prime desideratum.

If we opt for this definition – a democracy which is genuinely parliamentary, indirect and representative rather than direct and participatory – then we will approach the reform of Parliament with a much clearer and more confident sense of what needs to be done. We will want Parliament, among other things, to deploy a second-thoughts capability to correct and improve on the first impulses of public opinion and the first political responses to those impulses. We shall want to give MPs powers to amend or resist the more overweening or ill-considered interventions of government, however garlanded with mandates from the previous general election.

Public opinion in a parliamentary democracy is not to be regarded, in Wyndham Lewis's phrase, as 'a many-headed baby', incapable of appreciating argument or of modifying its first cries of protest or desire, but – if personalised at all – as an adult voice, fallible, sometimes ill-informed, sometimes wholly or partly mistaken, but nevertheless to be answered and taken account of. That, after all, is the purpose for which these elaborate procedures have been developed over the centuries.

What devices, old or new, need to be considered as aids to the revival of a truly parliamentary democracy? There are perhaps five relevant areas to be looked at: (1) The system of election to Parliament. (2) The procedures of the House of Commons. (3) The Second Chamber. (4) The role of entrenched statute. (5) Other legislatures or assemblies. Each of these areas occupies a formidable acreage; luckily, in each, we are likely to find only one or two usable devices of serious significance and the pros and cons of each device may be roughed out quite briskly.

The system of election

Is there any way of altering the rules by which the House of

Commons is elected that will add to the independence of its members and the authority of its deliberations – without at the same time undermining the prospects of reasonably coherent and effective government? That seems to be the question as precisely as we can state it. Quite clearly, there can be no question of forbidding candidates to declare their party allegiance in advance of election; nor is it easy to see how we can, through the system, persuade constituency or national parties to relax their hold on their representatives. Most methods of Proportional Representation, for example, actually increase the power of the party; in the West German system it is the party headquarters which adds its own nominees to the MPs elected by the constituencies so as to achieve proportionality. This power to fill up the list not only makes the 'fillers' themselves likely to be subservient to the party bosses; it encourages a general atmosphere of docility, for who knows when he or she may not need a place on the fill-up list?

The question, it should be emphasised, is not whether Proportional Representation is in some profound sense alien to the British tradition. We could switch over to any system of PR overnight without losing that night's sleep if the system in question appeared to offer practical advantages. Parliament did not hesitate to introduce Proportional Representation for the Irish elections in 1919, and subsequently for elections to the new Stormont Parliament until 1929, and more recently in Northern Ireland for elections to the European Parliament.

With that purposeful amnesia which underpins our constitutional tradition, we have chosen to forget, not only the passionate agitation in favour of Proportional Representation in the nineteenth century but also the fact that, between 1867 and 1885, there actually was an element of Proportional Representation inserted into the system. With the aim of improving the representation of minorities, Disraeli's Reform Act of 1867 provided that, in three-member constituencies, each elector was to have only two votes, so that by careful organisation a two-fifths minority might gain one seat instead of the largest party winning all three. As far back as 1831, the poet-politician Winthrop Mackworth Praed had spoken up for the rights of the minority. Praed, speaking in Committee on the Reform Bill, had put the same argument that is still being put today:

> What do we understand by the very word 'representation'? If we desire that the representatives of a numerous constituency should come hither merely as witnesses of the fact that certain opinions are entertained by the majority of that constituency, our present system of election is certainly rational. . . . But if we intend, as surely we do intend, that not the majority only, but the aggregate mass of every numerous constituency should, so far as is possible, be seen in the persons, and heard in the voices, of their representatives . . . then, Sir, our present rule of election is in theory, wrong and absurd.

A constituency of 12,000 in which a bare majority of 6001 might return 'the whole allotment of representation' would leave 5999, if not exactly '*un*-represented', at least '*mis*-represented in the grossest manner'. [53]

Lord John Russell's Bill of 1860 included the provision that was to be adopted in 1867 – and then repealed again in 1885, for precisely the same reasons that traditionalists oppose Proportional Representation today, that it increased the power of the already unpopular party caucus, which had to organise the party's vote to get as many of its candidates in as possible. This applied to the majority party as well as to the minority party. If, say, all the Liberals' double votes were carefully distributed among their three candidates, they could still manage to secure the return of all three. What strikes one in these old debates is not merely how closely they mirror the modern arguments for and against PR but also how uninhibitedly the Victorians contemplated every kind of alteration to the electoral system, with apparently very little sense of guilt or foreboding about tampering with fundamentals. Victorian pride in our Constitution – and a strutting peacock pride it often was – did not, it seems, entail any unbudgeable adherence to the details of the arrangements by which the electorate was at that moment being represented.

But does Proportional Representation as a general principle

encourage Parliament as a whole to become either more independent-minded, or more level-headed, or more fully and fairly representative of public opinion? Before trying to answer this, we should note that the virtues which Proportional Representation in all its forms is alleged by its supporters to possess are not necessarily compatible, one with another.

Hitler came to power under a very sensible system of Proportional Representation. Does that make Proportional Representation responsible for Nazism and the Second World War? Of course not, though we might suspect that this notorious example does demonstrate one of Proportional Representation's alleged virtues; the speed with which the Nazi vote grew over the elections of the late 1920s and early 1930s did accurately reflect the growing frustration and resentment of the German people – and perhaps reflected it more swiftly and directly than the first-past-the-post system might have done.

Is the instability of Italy's post-war politics due to its system of Proportional Representation? No, of course not. The prime root of that instability lies in the fact that during the war the Communist party won a certain historic legitimacy to represent the left in Italy and, therefore, the unacceptability of a Communist government dictated that Italy be governed by a succession of coalitions centred on the Christian Democrats. Only in the late 1980s, when the Communist Party signalled its willingness to become respectable and even to change its name, did two-party politics become a realistic prospect. One cannot blame Proportional Representation for the lopsided political legacy of the war, although it might be possible to argue that first-past-the-post voting might have brought about a speedier coalescence at both ends of the political spectrum.

Nor is it entirely clear whether the greater importance of the smaller parties under a system of Proportional Representation leads to a steadier, less immoderate government. This may be true when the smaller parties in question are inoffensive liberal or agrarian parties, but in Sweden the most crucial of the smaller parties has often been the Communists who, when in coalition, were able to drag their Social Democratic partners to the left.

In Israel, the indispensable support of the smaller religious parties is often decisive in securing the rejection of peace proposals. In Britain, the Scottish and Welsh nationalists, in return for sustaining the Callaghan government in office, insisted on early legislation to introduce Scottish and Welsh assemblies which was not much wanted by English voters, nor, as it turned out in the referendum, by Scottish or Welsh voters either. Under any plausible system of Proportional Representation, the chances of regional or extreme single-issue parties being required to make up a coalition could only be increased. One can imagine an anti-immigration party demanding an unpleasant price for its participation in such a coalition. No doubt every decent-minded party would refuse to conclude a bargain of that sort, in which case the prospects of securing any kind of stable majority would be reduced to the extent of the number of MPs who would be unusable because they were unspeakable.

This is not to argue that the effects of this or that system of Proportional Representation always contain a malevolent snag of this sort; it is merely to say that the effects are unpredictable and contingent on the political legacies and tendencies of the time, and in this respect are no more predictable or controllable than the results of first-past-the-post elections. Let us suppose that, under some system of Proportional Representation, the Alliance had gone into coalition with the Labour Party in the Callaghan-Foot era. For a time, no doubt, the future of the Alliance would have seemed even rosier than it did in reality during those years. Yet the problem of trade union power would still have loomed as large; there might still have been a Winter of Discontent (since the Alliance were at that time even keener on an incomes policy than the Labour Party), and the government might still have been flung out, exhausted and discredited, only this time carrying with it an equally exhausted and discredited Alliance. Political realities have a habit of breaking in upon the most elegantly designed electoral systems.

It is not even self-evident that Proportional Representation is fairer. As a rule, it transfers the power of making and unmaking governments from the most committed to the least committed.

The candidate who gets most first-preference votes may be dethroned in favour of the candidate who gets most second and subsequent preference votes. The most-desired is to be defeated by the least-objected-to. Is that really fairer, and is it always advantageous?

All large political parties are coalitions; and the rise and fall of moderate or immoderate tendencies within those coalitions are hastened or decelerated by comparable changes in the public mood, which are reflected, in Britain, in by-elections and opinion polls as well as general elections. The pursuit of power infuses political parties with a dynamic which is both calculated and instinctive; parties ultimately go where the votes are, or go as far as they can in that direction without enraging their committed supporters. Advocates of Proportional Representation often seem to take a somewhat static view of the political process and regard the making of post-election coalitions as a matter of bolting together stable bodies. In *Parliament for the People*,[54] Joe Rogaly argues that the open coalitions which naturally tend to result after elections held under PR 'would be better than the submerged coalitions we now get under the labels "Conservative" or "Labour" ', in which 'the party factions do their secret deals behind the scenes, leaving the voters in ignorance and therefore relatively defenceless'.

But the dichotomy between 'open' and 'submerged' is not so clear-cut. Within and between the parties under Proportional Representation, after all, there is a good deal of submerged activity – eddies, undertows and backwaters: what compromises are to be made, what unpalatable policies from the other parties will have to be swallowed, and so on. There is nothing discreditable about such dealings; they are part of the inevitable brokerage of democratic politics. But we cannot allow the Proportional Representation supporters to monopolise the shining armour. One can construct an alternative rhetoric denouncing the 'shabby deals', the 'kaleidoscope politics' of Proportional Representation.

If all this sounds somewhat negative, I hasten to add that many countries with Proportional Representation often produce admirable government over a considerable period; in a nation which has the good fortune to be in an historically stable mode, politics will adapt to take care of the quirks and weaknesses of its particular system of election, whether it be proportional or first-past-the-post. I have been eager to point out the quirks and weaknesses of Proportional Representation only in order to deflate the hopes that the adoption of PR would by itself restore the constitutional architecture to its former balance and proportion.

In particular, it would, I think, be a bizarre way of increasing the independent-mindedness of members of Parliament to break the constitutional link which at present does give them a genuine (if vestigial) sense that their duty is to represent all the people of their constituency, and not simply those who voted for their party.

It is this sense that the member is 'returned' from Loamshire by a spontaneous act of the people of Loamshire which we surely wish to reinforce. And with that in mind, we might do better to concentrate on the other main idea for reforming the system of election: fixed parliaments. This notion has surfaced at intervals throughout the last three centuries; the period for which the parliament ought to be fixed has varied from seven years to the single year demanded by the Chartists; modern proponents mostly plump for four years, probably influenced by the model of the American Presidency. But the reasoning behind the idea has remained constant, namely, that the summoning of Parliaments ought to be 'somewhat unalterable' and beyond the manipulation of monarch, faction, party or Prime Minister. The fixed periodicity dignifies the people's choice; the result of the election is the outcome of a regular constitutional process, instead of, as at present, a more or less successful confidence trick by the Prime Minister of the day. Most political economists would, I think, argue also that, over the long run, fixed parliaments tend to improve economic stability. Manipulation of fiscal and budgetary policy for electoral ends continues, but only in the run-up period to the election, which is a predictable and recurring period. The objection that fixed terms are a mistake 'because the Americans are always campaigning' ignores the fact that it is the off-year elections for the House of Representatives and part of the Senate which keep the campaign pot bubbling.

The more serious objection to fixed parliaments remains that, without a power to dissolve, minority governments may limp on for years until the next election date. For this reason, in many if not most Western parliamentary systems (Norway and Switzerland appear to be the only exceptions)[55] there is a provision for early dissolution. On the other hand, it should be pointed out that minority or coalition governments are not exactly unknown in twentieth-century Britain; we were governed by one or the other from 1910 to 1922, from 1923 to 1924, from 1929 to 1931, in 1974 and from 1976 to 1979. Nor has an early dissolution, even under our first-past-the-post system, always produced a fresh government with a satisfactory overall majority; it did not do so in 1910, and it only just managed to do so in October 1974 – and, within two years, by-election losses had destroyed the tiny majority Labour had then managed to extract from the electorate. It may be true – although the evidence of opinion polls does not always support the contention – that 'England does not love coalitions,' but even if it is true, this dislike relates to a system in which a dissolution and fresh elections are an ever present alternative to trying to make the coalition work. The existence of this alternative is bound to undermine the coalition's prospects of success, since all parties to it are presumed to be jockeying for position in and trying to control the timing of the general election which everyone believes to be just around the corner. The break-up of all twentieth-century British coalitions has been attended by dismal chicanery and squabbling and desperate attempts at bribery – none more desperate than James Callaghan's efforts to cling on to the Scottish, Welsh and Irish nationalists in the dying months of his government. In a genuinely fixed parliament, all the pressure is on parties to the coalition to make it work and to make a distinguishable contribution which will redound to their credit when the term is up. The presumption of stability tends to enforce co-operation.

In favour of fixed parliaments, it is often also said that they make it more difficult for governments to stage election booms which then go bust with embarrassing rapidity after polling day. Again, the experience of other countries, such as the USA and Australia, does not wholly confirm this. Our own fixed 'local parliaments', with their elections held every three or four years, are notorious for the way in which the ruling party raids the reserves in order to keep the local tax down in the year leading up to elections.

Nor does the provision for an early dissolution of Parliament invariably work smoothly. West Germany is an interesting example.[56] The Germans had had a miserable experience of early dissolutions under the Weimar Constitution, which gave the President, under the notorious Article 48, the right to dissolve the Reichstag more or less at will. As a consequence, between 1920 and 1933 all seven Reichstags were dissolved prematurely. The framers of the new Basic Law in 1949 were determined that neither the President nor the Chancellor should enjoy untrammelled use of this power. The only circumstances in which the President may now dissolve the Bundestag before the normal end of its term of office are if the Chancellor fails in a vote of confidence and requests a dissolution, or if no candidate for Chancellor can obtain an absolute majority in the Bundestag. As a result, since 1949 only two Bundestags have been terminated prematurely, in 1972 and 1983. In both cases, there was a certain amount of jiggery-pokery; in the first, seventeen out of eighteen Ministers deliberately abstained on their own motion in order to secure its rejection and open the way to fresh elections. That was not so underhand as it may seem, since the vote on the Budget, which was tied, had shown that the government really had lost its majority. On Chancellor Kohl's confidence motion in December 1982, the members of the government parties abstained, thus ensuring an opposition win. President Carstens then accepted the request for a dissolution, arguing that it was not for him to go behind the vote and try to distinguish a genuine from an artificial rejection and, in any case, the government did not really have a majority, since the Free Democrats had only offered their support in return for fresh elections. Four members of the Bundestag submitted this some-what inconsistent reasoning to the Federal Constitutional Com-mittee which, in a significant judgment of February 1983, backed away from declaring this particular dissolution invalid but declared that any future dissolution in similar circumstances would be likely to be unconstitutional. Thus the Constitution avoided the political confrontation and turmoil which would have been caused by declaring an election invalid just before it was about to take place; but at the same time it made quite clear that, in future, fictitious defeats to secure a premature dissolution would be void.

The Times (24 June 1991) argues against fixed-term parliaments on the grounds that the Prime Minister would simply instruct some of his MPs to vote against the government on a no-confidence motion and gain a dissolution in the West German style. That might be possible if constitutional practice remained unchanged on the introduction of fixed-term Parliaments. But it would have to change, and, once installed, the new practice would be as binding as any other procedural rule. Dissolutions would be more sparingly granted, and the monarch would need to be fortified with organised advice to ensure that the terms of the new law were being honoured.

If, for example, it were the practice of the Crown to consult the Judicial Committee of the Privy Council, as well as the leaders of all parties in Parliament, before deciding whether the objective conditions for a dissolution – that the government had lost its parliamentary majority and that no other party or combination of parties would be able to command the support of the House – had been satisfactorily met, then Prime Ministers would soon abandon any hope of fiddling a bogus dissolution; not only would they run the risk of being publicly branded as deceitful, the dissolution would not be granted. And even if, according to some calculations, the government had genuinely lost its majority, the Prime Minister might well prefer to hang on rather than resign and risk allowing the Opposition to gain the authority of office without having to win a general election.

In the tailor-made West German constitution, although politicians can wriggle round the fixed pillars of the system, it is perfectly possible for a constitutional court to put up barriers to stop them getting through the same way in future. By removing from the Chancellor or Prime Minister the right to dissolve, we do remove from his hand one important lever, the manipulation of which otherwise absorbs a huge amount of his attention and energy.

The best argument in favour of fixed terms is the general air of stability which they impart to political life. Among all the many other imponderables making for uncertainty, the date of the next election is then not one; public and private bodies no less than individuals have at least one established grid on which to sketch out their plans. In examining the United States, one cannot help noticing the contrast between the frenetic non-stop political campaigning (which no doubt arises partly from the extreme brevity of the two-year term endured by Representatives) and the stately, even somnolent tenor of non-political life and the extreme conservatism of attitudes and practices which belies the conventional view of American addiction to novelty. Has this something to do with the extreme fixity of American constitutional arrangements and the inconceivability, even in time of war, of postponing the elections? No doubt there are a dozen other reasons – the consensual nature of American society being one – but it is at least plausible that the fixed grid helps to give people a sense of knowing where they are. In the UK, by contrast, *bunched* elections – 1910, 1923–4, 1929–31, 1950–1, 1964–6, 1974 – may be symptoms rather than causes of political crisis, but they are not always successful in removing the underlying cause of the crisis, for the second election does not always produce the clear majority which it was intended to produce. It is arguable that the occasional minority government –which a fixed-term system will inevitably bring and offers no immediate way out of – may be a least bad way of exhausting the party discord and teaching the different factions to combine to produce a serviceable policy. In this sense, a fixed-term system may have some of the virtues of a Proportional-Representation system, without making it so difficult for a single party to gain the kind of overall majority which would be needed to drive through a programme of radical reform.

It is this combination of the existing first-past-the-post system with fixed parliaments which seems to me to offer the highest probability of government which is both stable and effective; the first-past-the-post system offers the best likelihood of majority governments, but the fixed term of the parliament will build up a tradition of party co-operation within those parliaments in which no party enjoys an overall majority and which are bound to crop up now and then.

Procedure

Advancing gingerly within the precincts of the Palace of Westminster, we have first to recognise the intrinsic limits on the capabilities of Parliament, perhaps of all parliaments. A useful starting-point is to be had from Leo Amery's remark in *Thoughts on the Constitution*, his 1946 Chichele lectures, which, in brief compass, strike more precisely at the heart of many of the problems than treatises of three or four times the length. 'The main task of Parliament', Amery argued, 'is still what it was when first summoned, not to legislate or govern, but to secure full discussion and ventilation of all matters, legislative or administrative, as the conditions of giving its assent to Bills, whether introduced by the Government or by private members, or its support to Ministers.'[57] It is a body to be wooed, cajoled, consulted, enthused; it is not an authority to issue commands, conceive long-range strategies or handle a fast-moving crisis. This character and these limitations it has, not because of the imperfect development of democracy in Britain, but because that is of the nature of a Parliament with over 600 members, all equal in their status as members but differing wildly in their opinions and allegiances. By contrast, a government, like any executive body, must exhibit a degree of coherence and hierarchy (as even the Chinese Red Army was to discover); there is no other way of ensuring a series of effective and consistent decisions.

When we use the phrase 'accountable to Parliament', we must not try to read more into it than is naturally there. Ministers must present an account of their actions to Parliament in a form which permits Parliament to express its views promptly and effectively (otherwise the accountability would be a hollow charade); but, however helpfully this procedure is carried out and however forcefully Parliament responds, it will remain the Minister who conceives and executes the policy. So, for example, Parliament will expect the Minister of Health to present his proposals for altering the health warning on cigarette packets in good time before the proposals are set in concrete and put before the European Council of Ministers; if Parliament's procedures mean that MPs are always presented with *faits accomplis*, then the procedures need to be altered (as they have been over the last year and will continue to be). But it will never be Parliament's task to conceive the wording of the health warning, although there is nothing to prevent the government *borrowing* the wording from an unusually intelligent back-bench amendment, if it feels so inclined.

Rather than campaigning for more power for Parliament in an undifferentiated sense, we need to look more specifically for ways and means which will enable Parliament to fulfil its traditional role; and the twin criteria here are *promptness* and *effectiveness*. The views of the House must be heard in good time, and, when the views are strongly held and shared by significant numbers of MPs, they must be listened to.

Most modern allegations of the lamentable impotence of the House of Commons do not test their conclusions properly against these criteria. Such allegations were, in any case, made to look a little silly by the events of the 1970s; in the bleak spring of 1974, there was Mr Heath immured in Downing Street making awkward and unavailing overtures to the handful of Liberal MPs, all too well aware that, even with their support, he would not have been able to command a majority without the added support of the Ulster Unionists, whose ancient links with the Conservative Party his own actions in Northern Ireland had so blithely snapped. Thereafter, for most of the succeeding five years, the Labour government was paying no less frantic homage to all the minority parties in the House in order to stay afloat. The fact that, for most of the century, governments have sailed on with robust majorities makes their agonies when they have no secure hold on power all the more pitiful.

Similarly, the fact that government measures which are brought before the House usually sail through never leads old parliamentary hands to forget the times when the House has turned nasty and dug its heels in. Nor do most accounts of parliamentary impotence mention the huge number of possible proposals which might appeal to enthusiasts in the governing party but which are never brought forward because they would be so repugnant to a large number of MPs who represent a significant section of public opinion or of the relevant vested interests.

Take the causes of denationalisation and the abolition of trade union legal privileges. Both would have provoked hearty enthusiasm at any Conservative Party Conference from 1945 onwards, and often did. But, until the 1970's, no Conservative government felt confident of framing any such measures which would carry Parliament and the country. Controversial measures have to wait for a sea change in public opinion. Consider the abolition of public subsidy for planting conifers in upland areas. When this was proposed for England, it was accepted as right and timely; when comparable measures were proposed for Scotland, Mr Malcolm Rifkind, the Scottish Secretary, was howled down by Scottish MPs, who were fearful, whether rightly or wrongly, about the consequent effect on local employment. Here, as with many such measures, a relatively small number of MPs can block a measure; sometimes even the fear of such a humiliation will cause the Chief Whip to report to Cabinet that he cannot guarantee to deliver a majority. Sometimes, the passage of time will erode the body of opposition; for example, the decline in the numbers employed in agriculture and hence the decline in the agricultural vote in rural constituencies – together with the rise in the conservationist revolt against artificial fertilisers, pesticides and the grubbing up of hedges – made it possible, in the later years of the Thatcher government, to begin dismantling some of the public subsidies available to agriculture, with only a whimper or two from backbench Tory MPs. Occasionally, the government in general, and the government Whips in particular, underestimate the number of diehards on a particular question, and government measures suffer a humiliating rejection, as they did on the Sunday Trading Bill, a measure which no government had previously dared to bring forward on its own account. The same very nearly happened to Mr Heath on the Bill to abolish resale price maintenance, another rational, modern-minded measure which underestimated the ferocious resistance of small shopkeepers.

Some of the measures mentioned above take the form of

legislation; others take the form of Orders in Council, or simply of ministerial announcements under powers granted by statute. There is no reason to think that, in this sort of work, Parliament is any more impotent than in the past. Nor is the government's sensitivity to the need to maintain a reliable majority in support of its general line of action restricted to home affairs. We have already seen, for example, how the fury of a handful of backbenchers at Mr Ridley's proposal to negotiate a leaseback arrangement with Argentina shaped the policy of the British government and then helped to provoke the Argentinian invasion; and how MPs' response to the invasion shaped, not only the sending of the task force, but also the counter-invasion. More subtly, it was possible to note a distinct modification of Mrs Thatcher's blanket support for Mr Reagan's bombing of Libya after the first hostile reactions in and out of Parliament.

In all these affairs, we can sense no lack of opportunity for MPs to put their objections, to gang up against an emerging government policy or to threaten to withhold their support if the policy is persisted with. The one recurring exception is in the conduct of European Community business; in fact, this exception tends to sharpen the outline of the rule. It is because there is so much horrendously detailed European business and because the House of Commons had until recently maintained a proud and jealous indifference towards EC activity that the inescapable processing of the business was relegated to the small hours and to a handful of obsessives; more seriously, much of the processing was of *faits accomplis*; and, when the House did hold one of its twice-yearly general debates on the Community, it was usually too late to shape the more general lines of approach. The Commons Procedure Committee has made reasonable haste to suggest improvements. Our concern here is not with how effective the new procedures are likely to be in practice but with the clear understanding that both the Committee and the House as a whole have their right and their duty, which are, above all, to be timely in their criticisms.

That clarity of understanding is also behind the recent development of a network of Select Committees to cover virtually every area of policy. Old parliamentary hands sometimes sneer at these new creations – first adumbrated when R. H. S. Crossman was Leader of the House and later coming full-blown in the leadership of Norman St John Stevas. These Select Committees, it is argued, distract attention from the serious business taking place on the floor of the House; they are a puny and impotent imitation of the congressional committees which enjoy real power in the very different system of the United States; their irrelevance to the British system is shown by the rarity of and poor attendance at parliamentary debates on their reports.

But this criticism, I think, misses the main purpose of setting up the network of Select Committees which was to place a body of information at the fingertips of a number of MPs, information from ministerial departments, in particular, which was not otherwise easily extractable through the traditional medium of parliamentary questions and interventions in debate; Ministers and senior officials were summoned to appear before these committees and argue in some detail during sustained bouts of questioning about their reasons for doing this and not doing that. The right of MPs to gain access to the more intimate passages of departmental thinking was in no way novel; Select Committees and their powers have a venerable pedigree. But by extending this routine of continuous quizzing and monitoring to the whole field of government, MPs now are in a position, if they are willing to do the donkeywork, to gain a genuine mastery of their chosen subjects, and so to become equipped to ask the right questions, if not always to secure the full and true answers.

What then is missing? In what way is the modern House of Commons underpowered or frustrated from carrying out its proper functions? Is the personal frustration undoubtedly experienced by the average backbencher after the first thrill of election has worn off a reflection of some systemic weakness?

The conventional complaint from outsiders (it is less often heard from MPs) is that the closed and secretive nature of British government is seriously damaging to the public good, from the moral point of view no less than from the point of view of efficiency. 'Open government', in the most generous possible sense, would make the United Kingdom a happier and better-run country. The Official Secrets Act 1911 was a ball and chain; and Mr Hurd's recent successor, the 1989 Act, is no better, some would say worse. In almost every field of government, the public is deprived of valuable information to which it is entitled by right. This argument is one of the principal thrusts behind the recent campaigns for constitutional reform, most notably that of Charter 88. Detailed proposals for opening up the operations of government to public inspection, on the lines of the Swedish model or the American Freedom of Information Act, bulk large in the books and pamphlets now being published.

If they receive somewhat cursory treatment here, it is not because I believe such arguments to be mistaken or broken-backed – there is clearly a serviceable logic behind them – but because I believe that their importance is hugely exaggerated. First of all, a vast amount of useful information is already publicly available; as any competent spy knows, the first resources to be tapped are the government's own publications and the daily newspapers. Secondly, the amount of such information has been growing steadily ever since the Second World War – without any discernible improvement in the quality of our government. Thirdly, the ways in which British government *is* more secretive than, say, government in the United States are less substantial than theory pretends. Authorised off-the-record briefing, by Ministers and their officials – otherwise known as official leaking – is on such a gigantic and systematic scale that the theory laid down by the old Official Secrets Act was daily mocked a thousand times. The systematic nature of the leaking system is shown by the fact that security matters (even without the support of the D-notice system, by which newspaper editors voluntarily agree not to publish a military or intelligence secret on the advice of the government) usually remain tightly held, thus showing that the government can keep a secret if it wants to.

One may legitimately abuse this leaking as furtive, hypocritical and graceless. But no sane observer of Westminster and Whitehall can deny its all-pervasive incidence. For that reason, although one may heartily welcome the release of further categories of information into the legitimate public domain, and the withdrawal of criminal sanctions in certain other categories, it is unreasonable to argue that the Hurd Act or any improvement on it represents or would represent a tremendous jump in the amount of useful information to which we have access about the way we are governed. We may or might know more officially, but it would be unrealistic to talk of a transformation in the total quantity of available information. The more solid hope is that a Freedom of Information Act enacting a positive right to know might transform the *attitudes* of officialdom, although I have my doubts about that too.

A more genuinely productive approach for Parliament-improvers might be to examine those areas where it is not information but *influence* that is denied.

It is in parliamentary discussion of legislation that the influence of backbench MPs is most consistently blocked by the whipped majority. We have already seen how successive governments since the war have been ever more impatient to resort to the guillotine to cut short tiresome debate on government Bills. Even within that process of debate, the government has been less and less willing to change its mind in response to backbenchers.

In three sessions during the 1964 Labour government, for example, of 3510 amendments moved by backbenchers in Standing Committee only 171 carried, whereas of 907 amendments proposed by the government to its own Bills all save one carried.[58] This pattern is typical of all post-war governments. Thus the Committee stage is useful almost entirely as an opportunity for the government to inject its own second thoughts – often in response to pressure from outside vested interests and professional advice – and very rarely as an opportunity for Parliament to improve the Bill. It is scarcely an exaggeration to say that, with many Bills, the government is likely to listen to almost anyone except the backbenchers on the Standing Committee which is examining the Bill.

Yet it is the Committee stage which is supposed to be the heart of the scrutiny. What can be done to make the reality conform in some degree to theory? At present, there are three main types of parliamentary committee: the Select Committees, each covering a specific area such as Agriculture or Foreign Affairs; the Standing Committees to which most Bills are sent 'upstairs', each known by a letter of the alphabet, running at present from A to E; and the Special Standing Committees, an experimental innovation dating only from 1980 and used only rarely since, which combines the Standing Committee's function of scrutinising legislation with the Select Committee's power 'to send for persons and papers', that is, to take evidence from expert witnesses and examine or commission research.

It is in this third category (enthusiastically endorsed by the Second Report from the Select Committee on Procedure, 1984–5) that the seeds of the solution may lie. If the three types of committee were amalgamated into one type, established on the lines of the Special Standing Committee, then immediately the scrutiny of legislation would take on a more deliberate and expert character; the use of the guillotine, except in cases of national emergency, would become more obviously scandalous; the committee chairmen and vice-chairmen, especially if selected for the duration of a parliament rather than a session, would take on something of the authority enjoyed by chairmen of congressional committees in the US, while not being weighed down by the old American seniority system which rewarded longevity rather than merit. The committee would then conduct investigations as well as examine Bills and so be in a position to question the arguments supporting the government's proposals more carefully and authoritatively.

But would not this slow down the whole business and deprive our legislative process of the speed and flexibility on which it prides itself? Of course it would. That is precisely the purpose. Government would have to consider its proposals more carefully before presenting them to the House; and it would have to content itself with a smaller legislative programme.

That would be entirely to the good. Nobody who has contemplated, for example, even a fraction of the incoherent, disreputable, ineffective and constantly reversed legislation relating to the financing and structuring of local government over the past thirty years would wish anything different. It is futile to expect modern governments with ambitious Ministers to keep to some self-denying ordinance. It is only if Parliament systematically, deliberately and justifiably *slows down* the process of making laws that we can hope to improve the quality of the legislation.

This objective of slowdown must be openly proclaimed and pursued. No one who refuses to subscribe to it can claim to understand the true meaning and purpose of constitutional reform or to be a genuine supporter of that cause.

In according proper priority to this objective, we must beware of wasting too much effort on desirable but secondary objectives, such as open government or the proportionate representation of women (or Liberal Democrats or ethnic minorities or any other sector of the nation) in Parliament. The House of Commons remains as great a remonstrator as it was in the days of the Plantagenets or the Hanoverians. It has become an abysmally ineffective scrutineer.

Reforming the House of Lords

Another desirable but secondary objective is reform of the House of Lords, at least reform as it is usually conceived. From Bagehot onwards, it has been correctly understood that the unrepresentative nature of the Upper House prevents it from playing a substantial part in the body politic; hereditary peers may spawn a sufficient crop of elder sons of enough ability to constitute an unambitious revising chamber. But, even after being reinforced by life peers, as recommended by Bagehot, Leo Amery and many others and finally implemented by Harold Macmillan, the House of Lords has never managed to muster the authority effectively to overrule the elected House on any question of real importance.

Public opinion towards the House of Lords, on the whole, seems to remain slumbrous and amiable. Most people share neither the rancour of the abolitionists nor the complacency of those (frequently peers and their friends and relations) who claim that debates in the Upper House are wiser, wittier and better informed than the goings-on in the commoners' bear-garden. But in decisive confrontations – in 1832, 1911 and 1949 – the public has shown no great desire to come to the rescue of the Lords. It was noticeable, too, in the recent argument about the War Crimes Bill that, while all the weight of expert legal opinion and a good deal of the press supported the arguments so eloquently put against the Bill in the Lords, the opinion polls recorded that a majority of the public supported the determination of the Commons to pursue alleged war criminals 'with the full rigour of the law', however slight the chances of justice being done to them.

Lord Carrington and his fellow reformers of the late 1960s were entirely right in arguing that, if the House of Lords was to have lasting and substantial authority restored to it, its composition must be changed. The hereditary element need not be abolished, but it must be reduced. The party composition of the Lords need not exactly reflect the party composition of the Commons, but it should not violently contradict it. We should be looking for some mixture,[59] therefore, of a representative selection of the hereditary peerage with a quantity of life peers reinforced perhaps by representatives of the counties or regions or even, though this would be more controversial, some representatives of the modern 'Estates of the Realm' or, in EC jargon, of the 'social partners' – the CBI, the TUC and so on.

This last suggestion has provoked mutters of 'Mussolini-style corporatism', but, as with the other proposals, there is no awesome novelty in it. Over the centuries, the monarch has summoned peers to Parliament on every kind of basis: geographical, for life, hereditary, by virtue of their office or calling, even by election in the case of the representatives of those Scottish or Irish peers who do not also enjoy United Kingdom peerages. If it is agreed that reform of the composition of the House of Lords would be a profitable exercise, then it should not be too difficult to work out a solution which satisfies most criteria.

But what would the House of Lords be reformed *for*? What tasks would it effectively perform that an unreformed House can perform only partially or not at all? In answering these questions, we come immediately up against two questions which must be answered first (which is why I describe reform of the Upper House as a secondary or consequential question).

If the House of Lords is to be a full-scale, fairly uninhibited revising Chamber – and one whose revisions are taken seriously and, as often as not, accepted by the government of the day – then the House of Commons must be an equally uninhibited revising Chamber too. For, however reformed the Lords may be, we must expect that it will always remain less directly representative of the electorate than the Commons; indeed, that is our express intention, because we want the Lords to be a little removed from the hot breath of the voters. That being so, MPs will never accept the superior claims of the Lords to revise Bills as they please, while they themselves are whipped through every vote on Committee. The Lords will be allowed to become a serious revising chamber only after the Commons has itself become one. Contrary to the conventional wisdom, reform of the Lords can arise only out of reform of the Commons.

The other answer often given to the question – what are we to reform the Lords for? – is that we may want it to fulfil certain constitutional functions, to act as a constitutional court of last resort in which government actions or Bills may, in some clearly defined circumstances, be challenged. According to this line of approach, a judicial committee of the House of Lords might be set up as a Council of State, or some other title of comparable splendour such as is often found in written-constitution nations, and be empowered to pronounce on the validity of what the government had done.

But, if the Law Lords are to assume or (as some lawyers say) resume this great function, they will want to know their terms of reference. Valid in terms of what? A written constitution? Certain entrenched statutes? The principles of common law or natural justice, but how and where reliably defined? We shall consider the possibility or impossibility of these criteria a little later on. But, at the moment, all we need to note is that, with the judicial as with the legislative reform of the functions of the House of Lords, there is little point in discussing the minutiae until we have settled much more major questions about the relationships between the government, the legislature and the judiciary. It is, however, worth saying at this point that, if we did settle those questions, previous experience suggests that the minutiae of organisational reform might not be forbiddingly hard to complete.

Entrenchment

Would we be freer if our freedoms were protected by certain special laws which could not be repealed or eroded by an ill-intentioned government, or only with the greatest difficulty? Would it help MPs to protect our liberties if there were certain basic laws to which they could appeal in denouncing some fresh threat as 'unconstitutional', laws which were so firmly dug in or 'entrenched' that they could be uprooted only with the overwhelming support of public opinion?

It is hard not to answer yes to such questions, whether they are thrown at us in a sweeping emotional fashion or couched in precise legal phrasing. To put it at its lowest, it is difficult to imagine that we would actually be worse off if, say, the American Bill of Rights (with a few modest amendments – we might not insist on the right to bear arms) or the European Convention on Human Rights were part of English law. It may be that, in most cases, most of the time, the wisdom of the common law and the sense and probity of our judges do protect us well enough, but the weather might turn darker, and, even now, there may be gaps in the fabric of our liberties which a written convention could effectively seal off.

To these alluring possibilities we tend to be given two objections which have a faintly contradictory ring. First, we are told, quite rightly, that English law already contains quite enough Great Charters and Petitions and Acts of Settlement and Bills of Right. These glorious documents have, in practice, endured centuries longer than these written constitutions and codicils of which foreigners are so proud – and survived not merely as historic relics but as living embodiments of justice. As often as not, their framers and signatories intended them to have a ring of permanence about them and, indeed, they do have, after shedding one or two anachronistic or mistaken clauses – a shedding which our flexible arrangements readily permit, but which is not available in rigid written-constitutions states, where they remain stuck with outdated or positively dangerous impedimenta, such as the right to bear arms or the Irish Constitution's claim to the whole island of Ireland.

The second answer to a plea for the entrenchment of our liberties is a more straightforward 'No, you cannot have it, because the beautiful flexibility of our system insists that any provision may be overturned as soon as Parliament wills it and that no Parliament may bind its successor.' Or, in Sir William Anson's words, 'Parliament therefore is omnipotent to change, but cannot bind itself not to change, the constitution of which it forms a part.'[60] To tamper with this flexibility would be to strike at the heart of the sovereignty of Parliament by imposing a fresh sovereign, for the entrenched clauses would have to be entrenched by somebody and de-entrenched for amendment by that same body, whether the body is to be the whole electorate in a referendum or a small body of elderly judges (judges are always referred to as elderly when they are to be thought incapable of performing some task, although it is rare, even today, that any commentator has the temerity to call for vibrant younger judges).

Seen from the outside, this would seem to be a bizarre situation. We see – or think we might see – a way of entrenching our liberties more securely, but we are told that we cannot have access to that way without destroying the whole neighbourhood. This, on the face of it, would seem a little implausible. And so it is.

What has gone wrong with the conventional argument here is yet another variant of a confusion with which we are now becoming familiar, the confusion between power and law.

In their obsession with the principle that no Parliament has the power to bind its successor, old parliamentary hands have lost sight of the equally important principle that Parliament must act according to law. In fact, the latter principle must be prior, since, in exercising its power to overturn its predecessor's acts, each Parliament has to respect the law and custom which that predecessor has bequeathed to it. If the first Parliament passes a Bill stating that all Bills of a constitutional type (including the Bill itself and any Bill to repeal or amend the Bill itself) must in future secure a two-thirds majority in both Houses in order to become law, that law will bind the second Parliament until it is repealed; and the repeal Bill will itself require a two-thirds majority. No doubt a wilful second Parliament might try to find ways round the dilemma by asserting – in defiance of the original Bill's wording – that the repeal Bill was not itself a constitutional Bill within the meaning of the Act by finding some other defect. But, if it was felt that liberty was at stake, then the public uproar would prevent the rascals from getting away with it.

This is not a far-fetched legal quibble. It is, in practice, the habitual protection of any written constitution. Suppose that a majority in the US Congress wanted to do away with the old laborious procedure for amending the American Constitution – which under Article V of that Constitution involves securing the amendment's passage in three-quarters of the state legislatures or by Conventions in three-quarters of the states (after the amendment has been passed by two-thirds majorities in both Houses or applied for by two-thirds of the state legislatures) – and proposed to substitute the 'streamlined', 'flexible' procedure of a simple majority in both Houses of Congress. There is nothing to prevent Congress from attempting this 'reform', except that the attempt would have to be made through the existing laborious procedures and would ignominiously fail.

Parliament is the master of its own procedure, but it is, at the same time, the servant of its own procedure. The point is blissfully simple, and obvious to anyone who has ever served on any rules committee: the rules can only be changed according to the rules as they stand.

I do not think that even constitutional lawyers are fully seized of the seriousness with which Parliament treats its own procedures. After all, as the saying goes, procedure is the only constitution that MPs – or the rest of us, come to that – have got. Religious adherence to the rules as they stand is not simply the enthusiasm of a few pettifoggers. It is the heart and soul of parliamentary practice. And 'parliamentary sovereignty' necessarily implies 'Parliament as duly constituted and as acting in accordance with its own procedures'.

This must be said emphatically, since even eminent legal authorities seem puzzled by the point. The basic principle of the law of Parliament must be acceptance and observance of the rules of parliamentary procedure as they stand; it is that acceptance and observance which constitutes the continuity of Parliament, this great boasted rolling tradition.

By contrast, an assembly which sits down the day after its members have been elected or selected (or have fought or bribed their way to membership) and makes up a complete fresh set of rules *de novo* is not a parliament; it is a constituent assembly, and its calling together is a visible token of the fact that a revolution has taken place – and one which will, as likely as not, require a Basic Law or written constitution in order to re-establish, visibly and durably, the rule of law which has been violently ruptured.

In this procedural sense, far from it being the case that 'no parliament can bind its successor', *every parliament cannot help binding its successor*; the binding is what defines its successor as a true parliament and endows its decisions with proper authority. To take the most obvious and recurring example of the last century and a half, every time the House of Lords threw out a Reform Bill or a Parliament Bill, the House of Commons could have voted an order declaring that this type of Bill did not require the assent of the Lords and so could become law straight away. But that declaration would not have been valid; its issuing would have been a declaration of anarchy, and anyone would have been quite entitled to ignore or defy it. Their Lordships had to sign their own death warrant each time to make that warrant legal.

Thus, as Heuston suggests, 'It has been discovered that we have been asking the wrong sort of question. Instead of asking "What can Parliament do?" or "Can Parliament bind its successors?" we should rather ask "How is Parliament composed?" or "How does Parliament express its will?" '[61] The rules which identify the sovereign are as important as the sovereign individual or institution so identified; if we doubt this, Heuston invites us to consider this simple question: 'Where is the sovereign between the dissolution of one Parliament and the election of another?' It must be an incomplete statement to say that such and such an assembly of human beings is sovereign. It can be sovereign only when acting in a certain way prescribed by law. Some rudimentary manner and form are indispensable; 'the simultaneous incoherent cry of a rabble, small or large, cannot be law, for it is unintelligible.'[62] The rules – for the election of a chairman, for deciding what is to count as a yes vote (simple majority or a two-thirds majority), for defining a quorum, for determining the type and number of stages which a Bill must go through – these also go to define the sovereign. The 600-odd persons who are entitled to put MP after their names are no more the sovereign than the Pope is to be regarded as infallible when he tips Poland to win the World Cup.

Let us then continue with our example of a Bill to specify a two-thirds majority in both Houses of Parliament for certain 'constitutional' categories of Bill, including the Bill itself. Other objections might be brought forward, such as that a simple majority of those voting had been the rule from time immemorial. But even that rule has been subject to qualification, for example, about the number of members needed to constitute a quorum. It is no more immutable than the system of first-past-the-post for electing members to Parliament. In the European elections, Parliament has already specified a system of Proportional Representation for Northern Ireland, as it had in 1920 for elections to Stormont; the Labour Party is inclining towards its use throughout the UK; nobody would dream of pretending that there is any *legal* barrier to adopting a similar system for Westminster as well. In the 1979 referenda for Scottish and Welsh devolution, Parliament, at the urging of a determined band of opponents led by Tam Dalyell and George Cunningham, insisted that the Scottish and Welsh assemblies would count as having been approved only if a majority of those entitled to vote voted yes – the absentees thus counting as no votes. This stiffened hurdle brought about the defeat of the Scottish Assembly, although a narrow majority of those actually voting did vote yes.

But suppose that, rather than try to clear the hurdle of the two-thirds majority, a different government returned at a subsequent general election tries to dodge round it, passing, by the usual simple majority, a Bill which has or might be held to have the effect of undermining one of the entrenched provisions.

O. Hood Phillips' *Constitutional and Administrative Law*

summarises the old conventional view, that no Parliament can bind its successors, even as to the 'Manner and Form' of legislation, that is, as regards its own procedure.[63] The courts, faced with a conflict of laws, would simply accept the later Bill rather than feeling bound to administer the law according to the earlier Bill. 'The courts will not concern themselves with the *procedure* by which a Bill passed through either House,' as the judgment of the House of Lords in *Pickin* v. *British Railways Board*[64] demonstrated. Mr Pickin pleaded that the British Railways Act of 1968 contained a false recital, that the Board had misled Parliament and that therefore the Act should not deprive him of his land, but the House of Lords ruled that the courts could not go behind the wording of the Act to examine proceedings in Parliament. Lord Reid said that the court had no concern with the manner in which Parliament or its officers had performed their functions, thus overruling Lord Denning in the Court of Appeal, who had argued that justice demanded that, if the court had no such concern, then it jolly well ought to have.

We shall pursue Lord Denning's line later, but we also need to note here the grotesque incompleteness of the textbook approach. The question is not simply whether the *courts* have the right to declare void such an Act. The question is whether MPs would be right to resist a flagrant attempt to breach their own procedures and also whether the 'political sovereign', the people, would be justified in offering the most vociferous opposition to such a move.

In dealing with the breach of a convention rather than a law of the Constitution, we have to resort, rapidly and brusquely, to sanctions outside the courts. Suppose the government of the day proposed to use its majority to pass a Bill decreeing that in future all Bills should be passed on a single reading without debate, the proposal would provoke a universal outcry, and there would not be a hope of passing the Bill itself in that truncated fashion. Opposition MPs would seize the mace and break up the proceedings; there would be uproar in the country. The proper forms of procedure have more sturdy protection than even the courts.

There does, in fact, exist a statute comparable to our hypothetical 'two-thirds law'. The single-chamber New Zealand Parliament is not limited by a higher law, but, in 1956, it did pass an

Electoral Act that included a section 189 which stated that certain provisions relating to the life of Parliament, the franchise and secret ballot may not be repealed except by a 75 per cent majority of all the members of the House of Representatives or by a simple majority of voters in a referendum. Now section 189 did not itself require this special procedure to be repealed or amended, so that it could presumably be repealed by a simple majority. But it is now generally regarded as a binding 'redefinition' of Parliament in dealing with such constitutional matters. We are told[65] that the legislature did not try to 'entrench' section 189 itself because 'it recognised that such an attempt would be ineffectual'. This seems implausible. If the three-quarters rule really has taken root, then any attempt to dig it up by repealing section 189 would be vigorously resisted, and entrenching section 189 would have tended to stiffen the resistance still further.

To make an end of all these hypotheses, the situation is, I think, fairly summed up in de Smith and Brazier's *Constitutional and Administrative Law*:

> None the less, there is no *logical* reason why the UK Parliament should be incompetent so to redefine itself (or redefine the procedure for enacting legislation on any given matter) as to preclude Parliament *as ordinarily constituted* from passing a law on a matter. (There are, of course, doubts as to the jurisdiction or willingness of the courts to intervene). If Parliament can make it easier to legislate, as by passing the Parliament Acts or abolishing the House of Lords, it can also make it harder to legislate.[66]

There is no doubt, however, that it would help to embed such an entrenched statute if there existed some accepted legal method for settling any conflict of laws which might arise. This could no doubt be done through the existing machinery of justice. The High Court is already being asked to judge whether certain actions of the British government contravene the superior authority of Community Law. It is the 1972 European Community Act which gives Community law that superiority, and so the High Court is indirectly being asked to decide between two rules both originally stemming from the UK Parliament – as, indeed, it would be asked to do in our hypothetical 'two-thirds Bill' case.

The more often that the courts are faced with such putative conflicts, the more logical it would seem to set up a 'Court of Conflicts' on the French model, to develop a body of expertise and case law and, in so doing, to reinforce the entrenchment of the entrenched clauses. And it would be easy enough to hive off a court of this sort from the existing judicial machinery of the House of Lords and so to institute the House of Lords as a constitutional court. None of this would come as a shock or novelty to British judges. The Judicial Committee of the Privy Council is well used to adjudicating on conflicts of jurisdiction, for example between the old Northern Ireland Parliament and the UK Parliament and between colonial jurisdictions and the UK Parliament. There is no need to treat the British judiciary as too ill-equipped with case law or as personally too inexperienced to handle the large matters which come to a conflicts court.

But suppose our hypothetical wilful government wished to override the judgment of the 'Court of Conflicts' by passing yet another law, declaring that this second law did not infringe and was not covered by the provisions of the original entrenching Bill. It would be quite entitled to try, and Parliament would be quite entitled to pass such a third Bill – but, once again, it would have to pass it by a two-thirds majority – or, once again, the highest court of law would rule the law invalid. By this time, the country would presumably be in an uproar, and the government would have to back down if it was not to do itself severe political damage.

I am labouring the point, but only because much modern constitutional argument is reluctant to take full account of it. If we really wish to entrench Bills of a constitutional or liberty-protecting sort, the sovereignty of Parliament is not a genuine obstacle to our wishes.

Other legislatures or assemblies

The first commandment of parliamentary monotheism is that thou shalt have no other gods but me; parliamentary sovereignty is a jealous god. Throughout this century and the latter part of the nineteenth century, it has been held as axiomatic that, if the Westminster Parliament is to enjoy the authentic sovereignty to which it is historically entitled, any other assembly, council or legislature within the United Kingdom must be subordinate. The very existence of these subordinate assemblies can be terminated overnight by the UK Parliament; any laws, by-laws and regulations which they may emit, they emit under authority conferred on them by the UK Parliament. Dicey, in order to shock the reader into recognition of what he regarded as both a central principle and an undoubted political fact, liked to declare that there was, in essence, no difference between a trivial by-law imposed by the Great Western Railway and a weighty edict from the panelled great chamber of some colonial legislature. All were equally derived from the authority of some Westminster statute.

The United Kingdom was, always had been and ought to remain a unitary state. The only alternative was a federal state in which the ultimate authority was a written document distributing powers between the federation and the states; as we have seen, sturdy British constitutionalists of the late nineteenth century and early twentieth century, such as Dicey and Anson, considered the federal form to be a weaker system; cannier traditionalists of today will concede that federal constitutions may be all very well for the Americans and the Swiss, with their very different history, but would be a recipe for disintegration if applied to the UK.

A secondary but frequent argument adduced here – although not always put in this way – is that federations, both in theory and in practice, must be *symmetrical*. Each state must exercise the same powers and stand in the same relation to the federal power. This, it is argued, is what makes the devolution of legislative power to Scotland, Wales and Northern Ireland such an impractical proposition; even if the same arrangements were applied to the Kingdom, the Principality and the Province, there would remain the problem of England. This argument has been put in various guises throughout the Home Rule controversy of the last century and the recent devolution controversy: if the Irish were to have their own Parliament again, in what circumstances, if any, would Irish MPs take part in proceedings at Westminster? Why should Scottish MPs continue to have a say in the domestic politics of England while English MPs would be barred from discussing health and education in Scotland? Gladstone found different answers in his two Home Rule Bills; Callaghan squirmed under the barrage of questions from Dalyell and Cunningham. The presumption that symmetry was indispensable has never lost its potency.

The primary and secondary arguments against federalism in this country are interlinked. We are asked to accept a supposedly inescapable dichotomy: either we live under a unitary system in which all power radiates from a single source; or we live under a federal system in which the power is equally and symmetrically dispersed under the authority of a written constitution. Nothing else, nothing in between. The beautiful simplicity of this dichotomy has never been more exquisitely deployed than by Mr Enoch Powell in his speeches on the Devolution Bills of 1979.

But is it true? Until the Act of Union of 1801, Ireland intermittently enjoyed its own Parliament; in Elizabethan times, the Irish Parliament's subjection to Westminster was at most debatable, at least vestigial; in the brief years of Grattan's Parliament before the Rebellion of 1798, the Irish Parliament was not really subject at all. Nor was the Scottish Parliament during the century between the Union of Crowns and the Union of parliaments. Naturally, good Unionists regard these unions as miraculous and precious achievements which must be safeguarded to prevent a return to anarchy; Dicey and Rait's book (Rait provided the research, Dicey the passion) is a continuous elaboration on this theme.

Other forms of asymmetry in our present arrangements are taken for granted. For decades, Scotland and Wales have been deliberately over-represented in Parliament, on the grounds of their distance from London and the sparsity of their populations; by contrast, until recently Northern Ireland, though equally remote, was under-represented, on the grounds that the existence of the Northern Ireland Parliament, subordinate though it might be, constituted a large measure of representation. This under-representation continued after the abolition of Stormont, until rectified by increasing the number of Northern Ireland MPs from twelve to seventeen. These asymmetries in representation are the unitary system's mimicking of the asymmetries which are built into many federal systems – most notably by the equal representation in some chamber of government, usually the upper chamber, of states of grossly unequal size. California with twenty-four million inhabitants and Delaware with 600,000 inhabitants both have two senators. In the German Bundesrat, every *Land* has at least three and no more than five votes – thus sharply narrowing the gap in representation between Bremen (654,000 inhabitants and three votes), Rhineland-Palatinate (3.6 million inhabitants and four votes) and North Rhine-Westphalia (16 million inhabitants and five votes).

It does not even follow from the claim that the achievement of the United Kingdom is a glorious one that it would be impossible to insert a second parliament enjoying a considerable degree of independence, whether *de facto* or *de jure*, somewhere into our system, even at the cost of asymmetry or imbalance of rights or representation as between one region or province and another; it may or may not be prudent, but it is not impossible, because we have done it before. Vestiges of the old patchwork of authorities persist in the Isle of Man, in the Channel Islands, in the separate systems of legal and ecclesiastical government in Scotland. Some, though not all, of these separate authorities are in law subject to the will of the Westminster Parliament, but that latter body would be extremely wary of expending its credit on attempts to enforce its will. Even in a part of the British system which was undoubtedly subordinate – the Parliament and Government of Northern Ireland – Westminster shrank from enforcement of certain measures repugnant to Northern Irishmen, most notably the abolition of capital punishment and a system of comprehensive schooling (which would have entailed the forced integration of the two communities).

The whole history of the Northern Ireland Parliament is a subject which Ulster Unionists are reluctant to examine too closely, since its peculiarities undermine their most profoundly held views. First of all, the Parliament was elected by Proportional Representation until the Unionists, finding that PR resulted in the inconvenient election of too many Nationalists, managed to introduce a first-past-the-post system in time for the 1929 Stormont elections. Residential and other qualifications for the franchise were more rigorous than those in the rest of the UK, in order to deter Catholic hordes swarming up from the South. And the theoretical subordination of Stormont to the Imperial Parliament was made virtually null by London's terror of stirring up a political crisis in Belfast. For nearly fifty years, the Unionists ran the show much as they pleased, *and* their MPs voted at Westminster as they pleased or when they bothered to turn up, regardless of the fact that much of the legislation didn't apply to Northern Ireland and that much of the comparable Northern Ireland legislation never came before the House of Commons. English MPs seldom if ever complained about this imbalance. Thus the practice of Northern Irish politics during half a century gave a clear answer to the question which had plagued Gladstone and was to plague Callaghan: in practice, asymmetricality in parliamentary representation doesn't really matter, so long as it is tolerated by public opinion.

But, if there are considerable vestiges of separate, independent authorities impairing the symmetry of our own unitary system, these asymmetries are as nothing to some of those in other countries. Greenland, although still under the Danish Crown, has voted to withdraw from the European Community; the Faroe Islands, also under the Danish Crown, never belonged to the EC. In Belgium, the 'community assemblies' for the Walloons and the Flemings are complicated by two further community assemblies for French and German speakers, which, unlike the first two, have no actual territory. The Northern Territory of Australia has been governed successively by the government of South Australia, by the Commonwealth of Australia and, since 1978, by its own government. Canada, like Great Britain, has two systems of law operating within its borders, the civil law in Quebec province and the common law elsewhere. The United States has progressively transformed its dependent territories into fully fledged states, the most recent being Alaska in 1959, but Puerto Rico and various other outlying islands remain in the embryonic condition; and the District of Columbia, although no longer denied self-government, remains a deliberate anomaly, as does the Australian Capital Territory. The progressively increasing grant of autonomy is not a trait confined to classically federal states; the autonomous regions of Spain are undergoing 'rolling devolution', acquiring fresh powers as and when they feel ready for them.

Some of these asymmetries are unsatisfactory, cobbled-together solutions to ethnic friction; others are comfortable accommodations to historical and geographical differences and cause little or no worry.

Any reasonably objective comparative analysis would, I think, conclude that it is not the symmetry or lack of it which determines the effectiveness of the arrangements but whether the peoples concerned find the arrangements convenient and congenial. Over-rigid symmetry may be a cause of rather than a solution to friction; governing both Catalonia and Castile even-handedly from Madrid might seem impeccably fair but not to the Catalans. Conversely, *untidiness* may be a characteristic of justice and a symptom of attentiveness and goodwill. An insistence on mathematical equality and symmetry may be less genuinely democratic, in that it betokens an indifference to the grievances of those regions or peoples who feel themselves unfairly dealt with by the application of unvarying rules. Without entangling ourselves too deeply in philosophic questions of desert and distributive justice, we cannot help noticing that no government which wants to survive can afford to treat people uniformly in matters, say, of social welfare. It is a consequence of paying genuinely equal attention to all citizens that we discover that some have greater needs or more unassuaged grievances and that therefore they ought to be treated unequally. Although it is a characteristic of rules that they should apply equally to similar cases, all corporate bodies have clauses and systems to cover exceptional categories, and constitution-making bodies are no exception. A society will, for example, permit members over sixty-five to pay reduced subscriptions without reducing their voting rights; similarly, a body of constitutional rules may build in or remove tiers of government or representational rights for a variety of reasons without worrying too much about the resulting patchwork effect.

As for the question of entrenching a structure of local or regional government, even in a unitary system, it may well be the case that a degree of entrenchment will turn out to be an important supporting characteristic of genuine devolution. If we were to include systems of local government or of regional assemblies under the definition of 'constitutional measures' in our 'two-thirds Bill', we might impart to those local and regional bodies qualities of responsibility and durability which could help to rebuild both local pride and the local fiscal base which has been so pitifully eroded by the tragi-comedy of the poll tax. The unbudgeable establishment of lower tiers of government in federal systems may be one of their principal virtues; even in the notoriously unitary system of France, it should be remembered that de Gaulle ultimately came to grief over local government reform.

At this stage, we want only to shake two widely held preconceptions: first, that parliamentary democracy cannot work without systems of local and provincial government which are tidy and symmetrical; second, that, in order to respond adequately to changing political imperatives and patterns of life, central government must be able to alter those arrangements at a moment's notice. It would be perfectly possible within our existing party system to signal the permanence of our local councils by affording their structures and financing a degree of entrenchment. Not merely would it have saved a huge quantity of public time and money if most of the local government legislation of the past generation had not been attempted; the greater stability of local government might well have improved its standards of economy and administration. After all, for 200 years Parliament barely intervened in local government at all;[67] there was no need to fly to the opposite extreme in the past thirty years.

The volume of legislation affecting the structure, function and finance of local government has been one of the most startling and dismal spectacles of the post-war era. In scarcely any aspect of local administration has there been any area of stability or agreed common ground. Should local government be freer or less free to decide what to spend their revenue on? Should the level of that revenue consume a larger or a smaller fraction of the Gross

National Product? Should a greater or a smaller proportion of that revenue come from the Treasury, or from business rates? Is the domestic rating system fair or unfair? Should local taxation be based on property values or on income or on expenditure, and, if on property values, how should it be assessed? Should there be one tier of local and/or regional government (that is, assuming we are to have regional government, yet another questionable assumption), or two tiers, or three? Should the areas of local authorities be larger or smaller? Should their boundaries correspond, as far as possible, to their historical boundaries, or is local government primarily a matter of effective administration rather than of local sentiment? Should local authorities manage virtually all local services (and if so, which ones), or should they merely see to it that decent services are provided, but not necessarily by themselves? And so on, and on, and on.

And we have not begun to answer all the separate but linked questions about the proper arrangements for Scotland and Wales. Some of these unanswered questions do arise out of genuine disputes about the scope and limits of the public realm versus the private realm, and also about the right way to embody and focus local loyalties and assuage local grievances. But a great deal of this frenetic and mostly futile legislative activity arises from the ease with which, under our system, governmental power can express itself in large-scale, impressive-sounding legislation and the difficulty of inducing our system to consider the constitutional architecture. Under a constitution which allocated powers clearly and definitively as between central and local government, there would be much clearer limits on the kind of alterations that could legitimately be introduced and hence fewer Bills and more stability.

In particular, the proportion of local authority revenue to be supplied by the Treasury would not zoom up and down as unpredictably as it has since the 1950s. Local authorities, even the most impetuous, free-spending councils, would clearly understand – as the typical American authority does, for example – that any extra expenditure would have to be financed, either by a rise in local tax or by issuing a fresh bond (both painful and unpopular measures). There would be less of this fruitless bickering and buckpassing. Reponsible housekeeping comes much more naturally in a stable and clearly understood system.

At this stage, we need not consider exactly how the functions and financing of local government could be given the much more transparent stable character which they seem to have in other Western countries, regardless of whether the constitutional architecture is unitary or federal. What is important, as a preliminary step, is to contemplate candidly the puzzled and demoralised state of local government in Britain and the lack of civic pride to which so many of our social problems are plausibly attributed and ask the simple question: isn't it rather likely that this depressing spectacle has at least something to do with the unsettled, badgered experience of local authorities over the past four decades? The community charge may have been one of the worst and most obviously doomed innovations in British political history, but other local government Acts have also combined the half-baked and the wholly futile. Supposing that governments over that period had not touched the system and had instead preferred to regard the existing distribution of functions and the rating system, with all its faults, as part of a constitutional settlement, would not the average local council today be in far better shape, with better control over its costs and revenues and over what was happening inside its schools and libraries?

In the next chapter, we shall consider some changing ideas of what local and regional governments are for and the new pressures to which those subordinate bodies must make their response. But the first thing to recognise is that successful constitutional arrangements tend to be *branched*. A bare-trunked tree is likely to be too rigid and to be unable to deflect and absorb the violent and unpredictable gusts of feeling and indignation that are an unavoidable part of the weather.

The law and the judges

Dick Crossman liked to shock almost as much as he liked to bully. It is not hard to imagine the relish with which he informed the audience for his Godkin lectures at Harvard that 'British politicians have no profound belief in natural law, largely because we have no written constitution or Supreme Court. If we don't like a law, we just change it.'[68] Such a disrespect for any idea of law, beyond the Acts of Parliament that are actually on the statute book, is not a figment of Crossman's sardonic imagination; it is the habitual, unthinking attitude of nine-tenths of the British political world. It is not that we are not law-abiding or that we lack an ingrained sense of the rule of law; it is rather that in our domestic political arguments we have been educated to keep the law out of it; the law is for law courts. In the indexes of constitutional treatises emanating from the British political world, the only entry under 'Law' is often 'LAW, Andrew Bonar'.

An American, or indeed a citizen of most other Western democracies, finds this combination surprising: a nation where the rule of law enjoys such a venerable tradition and where, at the same time, the subject is paid so little attention. The leading culprit is, I think, Dicey and his quirky but enduringly influential definition, not only of the rule of law (that has been lambasted often enough, most brilliantly by Jennings), but of what constitutional law consists in. Towards the beginning of his great work,[69] he lays down a distinction between two sets of rules which together make up constitutional law: the law of the Constitution and the conventions of the Constitution. Those rules which make up law may be written or unwritten, enacted by statute or derived from judge-made common law, but their distinguishing characteristic is that they may be enforced by the courts. Conventions, on the other hand, 'are not in reality laws at all since they are not enforced by the courts'.[70] These conventions may be extremely important, such as the convention that the House of Lords does not originate any money Bill, or the convention that when the House of Lords acts as a Court of Appeal only Law Lords take part, or the convention that Ministers resign office when they have ceased to command the confidence of the House of Commons. But they are not laws, and, because they are not laws, the constitutional lawyer has no business with them:

with conventions or understanding, he has no direct concern. They vary from generation to generation, almost from year to year. . . . the true constitutional law is his only real concern. His proper function is to show what are the legal rules (i.e. rules recognized by the courts) which are to be found in the several parts of the constitution.[71]

This self-denying ordinance which Dicey wants constitutional lawyers and judges in the courts to take to heart has a grander purpose behind it, which he unveils in its full majesty towards the end of his work:

> the one essential principle of the constitution is obedience by all persons to the deliberately expressed will of the House of Commons in the first instance, and ultimately to the will of the nation as expressed through Parliament. The conventional code of political morality is, as already pointed out, merely a body of maxims meant to secure respect for that principle.[72]

Thus Dicey's doctrine of the rule of law is inescapably a narrow, shrivelled thing. It applies vigorously enough to the rights of individuals in their dealings with one another and with the state, but it does not really touch the untrammelled quality of parliamentary supremacy. For Dicey, 'The conventional code of political morality' does not seem to be governed by the rule of law; if governed at all, it seems to be more by considerations of expediency; by behaving in a proper stately fashion, Parliament will maintain the respect of the people (the 'political sovereign') and so secure their obedience.

Dicey's difficulty is obvious enough. Any overarching concept of the rule of law – whether founded on divine law, on natural law or on any modern equivalent such as international conventions on human rights and the like – would interfere with and begin to gnaw at the unblemished wholeness of parliamentary sovereignty. So he would have none of it, even if his position meant holding the odd-sounding view that the 'conventional part of constitutional law' was not part of the 'law of the constitution' and so was not the concern of the constitutional lawyer.

The consequence of Dicey's position is clear too. It licensed the politicians to tell the judges to shut up. It was for Parliament, and Parliament alone, to define and redefine the Constitution; the judges were to know their place; they were mere legal artisans. These assumptions bred a generation of judicial passivists like Lord Simonds, who refused to be led 'by an undiscerning zeal for some abstract kind of justice to ignore our first duty which is to administer justice according to the law, the law which is established for us by Act of Parliament or the binding authority of precedent.' Reform 'is the task not of the Courts of Law, but of Parliament'.[73] Judges, even in cases involving the liberty of the subject – the heart and soul of common law – showed themselves, in Lord Atkin's famous phrase, 'more executive-minded than the executive'.[74] Judges like Hewart, who voiced their views off the bench, might let themselves in for a rebuke like Baldwin's, that 'it was obviously undesirable that His Majesty's judges should write for publication on matters of political controversy'.[75] The Kilmuir Rules, as late as 1955, not only forbade judges to be associated with 'any series of talks or anything which could be fairly interpreted as entertainment' but also placed overriding importance on 'keeping the Judiciary in this country isolated from the controversies of the day'.[76] This could obviously be taken to include controversies on major constitutional questions.

Although much modified by Lord Mackay of Clashfern's rewriting, within days of becoming Lord Chancellor in 1987, the spirit of the Kilmuir Rules still broods over the Bar and over academic constitutional law too. As recently as 1988, Rodney Brazier wrote in *Constitutional Practice* that Lord Hewart's *The New Despotism* – in its time, the only sustained and coherent counter-attack on the arrogance of the executive – was 'a vehement polemic unworthy of a judge'. Textbooks continue to deprecate any judicial ventures into constitutional theory. Recent editions of O. Hood Phillips's *Constitutional and Administrative Law* pour cold water on Lord Diplock's attempts to invoke the 'basic concept of separation of legislative, executive and judicial power as it had been developed in the unwritten constitution of the UK'.[77] It is difficult not to share Sir Ian Gilmour's fine excoriation of all this judicial abdication and retreat in *The Body Politic* (almost the only modern treatise written by a politician which places proper weight on the judicial leg of the tripod):

> Anxious not to offend the executive, the Courts got themselves so entangled in their own procedures, frictions and inhibitions that 'the rusty curb of old father antick the law' has curbed only itself, not the executive. They have slavishly worshipped at the shrine of parliamentary sovereignty.[78]

There is, as Gilmour says, a roll of honour, a list of judges worthy to follow in the steps of Bracton, Coke, Hale and Blackstone: Atkin, Reid, Devlin, Salmon, Radcliffe, Scarman – even Hewart, with all his faults. Above all, there has been Lord Denning, with all *his* faults, who has kept alive in the minds of Englishmen an idea of law which is broader and higher and more enduring than the ever fattening annual volumes of Acts of Parliament. Now and then, this aspiration has led Denning into 'making the law as it ought to be, instead of administering it as it is'. That was an accusation made by a pre-war Lord Chancellor against Lord Atkin, and it cannot altogether be dodged. But, as Gilmour points out,[79] the oath that judges take is to do justice according to law and, since they cannot help making law as well as administering it, justice requires that the law they make should be reasonable.

Moreover, it is not often pointed out – because politicians and political journalists like to think of themselves as self-propelled and not as having been prodded into action by mere lawyers – that, where judges have intervened emphatically, straying, as some would have it, far beyond their proper role, important and useful things have been accomplished. Constitutional reformers do not care to admit this either; they prefer to muse on the great things that 'a reformed judiciary' will accomplish in the future, largely no doubt at the promptings of the constitutional reformers. It is axiomatic that existing judges are stuffy bourgeois reactionaries, who are hostile to civil rights and have to be told what a bicycle is.

Hewart's polemic may have been too vehement for legal tastes, but nobody can doubt the long-term effect of this withering broadside against the growing tendency for the Minister to assume powers to 'do any thing which he may think expedient', and so to place 'a large and increasing field of departmental authority and activity beyond the reach of the original law'.[80] One may or may not be resistant to the rumble of Hewart's rhetoric, but this was not merely fogeyish bombast directed against the modern world. It was directed against a specific and ever advancing evil, the cumulative assumption by the government of powers which allowed the citizen no remedy against abuse of them. It was the work of the succeeding thirty years to provide rights of appeal, opportunities for judicial review, ombudsmen and administrative tribunals. Even today, sixty years after the publication of *The New Despotism*, we continually come upon situations in which Parliament has unthinkingly conferred powers upon the executive without providing proper opportunities for redress. And Lord Denning's what-the-law-ought-to-be judgments have played a leading role in prodding Parliament to change the law. His famous (or notorious) judgments in cases of trade union blacking and secondary picketing might be regularly overturned by the House of Lords, even after the first trade union Act of the Thatcher government,[81] but the point was made; the old immunities ceased to carry any moral authority after Denning had declared, in his eerily plain English, that they did not accord with common-law justice, and, in the end, the statute law was changed.

Denning makes no secret of his yearning to exercise the function claimed by Coke in *Doctor Bonham's Case* (1688): 'When an Act of Parliament is against right and reason, or repugnant, or impossible to be performed, the common law will control it and adjudge that Act to be void.'[82] Denning acknowledges that 'this sapling planted by Lord Coke failed to grow in England. It withered and died. But it grew into a strong tree in the United States.'[83] If any such extensive powers of judicial review are to be introduced, the American experience suggests that they can flourish only when 'right and reason' are defined in certain documents which enjoy an entrenched or special status. We already have several such documents in the shape of the Great Charters and the Bill of Rights; others are to hand, notably the European Convention. In fact, 'to hand' is a polite understatement of the reality. The Convention is already frequently cited in English courts; the tenor of its Articles is not necessarily upheld, certainly not where they conflict with the clear provisions of English law. But 'where our domestic law is not firmly settled' – to use Lord Fraser's words in *Attorney-General* v. *BBC*[84] – the courts seem to agree with Denning that 'our law should conform as far as possible with the provisions of the European Convention of Human Rights'.[85] Or in the formulation of the Vice-Chancellor, Sir Robert Megarry: 'The Convention is not, of course, law, though it is legitimate to consider its provisions in interpreting the law; and naturally I give it full weight for this purpose.'[86] Thus the Convention seems to be half-in, half-out of our law; most English judges no doubt share Denning's revulsion at its sweeping Continental statements of principle (and equally sweeping statements of exceptions), but they seem to find little difficulty in handling it, even in this delicate situation where the UK is a signatory but the Convention is not part of our law.

Nor will any fair-minded observer, I think, be much impressed by the argument now and then put forward – for example by John Patten – that 'to incorporate the broad provisions [of the Convention] into UK domestic law would be unnecessary. For our laws – common and statute – secure the freedom and rights set out in the Convention.' In that case, how is it that the European Court of Human Rights has found against Britain on, among other things, complaints about restrictions on the correspondence of prisoners, the treatment in Northern Ireland of suspected terrorists, birching by judicial order, criminal laws relating to homosexual conduct, the confinement of patients in mental hospitals, telephone tapping, and contempt of court in connection with press freedom? One may disagree with some or all of these findings, but one can scarcely maintain that, on the evidence so far, incorporation would make no difference to English law; nor that English judges would be incapable of absorbing this fresh body of law and adjusting their decisions in accordance with it.

I emphasise this adaptability of the much maligned English (and Scottish) judge as the first of three requirements necessary if we are thinking of embarking on a more ambitious programme of judicial review. First, the judges must have the right combination of intellectual energy and political modesty if they are to break out of their confinement and exercise something nearer an equal share in the upholding of our Constitution. This confinement has bred an excessive timidity in some but by no means all High Court judges since the war. There seems no reason to fear the capacity of the existing recruitment pool to supply enough judges of the right calibre to dignify any special constitutional court that might be required. The call for 'a reformed judiciary' is little more than a cheap attempt to arouse popular paranoia. If there are gaps in the citizen's defences against overmighty government, it is because of the legal restrictions on judicial review, not because of the social background of judges.

The second requirement is the existence of usable conventions and statutes to provide a sound basis for the judgments of constitutional courts. In Dicey's day, and even until quite recently, it was possible to dismiss such conventions and entrenched clauses as airy-fairy, alien devices which would not work here or of which we had no need, since the House of Commons responded to and ensured speedy redress of our grievances in a way which no paper blueprint could match. We are now less sure of that inherited superiority.

And the third requirement is that it should be possible without violent upheaval to fit such new systems and rights into the traditional system as we have inherited it. This is the last line of defence of those who defend the adaptability of the status quo, while denying that it could adapt in this particular abhorrent way: towards the limitation of parliamentary sovereignty, towards the separation of powers, towards entrenched clauses, towards ever widening judicial review of executive decisions. But this is, in practice, the direction in which adaptation has been taking place at an accelerating pace, ever since crusty old Hewart sat down to compose his first scorching sentences. In retrospect, we shall, I think, look back on the inter-war period as the high-water mark of executive discretion (and the low-water mark of the legal protection of individual liberty) in our recent history. Ever since, there has been a gathering recognition of the law's failure to defend the autonomy of the individual against the modern state and against the large institutions which modern society spawns. The pace of that gathering recognition is not likely to slacken now.

4

THE INCOMING TIDES

So far we have been discussing possibilities, not imperatives, the 'could' rather than the 'should' of constitutional development. It has been argued that many of the supposed principles governing our present arrangements are, in reality, corruptions or narrowings of our historical tradition; they cannot claim a permanent hold on our loyalties. Other ways of doing things would be quite consonant with our political history, have been tried before and could be tried again – or have not been tried here in the form in which they are employed in other modern nations but could be so tried if we had a mind to, without in any way doing violence to the framework of our political institutions.

Among the conventional maxims which have been challenged, in whole or in part, are:

that no parliament can bind its successor;

that the doctrine of the separation of powers is unBritish;

that federalism has no place in the British Constitution;

that Proportional Representation and fixed-term parliaments are unknown to the British Constitution;

that English courts are ill-equipped to interpret broad declarations of rights.

It may seem odd to have approached the argument this way round. In most controversies, it is, I suppose, more usual first to demonstrate the crying need for change before going on to consider the practicalities. But it is my contention that the shrivelled and corrupted understanding of the British Constitution is not merely an impediment to reform; it is also partly the cause of the degeneration of the institutions which are thus misunderstood. The Diceian misunderstanding first fixes our gaze on parliamentary supremacy and instructs our eyes not to turn elsewhere, and then bemoans the consequences (Dicey's later suppressed introduction to the eighth edition is a ripe example of this) without acknowledging that his own mind-set is to blame for those consequences. Nothing is less surprising than that parliamentary supremacy, if taken literally and unadulteratedly, would degenerate into elective dictatorship. Burke after all, prophesied the tyranny of the majority 200 years ago:

> Of this I am certain, that in a democracy, the majority of the citizens are capable of exercising the most cruel oppressions upon the minority, whenever strong divisions prevail in that kind of polity, as they often must; and that oppression of the minority will extend to far greater numbers, and will be carried on with much greater fury, than can almost ever be apprehended from the dominion of a single sceptre.[1]

Our first task then is to understand that parliamentary supremacy is neither the beginning nor the end of our constitutional history.

At this point then, but only at this point, it is right to consider the objections of those who are more or less content with the constitutional status quo. 'Could' certainly does not entail 'should'; it does not even suggest or nudge us toward 'should'; it merely advertises that other constitutional devices and principles are legitimate and available if required.

The case in favour of the status quo is a powerful one[2] and does not deserve the casual and sneering treatment it receives from full-time reformers. First of all, the case cannot be dismissed as complacent and prejudiced against reform of any kind. Parliamentary supremacy is so fluent, so effortless in its manufacture of fresh laws that parliamentary supremacists could more justly be accused of being too indulgent of change, too heedless of the virtues of stability and 'stickiness' in political arrangements.

In fact, the best case in favour of the present system relies on the long list of recent reforms that it can show as evidence that the system can respond to fresh challenges and dilemmas. Impressive lists are given in John Patten's CPC lecture, and in Philip Norton's collection of essays, *New Directions in British Politics*; most of the contributors to the latter argue that the last decades have shown that Parliament has demonstrated an undiminished capacity to generate new devices for improving the quality of democracy.

The House of Commons has, for example, introduced Select Committees to quiz the executive in almost every field of policy. The government produces a raft of Green Papers to enable both vested interests and the general public to be consulted at an earlier stage in policy formation. The Official Secrets Act 1989, in the government's view, shrinks the domain of secrecy. The House of Lords has introduced life peers to improve its representativeness and its expertise. Ombudsmen now provide a recourse against maladministration; and the grounds of appeal to the courts against ministerial decisions are constantly being widened.

The 1984 Data Protection Act gives individuals rights of access to information held on their files; the 1985 Local Government (Access to Information) Act gives rights of access to local authority meetings and to documentation and records; the 1987 Personal Files Act gives individuals the right of access to the files on them which are held by local authority housing and social services departments. The 1984 Police and Criminal Evidence Act, on balance, restrains police powers and affords suspects better defined protection. We have the Victims Charter, the Citizens Charter and now the Patients Charter. Rights are showered upon us in response to the complaints of an active citizenry.

Could any written constitution or network of entrenched clauses cope so smartly with an ever changing world? Surely it can be argued that recent decades, far from promoting the case for fundamental constitutional change, have given parliamentary supremacy a series of tests which it has passed with honour.

The defender of the existing system may then go on to suggest that the long and relatively peaceful history of parliamentary supremacy is no accident. Once the terms of the constitutional monarchy had been agreed at the end of the seventeenth century, our system has proved itself capable of dealing with the most violent societal shocks – most notably, war, ethnic conflict and the dislocations of the Industrial Revolution – while other systems have been blown away by the first crisis.

This is a formidable defence which should not be underestimated. Merely because the language of Hallam sounds sentimental to a more sardonic age, we must not dodge the fact that ours *has* been a blessed history by most standards ('ours' equalling well-to-do England's).

But the would-be reformers of Charter 88 and the like can certainly point to gaping weaknesses in this defence. While in the nineteenth century the challenges which the system was countering so successfully were from outside – notably the demands of the working classes to be admitted to the system – the challenge which the system has been countering recently has been internally generated, namely the corruption of parliamentary supremacy into something resembling elective dictatorship. The secrecy, the arbitrariness, the lack of scrutiny which have been complained of – these do not come from the outside world; they seem to be inherent in the system, and, while Professor Norton is right to remind us of the commendable efforts the system is making to get rid of these faults, only a blind optimist would claim that the pests have been totally or permanently got rid of. Deep in the inaccessible nooks and interstices of the fabric, the death-watch beetle bides its time. The Whips still control the choice of members for Select Committees; they still ensure that the Committee stage of Bills remains largely a charade; deprived of the sanctions of the criminal law (which were, after all, enforced only rarely), secrecy continues to contaminate Whitehall; Green Papers come increasingly to resemble White Papers, in that the government is reluctant to be budged from its first published intentions; Ministers who are reminded by their officials to go through the motions properly are rarely held by the courts to have exercised their quasi-judicial powers unreasonably.

I do not suggest that the reforms of recent years add up to little more than a series of inadequate palliatives; they often represent substantial advances in a direction in which further advances must and no doubt will be achieved. But I doubt whether even the most sympathetic observer would claim that these reforms had eliminated the systemic deficiencies of parliamentary supremacy in the

Diceian sense.

Still, if those deficiencies were all that we had to contend with, no doubt we could live with them; a sense of imperfection is the condition of human life. We might continue to look with the occasional stab of envy at other, more open, more balanced, more stable systems of government, while no doubt consoling ourselves with the thought that those systems have the defects of their virtues just as ours does – the insatiable legalism of the United States being a conspicuous example. But we might not fret too much.

Unfortunately, the internal corruptions of the system are not all we have to contend with. Constitutional reform can no longer be brushed aside as a middle-class hobby irrelevant to real politics, an activity somewhat comparable to growing organic vegetables. For our situation is not that of a ramshackle but pleasant old house, in a sheltered inland spot, with recurrent but not serious problems of rising damp and other fungal infestation. We are right out on the promontory, at the mercy of wind and tide. And it is the strength of these tides that forces us to look at our constitutional arrangements in a quite different spirit from the spirit of the later Victorians. Their anxieties were profound and inspissated; but they are not ours. And the fact that the huge and agonising adaptations they made to the system – the wholesale widening of the franchise over fifty years, the forty-year struggle for Irish Home Rule and eventually Irish independence – eventually created a fresh platform of stability should not lure us into thinking that this platform is therefore destined to last out the impending storms. Rotten timbers, however painstakingly lashed together, are unlikely to provide sure footing for long.

The European Community

Whatever may be said now, it was clear from the start that 'going into Europe' would have momentous consequences and was intended to have them. From the start, it was the fundamental thrust of opponents of British entry that our whole constitutional system would be undermined, if not swept away. If government spokesmen were more reassuring about the limited nature of the immediate consequences, nobody could be in any doubt that even 'co-operation' or 'even closer union' – let alone federal union – would make a huge difference to the way we had been governed. 'To enter Europe,' Dick Crossman told his Harvard audience in April 1970,

> is for us, in terms of constitutional methods, almost as difficult as making ourselves an extra State in the USA. . . It might be true that in our local British problems we could retain our British ways. But we couldn't possibly retain our fusion of executive and legislature in our relations with the rest of Europe.

Crossman said that, therefore, he would not predict that our existing system is 'going to last for ever. If we go into Europe, it probably won't'.[3]

We did, and it hasn't. In time-honoured British fashion, most of those directly involved in the political and legal worlds preferred not to recognise how the incremental change was building up into something monumental. Only those, like Mr Enoch Powell, who were acutely aware of the inescapable consequences of the 1972 Act because they feared and loathed those consequences have greeted the train of events without surprise and with a certain grim satisfaction. By now, it is clear to everybody what was clear to Lord Denning in 1974 that 'The Treaty is like an incoming tide. It flows into the estuaries and up the rivers. It cannot be held back.'[4]

It is clear, not merely that Community law is and must remain superior to English and Scottish law and must therefore take precedence over UK Acts of Parliament; it is also clear that the European Court of Justice is right to 'freeze' national law until its compatibility with EC law is tested. The *Factortame* judgment[5] granted a group of Spanish fishermen relief from the UK's 1988 Merchant Shipping Act, which had been introduced to stop 'quota-hopping' (the plundering of British fishing quotas by British-flagged vessels which had no genuine link with this country). The fishermen argued that the Act was incompatible with EC legislation and should be suspended until that compatibility was tested. Along with other MPs, Sir Teddy Taylor protested at this 'frightening' decision: 'It means the EC can suspend any British law it is investigating.' Mrs Thatcher said she was concerned, but concerned is all she could be, for the decision was a logical consequence of all that had gone before.

Lord Scarman said the decision 'exposes once again the necessity for a properly drawn, written constitution and a supreme court, one charged with the duty to interpret and apply the constitution'. It surely exposed something rather more than that – or rather different from that. The *Factortame* judgment reinforces the dawning awareness that the European courts, gradually, informally, but ineluctably, are themselves coming to make up a loose-knit sort of supreme court for us.

Professor Leslie Zines of the Australian National University remarks:

> Outsiders such as Australians see Britain in practical terms as having something in the nature of a Bill of Rights that is interpreted and applied by foreigners. Its procedures may, from the individual point of view, be highly inefficient, but the decisions, generally speaking, seem to be accepted. Laws and executive instruments are judged against an instrument declaring such rights. This goes beyond anything Australia and New Zealand have.[6]

And Zines draws the natural conclusion: 'It passes my understanding why the British do not see the virtue of having such questions determined by their own courts, initially at least.'[7] As Rodney Brazier remarks in *Constitutional Reform*: 'If that were done, enforcement would no longer be entirely a matter for a European Court and judicial system. Condemnations from abroad would be a thing of the past. The law would, once again, be in the hands of British judges'[8] – and incidentally, delays and costs would be reduced as a result.

Although not a member of a federation and still clinging to the doctrine of parliamentary sovereignty, Britain stands in relation to the Community in a position which strikes Zines as remarkably similar to the colonial federations that Britain itself created. The words of Lord Justice Bingham in the *Factortame* case have all the more resonance because of their discreet couching: where the law of the community was clear, 'the duty of the national court is to give effect to it in all circumstances'. That being so, one could not dodge the conclusion that 'to that extent a United Kingdom statute is no longer inviolable as it was once'.

If for a moment we put aside our British perspective and think about the personal situation of the litigants, the Spanish fishermen, then we might agree with Mr Hamish Adamson, Director of the International and Legal Practice Directorate of the Law Society, that 'if another member-state introduced legislation to put British firms out of business, surely we would be only too glad to be able to claim that its effect should be suspended until its validity had been tested before the court in Luxembourg'.[9]

The findings of the European Court of Human Rights, unlike those of the European Court of Justice, are not binding on the British courts, in theory. In practice, the moral authority behind them is now so powerful that the British government usually has no choice but to implement them, preferably after a dignified interval to save face; if it refuses, the Minister responsible knows that he will have a sticky time in the House of Commons and will incur the lasting enmity of the relevant pressure groups; as a consequence, he may be tagged in the media as 'accident-prone', and his career prospects may take a sharp downward dip. Thus the Court of Human Rights has, in practice, acquired something of the power of a supreme court to overrule cruel and unusual punishments.

But it is not simply the unchallengeability of ministerial decisions that has come into question. It is the legislative efficacy as well as the dignity of Parliament. It is part of the law of the land that, in areas covered by Community law, that law is superior to British law. But it adds insult to self-inflicted injury that the upstart European Parliament – which stalwart British parliamentarians like Mrs Thatcher have asserted not to be 'a real Parliament' at all – should, in fact, be more effective as a scrutineer of European legislation than the British Parliament is of British legislation. A high proportion of Euro-MPs' amendments are incorporated into European legislation; for British Opposition and backbenchers, the proportion of successful amendments is, as we have seen, extremely small. As for exercising influence over European legislation, we have seen too how disgracefully slow the House of

Commons has been to wake up to its responsibilities and opportunities; debates have been held in the small hours, attended only by a handful of fanatics, and often timed too late in any case to affect the UK government's negotiating position. Any chance of co-operation with British Euro-MPs, who have at least a sporting chance of seeing their amendments incorporated into the final legislation, has been put off by the refusal of the House of Commons to grant them any standing in the Palace of Westminster – although Euro-MPs have recently been admitted to the canteen, but not the bars. The Procedure Committee is finally dragging the House into some recognition of how damaging its childish pique has been; there will doubtless soon be some form of participation by MEPs in the work of Select Committees. But it has been a long and dingy business, which has seen this proud and ancient House at its most jealous and petty.

The notorious prophecy by Jacques Delors that within a few years 80 per cent of economic legislation, and possibly fiscal and social legislation as well, would originate from the Community,[10] sent British politics into a state of hysteria which probably triggered off the long process that ended in the fall of Mrs Thatcher. But the plausibility of the prophecy was scarcely challenged, certainly not by the alternative subsequently offered by Lord Young, then Secretary of State for Trade and Industry, that the real figure would be nearer 50 per cent.

Long before the political uproar surrounding the proposals for political union, the legal and political structures of this country were being remorselessly pounded by the European breakers. The responses demanded of those structures might well be just as formidable, with or without political union and EMU, however defined.

The shape of things to come had already assumed a hard outline. Already it was clear that British institutions stood in real danger of becoming dim and unavailing, piteously flailing at concrete realities rushing past them, unable and increasingly incompetent to formulate decisive and effective responses to events, bypassed not simply by forces in the outside world but – and this is the hardest to take – by their own citizens. Every time that a British citizen or group of citizen appeals to Strasbourg where he, she or they may have a remedy, instead of to the British courts where there is no remedy, British justice becomes a more insubstantial thing.

We have spoken intermittently of the recovery or restoration or revival of our Constitution. This is not simply a rhetorical trick to reclaim the cause of constitutional reform for the conservative tendency; it is an honest attempt to diagnose the degenerative symptoms of parliamentary supremacism. And, when we come to examine the European syndrome, we cannot fail to notice how those degenerative symptoms begin to gallop. Crossman, in his brutish, acute way, was right. The glueing together of executive and legislative which makes up parliamentary supremacism simply cannot hold in the European climate. Apart from the Low Countries, all other EC countries have some form of extra-parliamentary control of legislation. Ninety per cent of the rest of the Community is accustomed to some kind of court to determine whether or not a law is constitutional. The existence of such a court is intrinsic to written-constitution states and therefore comes naturally to a community preponderantly made up of such states.

The European Community has, in effect, endowed us with a written constitution and a Bill of Human Rights. The question is not whether we wish to have such newfangled things – we already have them – but whether we wish to *patriate* them, to incorporate some or all of their provisions into our own law. Similarly, in the case of parliamentary scrutiny, the question is not whether much or most of the legislation that affects our daily lives is to be scrutinised at European level – it already is – but whether our own Parliament can summon the wit and energy to patriate some of that scrutiny work, by organising itself to examine, promptly, expertly and uninhibitedly, some of the legislation which it now merely bleats and mews at *post facto*.

But is there not an alternative to this work of patriation? Instead of giving new life to our institutions by bringing home the methods and charters of European institutions, can we not restore the old life? We need, it may be said, to work closely together with our European neighbours; we need the widest possible free-trade area; we need to co-operate on a huge range of issues – environmental pollution, drugs, crime, transport. But Mr Norman Tebbit tells us,[11] international co-operation does not require all this supranational interference and this supranational take-over of our ancient institutions. To be free-standing nations standing together, that should be our healthy, limited and sensible ambition. We need to balance power, not to pool it in some Euro-cauldron which may eventually produce a mixture as unstable and explosive as that engendered by federalism in Yugoslavia and the Soviet Union.

Leaving aside the crucial differences between a voluntary and a coerced federation, we may concede the attractions of this alternative vision. Alas, experience has taught us that the trouble with the balance of power was that it never balanced for long enough; what one power perceived as balancing was always liable to be read by a rival power as stealing a march in terms of arms, territory or allies; one side's entente was the other side's encirclement. Blue land thinks it is only catching up with Red land, which believes that it is being overtaken and must therefore in its turn try to catch up, and so on until Armageddon. Since the late 19th century, at least, modern nation-states have been too prickly and self-conscious to allow themselves to be treated as inert weights to be tossed in a scale.

Today there are even less biddable forces emerging which make the alternative project – an association of nation-states – not so much unworkable as frail and insubstantial. When we come to define the qualities and principles of such an association, we may find that there is simply less *there*. Those characteristics which formerly defined independent nation-states with such a hard and brilliant outline are no longer consistently available.

Opponents of closer European union, however defined, often profess themselves baffled by the motives of its proponents (and vice versa). As for the mass of the population, they must have been somehow drugged or deceived into a state of demoralised inertia. Mr Charles Moore quotes Sir Walter Scott's verdict on England's attempt in the late 1820s to impose a single currency – gold – upon Scotland: 'Swift says that kingdoms may be subject to poverty and lowness of heart as well as individuals; and that in such moments they become reckless of their own interests and contract habits of submission.'[12] Similarly, it has been the constant burden of Mr Enoch Powell's later speeches that the British people have, so to speak, forgotten who they are; they are in a peculiar, numbed, unconfident state in which they allow themselves to be led up the blindest alley; but, sooner or later, they will, or they must, or he hopes they will, wake up to their true destiny.

This psychological explanation of the apparent relative indifference with which the British people have responded to the growing influence of European institutions over their lives is a rare instance of a right-wing doctrine of 'false consciousness'. It relies upon the (usually tacit) assumption that there can be no concrete, sensible reasons for accepting the Europeanising process, and that the process is itself the outcome of a deranged *fédéraste* mentality which has drawn utterly mistaken deductions from the past century of European history. Seen in this perspective, the Europeanising process is not so much an incoming tide as one of those artificial Water Paradises with elaborate chutes and whirlpools provided at huge expense by the local authority.

But the European project, with all its faults, cannot be abstracted in this way. It is part of the modern world, and the shape it has assumed is not the brainchild of some mad scientist, some Brussels Caligari or Frankenstein, but simultaneously the product and the exemplar of modernity. These are real tides. If we move further along the coast, they may be higher or later, but they will come in just the same.

At first sight, it may seem odd to identify the 'European idea' as the vehicle of modernity. The idea is, after all, as old as and closely linked to the idea of Christendom. In fact, though, it is precisely the modernising thrust of Christianity – its universalism, its individualism, its intolerance of local gods and time-honoured structures of oppression – which is at issue here. This can be seen vividly in the refusal of the Community so far to accept Turkey as a member, not on grounds of religious difference but on the grounds that civil society as we understand it has not fully taken root there; individual rights and democratic structures are built on the most shallow of footings, and the treatment of the Kurds advertises Turkey's failure to embrace racial equality.

Now, one would not dream of equating, in the manner of some eighteenth-century satirist, the political conditions in Turkey with those in the UK. Our purpose here is solely to draw attention to the modernising aspects of Community law, in particular its insistence that human rights are to be codified, entrenched beyond the reach of political rancour, made enforceable across national frontiers.

Human rights

The campaigner for human rights in a foreign country is attempting to 'get at' the foreign nation-state, to break through its shell of independence and untrammelled sovereignty. He is not only morally indignant; he is also in a condition of intense political frustration. Modern communications enable him to see, often in painfully vivid detail, the sufferings of his fellow beings the other side of the border, but modern border controls – electrified fences, armed guards instructed to shoot on sight, elaborate documentary requirements – all prevent him from charging to the rescue. He is in the situation of a Hitchcock hero: confined to a wheelchair while watching a murder being committed the other side of the street.

The barriers are not purely physical. The nation-state has also erected formidable doctrinal defences to protect its untrammelled autonomy against intervention. We cannot as individuals, and nor can our own governments, directly alter or influence events on the other side without resorting to acts that may be interpreted as warlike or at any rate unfriendly. Attempts to intervene on behalf of a person being tortured by another regime may create an 'international incident', even if that person happens to be one of our own citizens. The existence of the boundary magnifies the incident and engraves the memory of it, so that the incident, say, of the torturing of Dr Sheila Cassidy remains a factor in relations between Britain and Chile long after Dr Cassidy herself has been extricated. The impediments are not simply those posed by frontier guards and barbed wire but also the intellectual barbed wire of doctrines of non-intervention and national independence which are erected on both sides of the border.

The doctrine of non-intervention grows out of and is intimately connected with the idea of the nation-state. Throughout the

Middle Ages and well into the Renaissance, by contrast, intervention to punish wrongdoing was regarded as a moral duty. Even Grotius, in Book II of *De Jure Belli ac Pacis* (1625), still defended the right to punish wrongdoing wherever it might occur:

> It is also proper to observe that kings and those who are possessed of sovereign power have a right to exact punishment not only for injuries affecting immediately themselves or their own subjects, but for gross violations of the law of nature of nations, done to other states and subjects.

The medieval ideas of the just war and of the civilised world as *Respublica Christiana* outlived any physical remnants of a Christendom which was not divided into nation-states. But, as J. Bryan Hehir points out in his historical survey of the ethics of intervention,[13] Grotius was the last of his line. As soon as writers like Bodin began to concentrate on the idea of sovereignty, the days of interventionism were numbered. For, if supreme authority is located in the nation, then any outside intervention must be an insult to that sovereignty. The physical power of the nation-state secreted its own ideology. The Swiss jurist, Emmirich Vattel, in the *Law of Nations* (1758), enunciated the doctrine of non-intervention in its complete form little more than a century after Grotius:

> It clearly follows from the liberty and independence of Nations that each has the right to govern itself as it thinks proper, and that not one of them has the least right to interfere in the government of another. Of all the rights possessed by a Nation that of sovereignty is doubtless the most important and the one which others should most carefully respect if they are desirous not to give cause for offence.

Later this argument came to be given a liberal or liberationist gloss. National independence – meaning the liberation of people from some alien empire and their incorporation as a nation – was a form of self-realisation; liberty was, in one sense anyway, not freedom from government but freedom from government by foreigners. Peoples who had won their freedom were not to be lightly interfered with; the only kind of interference which might be legitimate was interference to protect people against interference. John Stuart Mill was dubious even about that: 'intervention to enforce non-intervention is always rightful, always moral, if not always prudent. . . .'

It is important to notice how far this kind of argument went. In 'A Few Words on Non-Intervention', Mill, in claiming that intervention was generally wrong, argued:

> The reason is, that there can seldom be anything approaching to assurance that interventionism, even if successful, would be for the good of the people themselves. The only test possessing any real value of a people's having become fit for popular institutions is that they, or a sufficient portion of them to prevail in the context, are willing to brave labour and danger in their liberation.

The free air one breathes in an independent nation is so precious that the benefits of any efforts from outside to remedy injustice, however kindly meant, are outweighed by the dangers of weakening the popular spirit of liberty. This argument may strike most people now as extreme. It is open to the obvious objection that, if the injustices which the outsider hopes to remedy are bad enough to be worth remedying, then the 'popular institutions' cannot be working properly and the spirit of liberty must be polluted already.

But what must be emphasised is the historical reality of Mill's passion for non-intervention. National independence seemed to nineteenth-century Europeans of progressive leanings to be something infinitely precious; such independence was both a consolation for the most wretched poverty and a token of the worth of every individual. Something like this passion, it is said, has been reproduced in modern Africa and Asia. Now that people of progressive sympathies in Europe and North America are turning back towards vigorous intervention to right injustices, it is worth recalling briefly the equally passionate belief in non-intervention of their great-great-grandparents.

It is tempting at this point to discuss the content of human-rights demands: should they be 'merely' demands for civil and political rights, or, if they are to have any serious impact on the target country, must they also include a minimum menu of economic and social rights? Or can economic and social rights be said to be rights at all, rather than desirable goals which may require not only goodwill but considerable physical and financial resources, as well as levels of individual competence and sophistication, to realise? I have argued elsewhere[14] that a campaign for the old human rights –the civil and political rights – is quite enough; it terrifies the wits out of tyrants as much as ever. The narrower definition of human rights at least implies and often explicitly affirms that personal and civil rights are *explosive*.

A regime which grants such rights cannot remain the same in any important respect as one which does not; certain measures of an economic or social nature *have* to follow. If they do not, if the regime continues to deny, say, land reform or some degree of equal access to schools and to medical treatment, then there will be protests which the newly 'civilised' regime must take account of. If the regime ignores the protests, then either it will be forced back into repressive 'incivil' measures – censorship, harassment and arrest of protesters, even torture – or it will be brought down by the new civil modes of change; fresh Ministers will come to power, fresh elections will be held. Personal and civil rights are not only a precondition of economic and social justice; they are pregnant with, and cannot help giving birth to, social justice.

In theory, the end-result of this pregnancy could be roughly the same as that of a full-scale programme of human rights in the broad sense, including economic and social rights, such as the radical priests in South America are demanding. But the process is entirely different, because the transformation arises out of the concrete experience of democracy and not from an imposed programme which may include unrealistic, illiberal or even totalitarian measures. The difference between the *liberalisation* which follows from a narrow view of human rights and the *revolution* which is implied by the broad view is the difference between enabling people to choose the form of a new society and imposing by force the new society that they ought to choose.

If civil rights were merely the kind of basic rights which led nowhere and which could be safely granted without endangering the tyrant's economic and social power and privilege, then we might expect him to yield to pressure to stop torture, arbitrary arrest and so on. In practice, tyrannical regimes will make only the most niggardly gestures of this sort and usually try to withdraw even those gestures as soon as the attention of well- meaning foreigners turns elsewhere. This suggests that the powers of torture, arbitrary arrest and censorship are essential weapons of social control, without which such regimes would collapse.

Thus the campaign for human rights, however narrowly conceived, represents a serious intrusion into the affairs of another country and not just an insult to the dignity of its independence. The narrow conception carries the added advantage of appearing to represent only the kind of basic minimum demands which no regime could dare to be seen resisting, while in practice prising open some of the tyrannous regime's most central armour-plating. Hence the tactical brilliance of the Helsinki agreements. Who can say if, even within civilised Western Europe, the apparently banal provisions of the European Convention on Human Rights are not beginning to have some modest success as tin-openers – not least in a nation like Britain, which prides itself on its heritage of common law justice and in which the Convention is not yet part of the law?

We have seen how English judges, so to speak, 'shadow' the provisions of the Convention – not relying on them to direct their judgments, but taking full account of them and trying as far as possible to establish a kind of consonance between the provisions of the Convention and the law of England.

Thereby the European Convention gains a growing authority and, with it, the findings of the European Court of Human Rights. Not merely are a growing assortment of litigants prepared to take their case to Strasbourg; the British government also finds itself unable to resist the findings of the Court, although Mrs Thatcher and several of her supporters never ceased to be darkly suspicious of it and to regard it as even less of 'a real court' than the European Court of Justice in Luxembourg. When Strasbourg issues a finding which reflects badly on English law or the British government, there is a dignified pause for reflection in London to demonstrate HMG's freedom of action; and then, a little shamefacedly and not without a good deal of grumbling behind the scenes, the finding is complied with. Thus, in a reluctant, informal way, not only the relevance of the Convention but its *superiority* is conceded. To hold fast to the nineteenth-century principles of non-intervention no longer seemed to be a politically stable option, even for the most robustly nationalist British administration since the war.

The consequences of this situation are clear. So long as the Convention is not actually part of our law but remains in this half-in, half-out position, a distant, shadowy but ineluctable authority, the majesty and authority of our own courts will continue to diminish. Judges will be looking, ever more nervously, over their shoulders at this alien code which must be referred to respectfully and accommodated as far as possible but cannot be robustly and openly interpreted, as it could be if it were part of our law.

It used to be said that the Convention could not be fitted in to English law because it was composed of high-sounding, typically Continental declarations of rights, and lacked the superb concreteness and specificity of English common law. Oakeshott wrote as far back as 1948: 'What went abroad as the concrete rights of the Englishman have returned home as the abstract Rights of Man, and they have returned to confound our politics and corrupt our minds.'[15]

But how unbridgeable is this gap between the concrete, inductive Anglo-Saxon and the abstract, deductive Cartesian, between the specific negative prohibition and the general positive right? In practice, English judges seem to move readily enough between the two; a cumulative series of negative prohibitions may in time come to form the outline of a positive right, just as a series of judgments stemming from a positive general right may in time provide a list of specific unlawful actions *à l'anglaise*. Might not the differences and difficulties dwindle with the years, as the law fills out with case law and statute law? It may have been only in the early years of the European Convention's operation that it appeared so foreign, so hopelessly alien to our own conceptions of how the law protects our liberties.

In practice, as we have seen, English judges have turned out to be a good deal more agile than they pretended to be, and they now seem to cope tolerably well with the far more difficult challenge of achieving harmony with a code which is not law, although it is subscribed to by Her Majesty's Government.

The conclusion surely follows that English judges would find their work easier, rather than trickier, if the European Convention were incorporated into English Law. They could then begin to build up a body of case law which would translate these Continental declarations into usable specifics.

The familiar argument that incorporation would diminish the relative importance of English common law seems to me precisely the reverse of the truth. That relative importance is already being overshadowed by European institutions and European law of all types. Paradoxically, only by incorporating the European Convention do we rescue and revitalise the common law tradition – in much the same way as it has been rescued and revitalised in earlier centuries by the incorporation of other great charters into our law. Strasbourg becomes merely a higher court within our own legal system rather than, as at present, an *alternative* source of law which is also a higher one. If this line of argument sounds perverse, we have only to refer back to the rights of appeal from the Scottish High Courts to the House of Lords and from Commonwealth High Courts to the Judicial Committee of the Privy Council. These rights of appeal have not, I think, made those courts seem less Scottish or Australian to their citizens.

But we should not dodge the fact that, if we take the final step of incorporation (or even if we don't and leave the authority of the Convention increasingly to overshadow the authority of the common law), we are still taking a dramatic and memorable step.

Not merely are we acknowledging and signalling an end to the era of non-intervention; we are also retreating from the long-held principle that the administration of law is a strictly national business, indeed, is one of the defining characteristics of the nation. The Queen's writ is no longer to run exclusively unaided or unfortified by external and higher authority, and precisely on those matters which Dicey saw as the prime constituents of the rule of law – freedom of speech and assembly, habeas corpus, due process and so on. It is public opinion which has forced political parties and governments, step by step, to accept this dilution of their power, and public opinion driven, moreover, by nothing more organised than a general sense of what is fair and reasonable (the bodies campaigning for, say, British adherence to the European Convention have remained virtually unknown to the general public). On such matters, it seems, there is some difficulty in persuading public opinion that we are being 'bullied by Strasbourg' or that 'Europe has no right to be judging our domestic concerns'; on the contrary, justice is regarded as so precious that it seems quite reasonable, even to the nationalist tabloids, that people should go abroad in search of it; the quest, in fact, tends to be presented as rather romantic and certainly admirable.

'Constitutionalist' arguments that acceptance of outside intervention in our judicial process undermines our nationhood seem simply puzzling to many people. We are already familiar with international regulatory bodies which enjoy a variety of disciplinary powers, especially sporting bodies, such as the International Olympic Committee, FIFA and the International Cricket Conference. Whatever the substantial differences in law, the European Court of Human Rights would seem in many people's eyes merely one more extension of the right to appeal to higher authority.

A return to hermetically sealed national legal systems looks no longer plausible. By contrast, a revival of the plural, overlapping jurisdictions of the Middle Ages appears to be an accelerating trend – which makes it more rather than less important that national systems of justice should be internally coherent and externally consonant with other systems. To satisfy the unvarying requirements of justice – clarity, predictability, stability – we need, wherever possible, to aim for explicitness and entrenchment, the tools of constitutional recovery. This incoming tide cannot be mopped away; it can be converted into tidal energy for domestic use.

The ecological imperative

The wave that literally laps our shores with our neighbours' scum and detritus bobbing in its eddies is the modern embodiment of the proposition that no man (or no island) is an island. We are involuntary partners in a Continental, if not global exchange of gases and garbage. It is no surprise, therefore, that the type of international intrusion which has been most readily and uncomplainingly accepted is that which attempts to regulate or prohibit noxious emissions and to control or reduce levels of environmental pollution. Opinion polls regularly show huge majorities of 80 per cent or more in favour of the European Commission's initiatives to reduce emissions from car exhausts and power stations and to clean up rivers and beaches. These initiatives naturally involve the EC in on-site inspections and in harassment of national governments to ensure that targets are met. Sometimes the harassment seems rather petty or unfair; the British government has a quite impressive record over the past three decades in clearing up the debris and pollution left behind by industrialisation and in making progress towards cleaner air and clearer rivers; this does not protect Her Majesty's Government from the orotund criticisms of Carlo Ripa de Meana, the European Commissioner for the Environment. Signor Ripa di Meana points out in return that he intervenes so often in British issues, not because Britain has a worse record in these matters – on the contrary, our record is far better than that of Italy and the other Mediterranean members of the EC – but because 80 per cent of all complaints to Brussels come from British complainants (*Times*, 25 November, 1991). But if politicians grumble at being chivvied along, the public seems, on the whole, pleased and feels quite unthreatened by these interventions.

In this respect at least, the EC and its agents seem to be active on behalf of the citizenry and to be consistently an ally of the consumer/client/customer against the producer/provider. By contrast, national governments are vulnerable to producer capture, as are national parliaments. Producers are, after all, characteristically clustered together; their interests are more intensely felt and can more easily be mobilised in a variety of ways – through lobbying organisations, through sponsorship of members of Parliament (although this somewhat eighteenth-century style of patronage is beginning to decline), through press and PR campaigns. Such methods are just as likely to be adopted by public providers, such as local councils and electricity and water authorities (before privatisation); the direct access to government departments usually enjoyed by such bodies has tended to ensure that the pace of environmental improvement puts no undue strain on their capital investment programmes.

By contrast, consumer interests are characteristically dispersed, intermittently experienced and of low intensity. A classic example is that of a bathing beach with a sewage outfall pipe in the middle of it; the pollution interferes with the pleasure of families on holiday for at most a fortnight a year; the money needed to build a sewage farm might cripple a small sewage authority's budget for years. The authority's interest in postponing the investment is likely to be robustly expressed in influential quarters and continuously pursued.

It would be absurd to pretend that the European Community is immune to producer capture: the Common Agricultural Policy is a glaring refutation of any such illusion. But the intervention of the EC, in many ecological issues, mobilises and unifies consumer interests in other countries to offer a stronger counterweight to place against national producer interests. For example, people living near a British power station may complain about the damage to their own local environment; but their distress will tend to be outweighed in the official balance by energy arguments advanced on behalf of the nation as a whole. But when local distress is reinforced by the outrage of Germans or Scandinavians complaining that their forests are being destroyed by acid rain from noxious British emissions, then the consumer interest begins to gather a political weight which becomes increasingly irresistible.

At the same time, producers who wish to fight back have to band together across national frontiers and develop techniques for lobbying the Commission and the European Parliament. If they merely wine and dine their own Ministers and parliamentarians, they may lose any serious chance of exerting critical influence on the decision, since the Minister's attention will already be turning towards deriving the maximum political advantage from the outcome in the European Council; he will wish to say that 'Britain leads the world in cutting its emissions' or that 'The Community has now adopted our standards.'

We cannot be sure that consumers will always be the net gainers by this transfer or political activity to Brussels. For example, if the decision on lorry axle weights were left entirely to British Ministers, mindful of the winding lanes in their constituencies, the limits would remain lower on average than with a Community-wide standard.

My point here is not to establish whether, on balance, the Europeanising of environmental controls benefits the private citizen (as it happens, I am convinced that it does). From the point of view of constitutional politics, what matters is that British public opinion now understands clearly that, in a considerable number of cases, making the environment a European matter does strengthen the hands of campaigners against pollution. When the 3,000 acres of Rutland Water were declared a specially protected area under EC rules, the manager of the reservoir welcomed the intervention on the grounds that its existing status under British rules as a site of Special Scientific Interest might not be sufficient protection: "The intervention of the EC means we have more muscle to resist any encroachment that would be harmful to the wildlife" (Daily Telegraph, 27 December, 1991). Thus the 'Brussels bureaucrats' are seen in this context, not as a threat, but as an additional line of defence against rampant, headlong industrialisation. They may be enlisted as potential defenders of parts of our heritage for which our own inherited constitutional system has been reluctant or impotent to offer effective protection.

Strong unitary government in these islands has not been over-attentive to the little platoons. Its preoccupations – with cheap energy, with the housing shortage, with better roads – have not been kind to the cherished nooks and vistas which illustrate our idea of England.

Instead, and perhaps partly as a consequence and partly as a cause, the British have spawned a huge variety of independent charitable organisations and campaigns, some national and permanent and professionally staffed on a large scale, others small, formed to fight some specific corner and staffed entirely by volunteers. The larger national organisations, such as the National Trust and the Royal Society for the Protection of Birds, have memberships running into the millions and are envied and, increasingly, imitated by those less happier lands which have no such bodies. Their enthusiasm, their expertise – whether in defining and protecting the habitat of the bee orchid or the breeding grounds of the dunlin, or in restoring tapestries, paintings, stonework and garden layouts to their pristine state – are rare and precious possessions.

But it should be remembered that, despite the ever growing land holdings of the National Trust and some of the naturalist trusts, they still lack the power of central and local government which, on the Continent, may be wielded so decisively to protect buildings and landscapes that are threatened. The British state, by comparison, is a philistine sluggard, and its sluggishness is due not only to its philistinism but to the shallow roots of its local government tradition. The structure and powers of British local authorities are constantly being cut off, uprooted and replanted in a different pattern. This lack of stability has left them ill equipped to represent our most ultimate local concerns and protect our best-loved surroundings with any semblance of tenacity.

The European Commission has, moreover, had the good fortune to arrive on the scene at a moment when a renewed indignation at the despoliation of the environment has come to the fore. The British House of Commons has remained curiously indifferent to these fresh concerns. Only a minority of somewhat quirky MPs have taken an interest in them; for Labour, social welfare, for the Conservatives, economics and foreign affairs have been much more popular fields. The EC has exploited the genuinely European dimension inherent in environmental issues and made itself the indispensable agent of environmental protection. These issues spread and leak into a variety of areas which national governments had hitherto regarded as their own exclusive domains, such as health and welfare and transport. The upshot is that, in trying to draw a line between those issues which are best handled at European level and those which should stay under the control of the member-states, it is increasingly hard to keep such a line firm or straight. Accordingly, it becomes increasingly difficult in constitutional negotiations to see the outline of an enduring constitutional settlement which would establish the division of powers for good and all. Yet there is no going back, because public

237

opinion is now convinced of the advantages of treating some at least of these issues at European level. Thus environmental control, which might at one time have seemed a fairly secondary policy area – and so one that could be safely conceded to EC scrutiny – has now become a principal implicating agent, leaving few areas of British policy unmarked by seepage from the Continent.

The Wealth of Nations revisited

At about this stage in the argument, the sceptic is liable to explode and repeat, with a vehemence reinforced by impatience, that all these considerations may, perhaps should, impel us to greater co-operation between neighbouring nations, but that does not entail submitting ourselves to supranational authority. It is not merely pride in our long history of independence that should make us prefer co-operation to federation in the American style; differences of history, language, religion, and culture make an American solution impracticable for the ancient nations of Europe. We should therefore content ourselves with close and amicable co-operation and adhere with tenacity and enthusiasm to the principles of free trade. The co-operative route is not only politically preferable; it is better from the economic point of view too. Freedom to alter the exchange rates of our currencies enables us to optimise our terms of trade; competition in, rather than harmonisation of, trading standards will lead to the adoption of the most apt set of standards right across Europe and so make European products more saleable both at home and around the world. Since the great 1979 *Cassis de Dijon* decision in the European Court of Justice, the Community itself, in theory at least, has recognised that if a product has, under Article 30 of the Treaty of Rome, been 'lawfully produced and marketed' in one member-state, then another member-state should be able to refuse entry to that product by invoking Article 36 (which permits exceptions on grounds of public morality, public health and the like) only if an *overriding* national interest is at stake.

Thus mutual recognition of one another's standards is at the heart of the 1992 programme, as it must be, even in the arrangements of existing federations. If one had to go through a fresh ceremony of marriage or divorce or take a new driving test every time one crossed a state line, life would become intolerable; the same is obviously true for manufacturers and for the providers of professional services, doctors, architects, lawyers, insurance brokers and so on. The spirit of Mrs Thatcher's Bruges speech is not, as its critics claim, a sour and isolationist one but an approach grounded in the practicalities of co-operation between nations; far from being 'a narrow nationalist', she was encapsulating the original spirit of the Rome Treaty, which was a freedom charter dedicated to free markets and the free movement of people and goods. There were concessions in the Treaty – escape routes, breathing spaces and bolt-holes – for those who were fearful of an open society or wanted time to adjust, but the thrust of it was essentially in the direction of freedom, and not in the direction of burdening the peoples of Europe with a fresh layer of government in the shape of the Brussels bureaucracy. Indeed, the whole thrust of modernity, as Mr David Howell argues in *Blind Victory* (1986), is to reduce the significance of governmental action and of mercantilist efforts to drive the national economy as if it were a motor car –with all the tired attendant imagery of steering, braking and streamlining. The newest technologies fragment and disperse knowledge and power far beyond the capacities of lumbering national bureaucracies reliably to track their activities, let alone effectively to control them. Meanwhile, the European Commission exhausts our patience by attempting to standardise the size of lawn-mowers.

All this adds up to an appealing reinforcement for those who instinctively recoil from the Community's most overblown pretensions. It is extremely tempting to mock those who make a simplistic link between the globalisation of the economy and the Europeanising of our Constitution. It does not directly follow that, because the volume of international trade is so vastly increased, we must therefore yield to European institutions the regulatory powers over trade and industry hitherto exercised by national governments and parliaments; similarly, it does not follow that, because wind and tide carry pollutants from nation to nation, we must set up international authorities to regulate environmental standards. These matters can surely be dealt with just as effectively between nations, and perhaps more amicably.

And yet the most devoutly Brugeist free-traders must concede a few difficulties in this argument, if presented in its full unblemished purity. Even Mr Enoch Powell has conceded (though it was not, I think, intended as a concession) that:

> if a distinction is now to be drawn, as a matter of settled policy, between on the one hand the surrender of political independence – by way of monetary union – by Britain to Europe, and on the other hand the continuation and extension of freedom of trade with that continent – in the breaking down of tariff barriers by 1992 – then a great quantity of tough intellectual work lies ahead. This work has been neglected during almost 20 years when freedom of trade and political imperialism were allowed and encouraged to be mistaken for one another.
>
> The work will involve a closer understanding and definition of freedom of trade than has previously been called for during perhaps the whole of the present century.[16]

But why should it require such a lot of work to 'deduce what conditions are necessary, and what conditions are not necessary, for freedom of trade'? Why has this work been so culpably neglected? It cannot be because there are so few free-traders with the requisite intellectual energy. The Institute of Economic Affairs has been by far the liveliest centre of economic and social thought for the past three decades. Yet, even among its human dynamos, one senses a certain listlessness when it comes to detailed examination of the precise arrangements which are required of government and public authorities to ensure the flourishing of free trade. The task of proclaiming the virtues of free markets and the vices of government ownership and control is altogether more exhilarating than that of setting out the legal framework – the weights and measures stuff – which is a precondition if the free market is to enjoy the political and moral acceptance which will enable it to survive. All those aspects which Adam Smith covered so scrupulously in *The Wealth of Nations* have tended to receive less attention recently – so much so that certain anti-free-marketeers have been emboldened to caricature Smith as an interventionist sort of social democrat, by concentrating on his careful attention to the legitimate tasks of government (which the followers of Hayek and Friedman often ignore).

Now, as soon as we follow Powell's advice and address ourselves to this neglected work, we find that the matter is not so simple and that we cannot exclude constitutional considerations. Can free trade really flourish for more than a short period without some overarching supranational authority to ensure mutual recognition of standards? If the European Court of Justice had not insisted, would the West German importers ever have been allowed to import from France a single consignment of Cassis de Dijon? Without some supranational enforcement, the Federal Branntwein Monopolgesetz would presumably have continued to specify that all spirits coming into West Germany must have an alcohol content of not less than 25 per cent (it was one of the peculiarities of the case that Cassis had been banned as being too *weak* to count as a spirit for the hard-headed Germans). It is hard to see how cunning and energetic national vested interests can be persuaded to accept foreign competition, without some supranational authority to give legal effect to the free-trade principles. Full-bodied and pervasive free trade must depend to some extent on some yielding of national sovereignty, whether tacitly through an agreement such as the GATT, or explicitly through the Treaty of Rome and the European Communities Act of 1972.

Moreover, competition in standards may work in the reverse direction. The commitment to free trade between member-states may expose and make transparent the difference in conditions of production to such an embarrassing extent that the more threadbare, low-cost producer is forced, by political pressure, to improve his standards of safety, hygiene and social security in a way which would not have been dreamed of in traditional international trade. The reality – and it is an experienced truth, not simply political cant – is that the more genuine and beneficial and amicable the association (we shall avoid the cloying word 'Community'), the more difficult it is, in the longish run, to avoid a degree of civic fellow-feeling, which is likely, in turn, to lead to some sense of mutual responsibility and therefore to social legislation which attempts to remove the most intolerable inequalities.

As soon as one witnesses any attempt to reclaim the lost sovereignty (or power – no need to bandy definitions here) while maintaining the benefits of the free-trade agreement, one instantly detects the implausibility, not to say the bad faith, of the attempt. For example, Dr Alan Sked of the LSE, in his *Proposal for European Union*, tries to rescue the sovereignty of the British Parliament by proposing that:

> If a majority of any national delegation [in the European Parliament] object to legislation proposed in the European Cabinet on the grounds that it undermines a vital national interest, and find their objections sustained by a majority in their national parliament, the proposed legislation, even if passed will not be applicable to the country concerned.[17]

This 'opt-out facility' would present a permanent opportunity to defenders of any national vested interest. They need only mobilise a bare majority of their own nation's Euro-MPs to vote against the proposal. This would build up pressure in the national Parliament to do the same. Once the commercial, industrial and professional lobbies had got the hang of the technique, the democratic deficit might be seen to have been remedied, but the principles of free trade would be severely dented. It could well be argued that, the more emphatically the principles of free trade are constitutionally entrenched and the less they are subjected to the day-to-day barter of the political process, the better their chances of being put into practice; one need only contrast the majestic freedom of the United States' internal market and the grubby protectionist tactics on the international front which offer an ambitious US Congressman an easy route to fame. A really dedicated free-marketeer surely ought to welcome the installation of a supranational legal framework which would take the principles of free trade out of reach of the political lobbyists. He would look for a constitutional settlement which would include assertions of principle on the scale of those contained in the US Constitution:

No Tax or Duty shall be laid on Articles exported from any State. . . . No State shall, without the Consent of the Congress, lay any Imposts or Duties on Imports or Exports, except what may be absolutely necessary for executing its inspection Laws: and the net Produce of all Duties and Imposts, laid by any State on Imports or Exports, shall be for the Use of the Treasury of the United States; and all such laws shall be for the Revision and Control of the Congress.[18]

Full Faith and Credit shall be given in each state to the public Acts, Records and judicial Proceedings of every other State.[19]

In default of other evidence, one must therefore suspect that the prime allegiance of many Brugeiste is to national sovereignty rather than to free trade.

A loathing of bureaucracy is compatible with either the pro- or anti-Community view. If the ideals of the Single Market are eventually realised, the European courts need to be no more choked with business than are the bodies regulating inter-state commerce in full-scale federations. It may be that the threat of court action and the growing authority of precedent will gradually create a climate of compliance. Or, to put it more bluntly, national governments and their local vested interests will come to accept that they cannot get away with it and that elaborate non-tariff barriers, such as the notorious 'Poitiers incident' (when France insisted, just before the 1982 Christmas rush, that all imported video recorders should have to clear customs at a single, small and unequipped customs post in Poitiers), will be dismantled by the authorities. But, without some kind of supranational legal resort, is it really conceivable that Britain would have been able to overcome, say, France's claim that British-built Nissans didn't count as European cars because they did not have 80 per cent 'European content' (by contrast, France is quite ready to consider the Airbus as European, although it has at least 30 per cent American content)?

On closer inspection, the claim to be a dedicated free-marketeer and yet to be opposed to British membership of the 'Common Market' or the 'European Economic Community', as persons of this persuasion prefer to call the EC, seems rather less highly principled; it must, after all, be honestly admitted that part of the effect, if not the intention, of retaining or re-arrogating a sovereign power to opt out of international arrangements will be to make it easier to keep foreign goods out.

There is a curious similarity here to the effect, if not the intention, of retaining or re-arrogating a sovereign power to opt out of European monetary arrangements. In this respect, there is no difference between our present membership of the Exchange Rate Mechanism and any prospective participation in a future European common currency. The only practical reason for opting out would be to accommodate our domestic inflation in a manner which seemed, for the time being at least, less painful; the prime purpose would be to devalue and so to revive our export trade and employment. It is theoretically possible that we would wish to opt out because we were dissatisfied with the monetary structures of the European Central Bank and wished to pursue fiscal continence on our own – but only theoretically possible. Even in the bloodcurdling warnings issued by Mrs Thatcher and Mr Ridley, it is the loss of the freedom to *devalue* that is clearly in question. In the notorious *Spectator* interview which was to cost Mr Ridley his job, he argues:

'The point is that when it comes to "Shall we apply more squeeze to the economy or shall we let up a bit?" this is essentially about political accountability. The way I put it is this: can you imagine me going to Jarrow in 1930 and saying, "Look boys, there's a general election coming up, I know half of you are unemployed and starving and the soup kitchen's down the road. But we're not going to talk about those things, because they're for Herr Pöhl and the Bundesbank. It's his fault; he controls that; if you want to protest about that, you'd better get on to Herr Pöhl"?'

There might be more financial discipline in a British economy run under the influence of men like Herr Pöhl, Mr Ridley agreed. But, he added, suddenly looking up at me through his bifocals, 'There could also be a bloody revolution. You can't change the British people for the better by saying, "Herr Pöhl says you can't do that." They'd say, "You know what you can do with your bloody Herr Pöhl." I mean, you don't understand the British people if you don't understand this point about them. They can be dared; they can be moved. But being bossed by a German – it would cause absolute mayhem in this country, and rightly, I think.'[20]

It would be barely relevant here to discuss the difficulties inherent in the transition to a common currency – the problems of achieving convergence between conditions in Düsseldorf and the Peloponnese and so on. What strikes us rather is that the powers which are liable to be surrendered in European economic union are the very powers to do things which robust free-marketeers abhor. By contrast, constitutional entrenchment of the economic principles which they hold most dear can, it seems, be achieved, if at all, only at European level.

The perversity of this campaign for the right to pursue economic policies which one regards as abhorrent is only a reflection of a similar but greater perversity in the political sphere – the determination to throw everything into the defence of a system which one recognises to be hideously flawed. For example, Mr Andrew Alexander, City Editor of the *Daily Mail*, ridicules the compromise on monetary union whereby Parliament would be permitted a final say.

> Well now, there is a kind of concession for you! The pound to be abolished only if Westminster approves!
> But even that formula is misleading. Ted Heath required 'the approval' of Parliament for joining the EC. Approval was achieved, not by some polite enquiry and a free vote, but by an exceptionally ruthless exercise in political pressure. Tory Members were given to understand that prospects, careers and honours depended on their toeing the line.
> It would be similar with EMU, once the government of the day had decided to join.[21]

So this is all that our precious parliamentary sovereignty amounts to then? This is what we are invited to die in the last ditch for – a Parliament which can be bribed, arm-twisted and steam-rollered into approving any calamitous scheme which happens to have taken the fancy of the Prime Minister of the day. From a distance, the last ditch may seem like a decent sort of place to make a stand from. It is only when we are pushed into it that we notice the mud and the stench.

The misuse of floating exchange rates, like misuse of parliamentary sovereignty, may be blamed on the folly or wickedness of the individuals in power at the time. But the purpose of constitutional design is to reduce (it can never hope to eliminate) the extent of that misuse. And given the frailty of politicians, unlimited sovereignty, whether political or monetary, seems unlikely to produce optimal results over the long run. Until recently, it was possible to contest this proposition in relation to the exchange rate; like many another scribbler, the present writer has in his time claimed that there is no difference between the price of money and the price of grapefruit and that both should be allowed to fluctuate freely. Zones of monetary stability, however organised, were regarded as an infringement of free-market principles. But in recent years allegiance to floating currencies has been eroded by the spectacle, both cataclysmic and comic, of vast lumps of speculative money hurtling around the exchanges of the world and causing dizzy-making jumps and plummets in exchange rates which bear little or no relation to fundamental realities. Hedging against movements so violent becomes prohibitively costly for many businesses; new entrants are discouraged by the total unpredictability of the return on exports. Money's function as a store of value begins to seem incompatible with total deregulation. Not merely do European businesses feel more confident with stable exchange rates, it is even suggested that the US dollar too should be linked to the ERM. Between the summers of 1990 and 1991, the mark/dollar rate moved from 1.70 down to 1.44 and back above 1.80 again; the dollar/pound rate from $1.60 to $2 and back to $1.60. Such turbulence produces in the stoutest free-marketeer a yearning for some kind of co-ordination, if not of a full-scale return to Bretton Woods.

The constitutional enquirer may wish to ask a different type of question: when, and for what reason, did the management of the exchange rate become the responsibility of national governments? Quite clearly, the outbreak of the First World War and the collapse of the Gold Standard governmentalised the business; the nationalisation of the Bank of England by the Attlee government merely formalised what had come to be the state of affairs, though it could certainly be argued that the formal subjection of the Governor to the politicians did remove one last barrier against the inflationary temptations, which were unhappily made more attractive by the nigh-universal adoption of vulgar Keynesianism.

But if we go back to the pre-1914 economy, we see bizarre echoes of the economy of the 1990s with all its swirling international currents and connections. And we may find it quite appropriate to recreate the effect of the Gold Standard by the constitutional means of a European Central Bank and eventually a common European currency. Whether these things do come to pass are matters of practical judgment and convenience; it would be hard to argue that they go to the heart of national sovereignty in quite the manner that Mrs Thatcher argued they did. To do so would be to argue that the countries that belonged to the old sterling area were thereby colonial dependencies, or that Ireland achieved proper independence only when the link between the punt and the pound was broken. Nobody could deny that exclusive management of one's own currency without having to refer to any other nation or international authority confers a substantial quantum of independent power; so do owning and managing one's own national airline and a dozen other large-scale activities; but co-operation in such matters is not subjection. The best argument, advanced by Mr Norman Lamont, is that no two countries, with the possible exception of Belgium and Luxembourg, have ever jointly issued a currency; but there are a lot of arrangements that no two countries have jointly operated before which are now being operated, for good or ill, by a dozen countries, ranging from a Court of Justice to a Common Agricultural Policy. The lack of precedent is a useful argument but not a clinching one.

At this point, an unexpected question suggests itself: if free trade and the free market do, in fact, not merely legitimise but demand some kind of supranational constitutional framework, how is it that the most intelligent free-traders and free-marketeers do not more often and more readily recognise this? If they have been deceiving themselves, what has led them to do so? I suspect that the root of the trouble lies with the now familiar villain: the confusion between engine power and constitutional architecture. Concentrating on the power that is draining away from national governments and national parliaments tends to induce a degree of paranoia; workaday political opponents like Jacques Delors are magnified into sinister villains; institutional blueprints which would, in other circumstances, have appeared benign and concordant with one's principles take on the appearance of enemy siege-engines. Instead of regarding the designing of European institutions as an opportunity for imparting some permanence to the fiscal and monetary prudence which, at present, can be blown away the day after a general election by a change of government, many leading British politicians, from Eden to Thatcher, have regarded the designs as directed at ourselves. That mood is fading; if not in at the creation, we are now in at the re-creation, especially in the designing of European economic institutions. And the more we approach the drawing board in a constitution-maker's spirit rather than a wheeler-dealer's, the better the chances of designing something that will last.

Little (and medium-sized) platoons

It is now commonly understood that movements for national independence tend to prosper when a threat is lifted or there seems to be a prospect of it being lifted. The threat may be one of physical terror, or of various combinations of poverty and insecurity, but the same phenomenon is observable: that the movement for independence (or autonomy, or devolution, or revolution, come to that) takes heart from the easing circumstances, begins to gather self-confidence and recruit new members, both from those who were too poor or too frightened to come forward and from those who were too comfortable in or too compromised by the status quo to risk their social secureness. From this point of view, maxims like 'England's danger is Ireland's opportunity', 'it's Scotland's oil' or 'the revolution of rising expectations' all depend to some extent on Tocqueville's insight, first applied to the French Revolution, that it is after a substantial period of improving social circumstances that a revolutionary movement will gather strength and that underlying aspirations to nationhood or feelings of exclusion from political power begin to take concrete shape. In our own century, the revival of nationalism in Scotland and Northern Ireland, no less than in the Baltic States, belongs to the same pattern; the threat of repression had begun to fade; it seemed safe to dust off the old hopes and give them an airing.

Thus in terms of effective political action, these movements are *externally led*. That is an unwelcome thought to the movements themselves; they prefer to see their resurgence as a spontaneous bubbling up of heartfelt aspiration. But the recent history of the UK, no less than the evidence of the Gorbachev years, suggests otherwise, and powerfully so. It was the appearance of Captain O'Neill's moderate Unionism and his meeting with the Taoiseach in 1965 which triggered off the revival of the Republican movement and the IRA; in Scotland, the revival of the economy in the oil years led to the fashion for devolution sweeping through all UK political parties. This is in no way to dismiss the attractions of a Scottish assembly; it is merely to repeat the lesson of the asparagus patch, that political opportunity is an indispensable accelerator of constitutional reform.

Now the oil is running out, but a different kind of opportunity has presented itself and has, rather clumsily, begun to be grasped and understood. The phrase 'a Europe of the regions' has a certain modish vacuity about it and slips all too easily into the windy rhetoric of Europhiliacs. But it does relate to a concrete political reality which will present itself with increasing insistence in most European countries.

Thorough-going, unitary unionism in multi-tribal nations – especially the UK – has survived and flourished partly because of external threat. In the sixteenth, seventeenth and early eighteenth centuries, France and Spain repeatedly tried to use Scotland and

Ireland *against* England. Union, whether achieved voluntarily or by force or fraud, was a defence mechanism. In the nineteenth century, Britishness became an offence mechanism for strengthening the Empire, for staffing its armies, its civil service and its commercial and industrial institutions. Britishness always contained a strongly imperial flavour, reinforced by the particular myths and migrations of the constituent tribes: the Scots in New Brunswick, the Irish convicts in Australia, the Welshmen fighting at Rorke's Drift. The British Union made sense of the farflung and heterogeneous nature of the Empire, so much so that a certain 'domestic imperialism' crept into our political arrangements back home. Devices and reforms which had first been tried out in the colonies were reimported to the Mother Country: PAYE was first tried in India; it was in India, a century earlier, that the first serious exercises in legal codification were carried out; the Northcote–Trevelyan reforms – entry by competitive examination and promotion by merit – owed a lot to the principles already in force in the administration of India. Many of the prominent reformers in British politics – R. A. Butler, R. H. Tawney, Sir William Beveridge – were children of the Raj. Many others – Churchill and Neville Chamberlain united in this at least – had spent a good deal of their early manhood fighting or administering in some part of the Empire. 'What should they know of England who only England know?' Kipling almost always speaks of 'England', but what he means by 'England' (and here he spoke for millions in his time) was a United Kingdom with a manifest global destiny. Compared with that, the Scottish nationalism being reborn during his lifetime seemed a weak and pitiful thing, a wraith of the Celtic mists, infected by myth and fancy (the first President of the Scottish National Party, Lewis Spence, claimed to be able to hear 'faerie singing, wordless, and of wonderful harmony'), certainly not a force to be seriously reckoned with.

The end of the British Empire, it can be argued, left the ordinary people of England relatively unaffected (the classes which provided soldiers, traders and civil servants were perhaps a different matter). But it undoubtedly gave the idea of Britishness a hard knock, removing, if not its reason for existing at all, at least its exceptionality, its scale and splendour. To many Scots, Scottish identity seemed to take on greater substance, or at any rate to offer greater potential.

At first, Scottish and Welsh nationalists inclined to an isolationist, 'ourselves alone' or Sinn Fein phase. They wanted to be separated from England to a greater or lesser degree; their identity was defined largely in terms of anti-Saxonism, as had been that of the newly formed Irish state. They were opposed to (or, in some cases, not much interested in) the then European Economic Community, partly because a large element in nationalist parties had a strongly ruralist, anti-modern tinge and Düsseldorf was as repellent to them as Birmingham or London.

But, over the last decade, the European opening began to become unmistakable, and, all at once, 'Scotland in Europe' – or, for some, 'an independent Scotland in a united Europe' – became a convenient and attractive slogan. In Northern Ireland, the Unionists, previously fiercely opposed to membership of such a Romish institution, began to see opportunities for protecting the separateness of their province. Only the stout, unyielding Unionism of Mrs Thatcher obscured the relative weakening of the United Kingdom as an idea.

At the same time and over much the same period, the destruction of the stability and authority of local government had left *all* the UK's subordinate institutions in a mess. It is fashionable to blame the Thatcher administration and Mrs Thatcher personally for all this; in reality, successive administrations and all three political parties have involuntarily collaborated in the process. The percentage of local expenditure financed by the Treasury remorselessly increased from a tiny fraction at the beginning of the century to about one-third in the 1920s and rose to a peak of 65 per cent in the late 1970s – the moment when Anthony Crosland, as the responsible Minister, said 'the party's over', the point being that the party, the huge expansion of local government spending, was being paid for out of national taxation. Correspondingly, the real independence of local authorities diminished, although by a series of complicated formulae – each one turning out to be less satisfactory than the last – they were usually able to tug the

Exchequer grant along behind them as they ventured (or, to be fair, were instructed by Act of Parliament to venture) into fresh fields.

Over the same period, strongly ideological local Labour caucuses aroused party-political dogfights wherever possible, especially in the larger boroughs. This ideologising of what in most places had been a relatively peaceful business of drains and libraries took a sourer turn in the 1960s and 1970s when those same Labour caucuses lost the mass support they had enjoyed in the late 1940s (the peak of party allegiance and membership in both the Labour and Conservative parties) and became an easy target for the 'bedsit militants', the 'loony left' or the 'incomers', as they were variously called. In the boroughs which they captured, the level of domestic rates soared to unprecedented and often unaffordable levels; Tory councillors in the shires, too, succumbed to municipal imperialism. The government felt compelled to take action, not least because the voters tend to punish the party nationally for its local sins. Rates were 'capped', then abolished, to be succeeded by the even more unpopular community charge, now in its turn to be replaced by the council tax. Even if the last-named does become acceptable (it is, after all, a reasonably fair property tax of a type that operates in many other countries), the authority and stability of local government have received a terrible battering over the past thirty years. Nor has the disappearance of familiar counties and borough authorities under the Heath–Walker reforms of 1972 helped to maintain the credit and tradition of local government in Britain. All the recent 'reforms' remain shallow-rooted and can be consigned to the rubbish heap with a flick of the legislative wrist and without a backward glance.

If the government is ready to backtrack to the extent of abolishing the poll tax and returning to a simplified version of the rates, not to mention abolishing Merseyside and Humberside and restoring some at least of the historic boroughs and counties, then there seems little obstacle to a similar change of heart on the question of Scotland and Wales.

It is worth briefly recalling that particular story so far, if only to admire the acrobatics of which political parties are capable when put to it by reverses in by-elections.

In June 1967, after a dramatic Scottish National Party victory in the Hamilton by-election, Mr Heath set up a Scottish Policy Group to 'examine the machinery of government in Scotland'. By May the following year, two centuries of stern Unionism had been briskly jettisoned, and Heath had committed the party to an elected Scottish assembly. By April 1969, Labour had panicked too and set up a Royal Commission on the Constitution, which, four years later, also recommended an assembly. In both the 1970 and 1974 elections, the Conservative manifesto promised an assembly; but then Mrs Thatcher replaced Mr Heath, Labour produced its Scotland and Wales Bill, and the Conservatives began a long about-turn which brought them back to the uncompromising Unionism from which they had departed a decade or so earlier. By 1982, the then Secretary of State for Scotland, Mr George Younger, was declaring that 'in spite of strenuous efforts by interested parties to re-start this debate, I do not believe most people in Scotland are any longer interested in this subject [the establishment of a Scottish assembly] as a practical proposition'.[22]

Meanwhile, the Labour Party had travelled at much the same speed in the opposite direction. Having started from an equally uncompromising Unionism, reinforced by a conviction of the universality and primacy of the task of achieving socialism, it has under Mr Kinnock's leadership become firmly committed to an elected assembly for Scotland and a senate for Wales – despite the fact that it was Mr Kinnock's firm and principled (and successful) campaign for an emphatic no to a Welsh assembly in the 1979 referendum which brought him to prominence in the party. The traditional view was represented by Labour's Scottish executive committee's assertion that any form of self-government was 'constitutional tinkering, which does not contribute to Socialist objectives'.[23] However, the party has always contained Scots with semi-nationalist hankerings; the prospect of a permanent Labour majority north of the border has its attractions. And the party seems to have found it as easy as the Conservatives to swing from one extreme to the other.

On both sides, although the policy changes have been driven primarily by the search for votes, there remains an uneasy consciousness of how shifting and unsatisfactory our arrangements have been and a somewhat incoherent yearning for some sort of structural permanence – what has been called here 'constitutional architecture'. It is not difficult to perceive a plausible blueprint for such architecture; it would combine, for Scotland, the proposals of the Conservatives' Scottish Constitutional Committee (the Douglas-Home proposals, March 1970) with the present-day proposals of the Labour Party or the Institute for Public Policy Research (autumn 1991): namely, a directly elected Scottish assembly to act as a 'third chamber' of the Westminster Parliament, with powers to question Scottish Ministers, discuss estimates and scrutinise legislation; it might be allocated a proportion of Treasury revenues to finance Scottish services, such as health, education and transport, and have, at the margin, a power to levy taxation but in a fashion delimited by the Westminster Parliament.

For Wales, the consensus seems to be for a more modest assembly without legislative powers, perhaps consisting of representative members from Welsh local authorities – a glorified metropolitan council, in fact.

In both Wales and Scotland, a move to unitary local authorities, largely based on the old counties, would reduce any political embarrassment involved, while ensuring that, in both the Principality and the Northern Kingdom, the people were not over-burdened by layers of government. Such a rearrangement would correspond more naturally and exactly to the hierarchy of felt loyalties than these arbitrary and administratively feckless entities such as Tayside, Merseyside and Humberside – which are patently river gods with no worshippers. Such a rearrangement could not only lay a respectable claim to historic lineage; it would have some prospect of enduring.

One objection – that such a rearrangement would be untidy and asymmetrical – has already been dismissed. Actual loyalties exhibit no God-given symmetry, and legislators should not attempt to invent any. There is no logical compulsion either to set up matching regional assemblies all over England; they are not wanted, and would serve no useful function. As for the 'West Lothian question', it is answered by existing practice. MPs are constantly voting on Bills which do not apply to them or their constituents. Membership of any political community entails acceptance of its anomalies; some of these anomalies may be the result of oversight or ill-considered legislation or administration in the past, and so removable, and part of the never ending quest for improvement which is inherent in political activity is to remove such anomalies. But other anomalies follow from the uneven, asymmetrical nature of all existing societies and so must be endured; the maturity of any political culture is to be measured very largely by the extent to which this is understood. That is not to say that sophisticated political cultures are complacent or blind to injustice; on the contrary, they will tend to be alert in the detection of injustice and active in its removal. But to understand that political arrangements at any given moment can never be perfectly harmonious and symmetrical in every respect is the condition of a durable polity.

It does seem likely that, if not this government, then the next government will find itself both willing and able to undertake some sort of regional settlement on the above lines. The old preconception that Unionism entails unwavering devotion to unitary government has largely wavered. Both major parties now have a record of at least temporary espousal of a new settlement; the minor parties have long sought one.

Above all, the encircling European girdle makes the UK *safe* for devolution. From the point of view of moderate Scots and Welshmen, the dangers of total separation are removed, since even their wilder compatriots no longer wish to float off into the blue yonder out of range of EC largesse. And the same assurance comforts the dominant English population against nightmares of a break-up of the United Kingdom.

5

SHAPES OF THINGS TO COME

We began by describing the progressive degrading and eroding of our old understanding of the British Constitution. If something of that understanding is now restored, we can advance, cautiously but not without a certain self-confidence that we know more or less what we are after, some ideas for restoring the architecture of the thing itself. This task of reviving or remaking the old checks and balances must be undertaken, not in a sweeping, blank-sheet fashion, but rather with a careful appreciation of practicalities: what will fit in with our parliamentary system, what MPs and public opinion will find fitting, what is consonant with national tradition and international obligation.

It may be helpful before we launch into this tricky final stage of the enterprise, to jot down five architectural principles, which ought to guide us (I mean here qualitative principles, not political ideals such as democracy).

First, *simplicity*. We do not wish to add to the burdens of government on the citizen or to those administrative complications which lend a frantic, incoherent quality to the business of government. Each extra tier of government increases the possibilities of bureaucracy, public expense and maladministration. The limitation of government must remain a priority. Thus if, in the quest for the reconciliation of Scotland and the greater dispersal of power, we choose to set up a Scottish Assembly, then we should compensate for this by removing a layer of Scottish local government; and we need not feel compelled to add a corresponding network of English assemblies if there is no demand for one.

Second, *stability*. We want a system that is more, not less steady and consistent in the legislation and administration that it delivers. Does Proportional Representation deliver that kind of stability better than first-past-the-post? It could be argued that a succession of coalition governments might, in fact, produce a greater consistency of policy than the more infrequent but more violent shifts which we have endured under the present system; on the other hand, *any* change of government must involve some increase in those marginal finicky changes in laws and regulations which make life so irksome and unpredictable.

Third, *separation*. Any reforms which help to entrench, clarify or widen the present separations between the executive, the legislature and the judiciary should be favourably considered, in the interests of improving both the protection of liberty and the transparency of government. Conversely, any proposal which would tend further to glue together our already over-fused branches of government should be looked at with a sceptical eye.

Fourth, *subsidiarity* (a more exact though even less elegant word than devolution). Functions should be exercised at the lowest practicable level of government; this rule applies pre-eminently to European institutions. The maximum dispersal of power tends to root the system more securely in the practices of ordinary life, as well as to intensify participation and representation; dispersal and democracy are intimately linked.

Finally, what I have called *patriation* seems to me distinct from subsidiarity, although, in many instances, the two qualities will overlap or run parallel. While subsidiarity is a constitutional expression of democracy, patriation gives constitutional expression to national pride and independence. That English and Scottish judges should be the prime protectors of our legal rights and liberties, that British MPs should be the prime exponents of our anxieties and grievances would help to provide a constructive remedy against that rebirth of fascism which Euro-sceptics like Mr Tebbit and Mr Nigel Lawson say they fear.

The fact that we have armed ourselves with these principles does not mean that we ought therefore to charge in with a ready-made New Constitutional Settlement, as recently offered by the IEA and the IPPR, not to mention the earlier version proposed by Charter 88 (all three blueprints have a good deal in common). On the contrary, it makes better sense to arrange the conclusions that have emerged from this book in clusters of political plausibility, starting with the tendencies that are *already becoming visible*, as it were spontaneously, with little or no intervention from constitutional reformers; then going on to the changes that are *likely soon*; before setting out the *long-term structures* which would bolt the earlier changes securely into place.

At first sight, this may seem a hesitant, even meandering way to approach the matter. Surely an at-a-stroke, big-bang charter is more likely to achieve a stable and comprehensive settlement of the constitutional question. To see why this is a shaky argument, we must return to the lesson of the asparagus patch. Big-bang charters require major political upheavals; they are fuelled by a shared sense of crisis which can be resolved only by a spectacular re-ordering of the polity. It would be an absurd exaggeration to pretend that such a sense of crisis is widely shared at present; there is a polite interest in the constitutional question, possibly a spreading unease, but little more than that. Moreover, the erosions and corruptions are various and not all easily reconcilable within a Grand Charter.

As to whether piecemeal, progressive constitutional change can add to a substantial transformation, I offer the example of our nearest, perhaps our only analogue on earth, New Zealand. New Zealand's Constitution has been described by Professor Leslie Zines as 'probably the simplest and most uncomplicated constitution in the democratic world . . . . its legislature is the very model of Dicey's notion of a sovereign parliament'.[1] In 1979, when Mr Geoffrey Palmer published the first edition of his highly successful *Unbridled Power*, the title did indeed describe New Zealand with its unitary Constitution, its single-chamber Parliament and its lack of a 'written' constitution. By 1987, Palmer (by then Minister of Justice and soon to become briefly Prime Minister of New Zealand) could write, in the introduction to the second edition, of the:

massive number of changes made to the system of government in New Zealand since this book first appeared. Almost nothing is untouched. In some areas, such as freedom of information and parliamentary reform, the changes have been fundamental. So great are the changes that for one delirious moment I thought of changing the title to 'Bridled Power', but I will leave that for the third edition!

In particular, the Constitution Act of 1986 was remarkable, not so much for having patriated the New Zealand Constitution (the same thing was happening in Australia and Canada); it also 'brings together in one enactment the most important constitutional provisions scattered around the statute book' – a feat which was not required in Australia and Canada with their existing written federal basic laws. The Act re-enacted, for example, those provisions of the Judicature Act 1908 which had come to New Zealand from the English Act of Settlement, providing that a judge of the High Court 'shall not be removed from office except by the Sovereign, or the Governor-General acting upon an address of the House of Representatives, which address may be moved only on the grounds of that judge's misbehaviour . . . or incapacity'. The 1986 Act also re-enacted the clause of the 1956 Electoral Act which semi-entrenched certain important provisions by requiring 75 per cent of New Zealand MPs or a majority vote in a referendum to approve any amendment or removal. I say 'semi-entrenched' because the clause was not itself protected by this special require-ment – although the later Royal Commission on the Electoral System suggested that 'the protecting provision should itself be protected in the same way'. At the same time, there has been substantial progress towards legislating for a new Bill of Rights for New Zealand.

Thus looking back to the high-water mark of the unbridled supremacy of the New Zealand House of Repesentatives, which can be dated at 1951, in which year the Upper House of the New Zealand Parliament was abolished, we see a piecemeal but probably irreversible progress towards a constitution which is *protected, collected* and *balanced* and which sets fixed limits to the legislating power of Parliament and imposes special conditions for the exercise of that power where the Constitution itself is concerned. Whether or not you care to call such a constitution 'written' is a matter of taste; but the set of arrangements would have certainly seemed to A. V. Dicey altered beyond recognition. It would be hard to maintain that what has happened in virtually the only country which has inherited arrangements so like our own could not happen in the United Kingdom too.

Becoming visible

It would also be hard to maintain that certain signs of a comparable process over here are not already clearly visible. Mr John Patten has already listed for us a ream of legislation which purports to open up the operations of government in various ways; and these new laws are significant as a token of what is now generally understood to be the right relationship between government and people, one in which prerogative is reduced to a minimum and accountability and openness are the guiding principles. But more constitutionally significant than these measures are those statutes and judgments which actually enlarge the citizen's rights to take action against the government and so institute checks to that unfettered discretion of Ministers which was Lord Chief Justice Hewart's prime target. A start was made with the Crown Proceedings Act of 1947, which abridged or abolished various legal advantages, privileges or immunities of the Crown and made the Crown liable in tort. A number of court judgments have further reduced the immunity that can be claimed by government departments in the public interest, notably Conway v. Roumer (1968), which, in de Smith and Brazier's words, 'has substituted absolute judicial discretion for absolute executive discretion'.[2]

In 1957, the Franks Committee on Administrative Tribunals and Enquiries went a long way to undo the damage done by the Donoughmore Committee on Ministers' Powers in 1932; Franks, unlike Donoughmore, rightly saw administrative tribunals, which by the 1950s had proliferated because of the huge growth of ministerial powers, not as part of the machinery of administration but 'as machinery provided by Parliament for adjudication'[3] – that is, as something separate from government and, in most cases, offering an ultimate right of appeal to the superior courts (though not in immigration or social security cases).

More important still, and more conclusive evidence of the revival of judicial activism, is the huge and benign expansion of judicial review of administrative action. This is a complicated subject in which an amateur must tread warily; the grounds on which an aggrieved person may ask a judge to quash an administrative decision are so various – that the decision was *ultra vires*, or wrong in law, or contrary to natural justice, or unfair or biased, or not a reasonable exercise of discretion – and the remedies so numerous – habeas corpus, certiorari, prohibition and mandamus, injunction, declaration and damages – that it might seem amazing that the courts were not always clogged with judicial reviews. The fact remains that they were not and that it is only since certain memorable cases such as *Laker Airways* v. *Department of Trade* (1977), *Ridge* v. *Baldwin* (1964), *Padfield* v. *Ministry of Agriculture* (1968) and *Secretary of State for Education and Science* v. *Tameside Metropolitan Borough Council* (1977) that the floodgates have really opened and fresh life has been breathed into the ideas of natural justice and fairness and reasonableness.

It was with a certain justifiable pride that the beleaguered Lord Chief Justice Lane recently retorted to his critics that applications for leave to apply for judicial review had risen from 491 in 1980 to 1169 in 1985, 1580 in 1989 and 2129 in 1990. 'The percentage of applications granted have remained fairly constant throughout, at around 50 per cent, so that increase is not accounted for by any percentage increase in maverick applications.'[4] This fivefold increase within a decade is little short of a judicial revolution. Zines, referring primarily to the Commonwealth, talks with some apprehension of 'the extraordinary upsurge in judicial boldness in challenging legislatures in the cause of individual and democratic liberties and the rule of law',[5] but recognises also the vastly increased checks that British judges too have imposed upon executive and administrative authority over the last twenty years or so. Even ten years ago, it would have been unthinkable for the Court of Appeal to find the Home Secretary guilty of contempt, as Mr Kenneth Baker was found guilty in 1991 on a contentious technical point in a deportation case.

In parallel, within Parliament we see a gradual but still timid peeping forth of backbenchers' confidence to examine the actions of the executive and, now and then, challenge them, despite the inbuilt government majorities on Select Committees no less than in the Chamber. Too much need not be made of this; there have been other false dawns for those who hope to see the Commons fulfil, energetically and promptly, its purported role of scrutineer. But the Select Committees, covering almost every field of government activity, still in theory liable to be swept away at the beginning of any Parliament, look increasingly like a fixture.

And one of the most important factors making for their permanence is the ever growing bulk of European legislation which now looms over Westminster. The changes in procedure needed to deal effectively with European proposals before they are set in concrete have only reached an embryonic stage. But it is clear that they can be scrutinised effectively only through a structure of Select Committees; and these Select Committees, being masters of their business, will govern a stream of increasing activity which is independent of the usual government channels with their ancient weirs and sluices.

Parliament is facing a choice which it has not, as yet, fully defined but which it is already conscious must be faced: either to become a dim and trivial chamber spluttering its pique at a series of *faits accomplis* or to become an effective critical forum operating in advance of the European Council and the European Parliament, shaping and exercising its veto over the national input to the European system. This choice confronts the Westminster Parliament more or less regardless of precisely what balance of power is arrived at among the institutions of the European Community (which is why this essay takes little note of the recent negotiations on political and economic union). Parliament has to gear itself, in ever growing measure, to the timetable and the agenda of the EC, and – a paradox with which we are now becoming familiar – that can only heighten its sense of having an independent mission.

Likely soon

Thus already we can see two of the three legs of the tripod being moved to assert a degree of activism and separateness which would have surprised the judges and MPs of the 1930s and 1940s. But these can at most be described as tendencies; they are not structural reforms of the sort which mark a turning-point as, say, the Act of Settlement did or the 1832 Bill did and was seen to do at the time.

One great turning-point has already occurred: the passing of the European Communities Act of 1972. That was unmistakably a major entrenchment of a superior source of authority, and was seen to be so at the time by its more perceptive critics and supporters alike; like all entrenchments, it can ultimately be overthrown by the organised will of the people. The fact that neither the Treaty of Rome nor the 1972 Act includes a get-out clause is a trivial technicality; even to hold the 1975 referendum on Britain's continued membership could be held to have been a breach of the Treaty, but it was not a breach that anyone felt like challenging, not least because the emphatic result of the referendum was further to embed the 1972 Act, so that it would be unthinkable to repeal it without another referendum. It may be that the degree of entrenchment had not fully sunk in for many people until the European Court of Justice ruling in the *Factortame* case[6] first forced a British government to amend an Act of Parliament in response to the ruling of an external court. But it was the 1972 Act that did the entrenching.

The weight of a superior external authority will, I suspect, be more directly and intimately felt when and if a future government incorporates the European Convention on Human Rights and so imports a set of general declarative principles into the branches of law that are most easily understood in human terms – those very realms in which Dicey saw *the* exemplars of the rule of law. It seems likely that, before the century is out, this incorporation will have taken place; there is so little now standing in its way. And, for all that government Ministers stoutly maintain that incorporation is quite unnecessary or would make no practical difference, there is no doubt that its principles would be ever present in the minds of any prudent law-framer – as its shadow is present already.

To hazard another couple of prophecies, I can see little to prevent an incoming government from inserting a Scottish assembly into the system and much to reward such an innovation, so long as it is carefully constructed on minimalist lines. Several developments have reduced the practical and theoretical objections; first, the discrediting of the new Scottish super-authorities offers an opportunity to insert some form of assembly on top of a layer of single authorities; the experience of capping local taxation makes it possible to guarantee that Scottish voters would not be overtaxed, if that was felt to be a further threat; and the intensification of the European Community takes the sting out of the fears of total separation from the rest of the UK.

The shock to the system by the introduction of such an assembly could be partially absorbed by a modest reform of the composition of the House of Lords; there could be peers chosen by one means or another to represent English and Welsh counties and give the Upper House an informal regional flavour, to supply the want – an unfelt want, as it happens – of assemblies in the regions of England.

To traditionalists, it can be pointed out that this pleasant tinkering represents more of a return to than a break with tradition; initially lords were, after all, of their essence regional; and a Scottish parliament under a United Crown is where we came in.

The case against depends on clinging to a geographical and administrative centralisation of a sort which, when encountered elsewhere, we disdain as brutishly Napoleonic. I doubt whether that kind of huddled-together centralisation can retain its old compelling appeal in the absence of an external foe.

In the longer term

What deters practical men of the Bagehot humour from taking an interest in these contraptions is a feeling that they are peripheral and likely, if introduced, to prove fashions as fleeting as the hula hoop. And the truth is that, for all their charm, they seem unlikely to survive in a harsher climate unless they are dug in on foundations of a deeper and sounder character. For those who seriously wish to see a restoration of constitutional habits of thought and action, there is ultimately no substitute for deep-dug, pre-stressed pillars which will withstand all weathers.

There seem to be three indispensable elements for a long-term structure within which the innovations already visible or recommended in these pages can expect a secure future:

an entrenchment clause covering certain basic essentials of the Constitution;

a supreme court which includes among its duties the interpretation and safeguarding of the entrenched provisions;

an entrenched provision prescribing a fixed term of, say, four years for Parliament with provision for early dissolution on certain objective conditions, but not at the wish of the Prime Minister of the day.

All three are familiar in most other parliamentary democracies. They would tend to impart a character of stability to government and to rob parliamentary life of some of its seedy (though vivid) manipulative quality – a loss for sketchwriters but a gain to the public esteem in which Parliament is held.

At present, after a century of indoctrination in the beauties of parliamentary omnipotence, these three things may seem unfamiliar, even alien to students of British habits. But, even in Britain, they seem like novelties only to our generation; they would be easily recognisable to reformers of the seventeenth and early eighteenth centuries, who would have seen such provisions as so many practical ways of realising the hopes implicit in the words 'constitutional' and 'settlement'; they had no allegiance to fluidity and flexibility, having had all too much experience of both.

When Burke declared that 'it has been the misfortune (not as these gentlemen think it, the glory) of the age, that every thing is to be discussed, as if the constitution of our country were to be always a subject rather of altercation than enjoyment[7]', he was assuming there was a stable, settled something there to be enjoyed.

At present, we are told – quite rightly – that there is little popular demand for such things; MPs who are themselves happy with the status quo point to the evidence of their empty postbags; years may pass without their receiving a single letter about a Bill of Rights. But it has been the burden of this essay that this apathy is a symptom of the decadence of British public opinion rather than of its creditable insouciance; deprived of serious constitutional conversation for nearly a century, the British electorate, on the whole, simply does not know what it is missing.

It is impossible to prove that the erratic and unstable conduct of British government since the war is a consequence of constitutional decadence; it can perhaps be argued that a decent Bill of Rights might have prevented the trade unions from wrecking Britain's industrial prospects for most of this century, including the duration of two world wars; it might even have done something to curb the high-handed methods of successive British governments, until the judges, under the noble, if occasionally erratic stimulus of Lord Denning, began to come back to life.

No written constitution or Bill of Rights can push a society beyond the limits of its prevailing world-view (which is why the US Constitution did not abolish slavery or introduce votes for women overnight, as its detractors claim it ought to have). But it can animate that society with a sense of what is right and instil into government an understanding of the proper limits to the exercise of power; above all, it can inform the conversation of politics with a sense of dispersed responsibility. In a country with a constitution which is both living (as ours already is) and secured (as ours is not), there can be no question of blaming everything on the government; the entrenched limitations on government secure the more even distribution of civic duties throughout society. In the age of Burke and Madison, this crucial association between the entrenchment of political arrangements and the dispersal of power and responsibility was well understood to be the foundation of civic virtue; it was what distinguished us from the irresponsible sloth which was bred by the unpredictable and overweening caprice of oriental despots. That understanding has gone astray. We are now perhaps within sight of recovering it. By the turn of the century, we may well be within touching distance.

Looking back on the hundred years or so just past, we may come to think of them as something of an aberration in our history. It has undoubtedly been a strange period – stretching roughly from the publication of the first parts of Bagehot's *English Constitution* to the lectures Harold Laski gave in Manchester shortly before his death, which were later published under the title of *Reflections on the Constitution*: parliamentary monotheism, the battering-ram view of political activity, judicial abdication – all these things and many other features of the period may come to seem profoundly odd, and even alien to our traditions. In the old Dominions, the business of collecting and protecting the principal elements of constitutional heritage is already well under way; in Britain, it has scarcely begun. Ironically, it is the supranational enterprise of the European institutions which may well accelerate the revival of our national pluralism. The solipsism of the Diceian dispensation may be superseded by rules and practices that would have been familiar to Coke and Blackstone, perhaps even to Glanvill and Bracton. Very little in politics is minted entirely fresh.

The alternative – if it is indeed a practicable alternative – is not exactly alluring: an increasingly irrelevant Parliament at Westminster spluttering unavailing objections to European decisions, a High Court timid and bewildered by an ever growing conflict between domestic and European law (a conflict which it is powerless to resolve), a disaffected Scotland, an emasculated structure of local government draining away whatever remains of civic and provincial pride.

Not merely does all this sound intolerable; it also sounds implausible. For whatever else may be said against the flexible temper of our constitutional history (and a good deal has been said in the preceding pages), it does not, on the whole, remain inert for long once it has perceived a challenge. We may, once again, be rescued – as in 1689, as in 1832 – by that ultimate and characteristic English paradox (for once, it is appropriate to drop the mask of Britishness): flexibility in search of permanence.

NOTES

Place of publication is London unless otherwise stated.

1 Delusions and Discontents

1 Swift, *Prose Works*, Oxford 1962, vol. V. pp. 193–4
2 David Ogg, *England in the Reigns of James II and William III*, Oxford 1957, p. 492
3 *Who's Who Magazine*, Summer 1991
4 Sir W. Ivor Jennings, *The Law and the Constitution*, 1933, 3rd edn 1943, p. 234
5 A. V. Dicey, *Introduction to the Study of the Law of the Constitution*, 1885, 8th edn 1915, p. cii
6 Ibid., p. c
7 John Morley, *Walpole*, 1889, p. 158
8 H. H. Asquith, *Fifty Years of Parliament*, 1928, vol. II, p. 185
9 W. E. Gladstone, *Gleanings of Past Years*, 1879, vol. I, p. 225
10 *Hansard*, 13 February 1893, col. 1251
11 Walter Bagehot, *The English Constitution*, 1867, Oxford (World's Classics) edn 1928, p. 35
12 Ibid., p. 259
13 Sir W. Ivor Jennings, *Cabinet Government*, Cambridge 1936, p. xii
14 Jennings, *The Law and the Constitution*, p. viii
15 *Hansard*, 8 February 1932, col. 531
16 Dicey, *Law of the Constitution*, p. 22
17 Henry Hallam, *A View of the State of Europe During the Middle Ages*, 1818, 12th edn 1860, vol II, p. 267
18 Dicey, *Law of the Constitution*, 1818, pp. 3–4
19 Graeme C. Moodie, *The Government of Great Britain*, 1964, p. 16
20 Ibid., p. 213
21 *Sunday Telegraph*, 23 September 1990
22 S. E. Finer, *Comparative Government*, 1970, p. 122. See also Stanley de Smith and Rodney Brazier, *Constitutional and Administrative Law*, 1971, 6th edn 1989, p. 8

23 See Mr Patten's CPC lecture, *Political Culture, Conservatism and Rolling Constitutional Changes,* July 1991
24 Jennings, *The Law and the Constitution,* p. xiv
25 *Foreign Affairs,* Spring 1991
26 See Barry M. Blechman and W. Philip Ellis, *The Politics of National Security: Congress and U.S. Defence Policy,* Oxford 1991
27 *Times Literary Supplement,* 1 March 1991
28 *The Law and the Constitution,* p. xiv
29 Ibid.
30 Sir David Lindsay Keir, *Constitutional History of Modern Britain (1485–1937),* 1938, 3rd edn 1946, p. 1
31 Ibid., p. 2
32 Ibid., p. 49
33 Ibid., p. 50
34 Dicey, *Law of the Constitution,* p. 18
35 Ibid., p. 10
36 Jennings, *The Law and the Constitution,* p. xiv
37 Edmund Burke, *Works,* 1808, vol. V, pp. 53–6
38 J. E. A. Jolliffe, *The Constitutional History of Medieval England from the English Settlement to 1485,* 1937, p. 431
39 Ibid., p. 432
40 Keir, *Constitutional History,* p. 364
41 Ibid., p. 549
42 Moodie, *The Government of Great Britain,* p. 20
43 John Mackintosh, *The British Cabinet,* 1962, p. 20
44 Harold Laski, *Reflections on the Constitution,* 1951, p. 14
45 Jolliffe, *The Constitutional History of Medieval England,* p. 306
46 Dicey, *Law of the Constitution,* pp. 183–4
47 Ibid., p. 14
48 Ibid., p. 69n.
49 Jeffrey Jowell and Dawn Oliver, *The Changing Constitution,* Oxford 1985, 2nd edn 1989, p. 5
50 Lord Scarman, *English Law: The New Dimension,* 1974, p. 16
51 See *DNB* entry on John Holt. Also Lord Chief Justice Lane's remarks on Holt, 7 November 1989, reprinted in *Graya,* No. 93, pp. 15–22
52 Scarman, *English Law,* p. 77
53 Ibid., p. 17
54 Ibid., p. 35
55 Gladstone, *Gleanings of Past Years,* p. 245
56 Lord Hewart, *The New Despotism,* 1929, p. 10
57 Ibid., pp. 16–17
58 Lord Radcliffe, *The Problem of Power,* 1953, reissued with new preface 1958, p. 33

59 Ibid., p. 59
60 Ibid., pp. 65–6
61 Ibid., pp. 68–70
62 Ibid., p. 73
63 Ibid., p. 76
64 Ibid., p. 96
65 Ibid., pp. 107–8
66 Ibid., p. 108
67 Ibid., p. 111
68 Ibid., p. 120
69 Ibid., p. 121
70 Ibid., pp. 123–7
71 *Observer*, 31 March 1991
72 *The Times*, 19 March 1991
73 Nevil Johnson, *In Search of the Consititution*, Oxford 1977, paperback edn 1980, p. x
74 Ibid., p. 29
75 *Independent*, 9 October 1991
76 Patten, *Political Culture*
77 Jennings, *The Law and the Constitution*, p. 140

2 The Three Great Simplifiers

1 Alastair Buchan, *The Spare Chancellor*, 1959, p. 52. This remains the best all-round book on Bagehot. *The Case of Walter Bagehot* by C. H. Sisson, 1972, offers an intense and vituperative version of many of the criticisms of Bagehot made in this chapter. The first *Life*, by Bagehot's sister-in-law Mrs Russell Barrington, is to be found in the tenth volume of the 1915 edition of Bagehot's works. Norman St John Stevas, now Lord St John of Fawsley, offers a brief biography, largely based on Mrs Barrington, in *Walter Bagehot: A Study of His Life and Thought* (1959), and another version in vol. I of his splendid *Economist* edition (1968–86, here *Works*). Lord St John also includes two shorter essays on Bagehot as a writer and literary critic and on Bagehot's religious views in vol. XIV. This latter volume contains biographical sketches of Bagehot by R. H. Hutton, Gladstone and others.
2 Buchan, *The Spare Chancellor*, p. 53
3 Ibid., p. 262
4 Bagehot, *Works*, vol. I, p. 268
5 Ibid., p. 271
6 Ibid., p. 274
7 Ibid., p. 283
8 Bagehot, *English Constitution*, p. 48

9 Ibid., p. 79
10 Ibid., p. 130
11 Ibid., p. 53
12 Ibid., p. 6
13 Ibid., p. 276
14 Ibid., p. 265
15 Ibid., p. 266
16 Ibid., p. 281
17 Jennings, *Cabinet Government*, p. 32
18 Ibid., p. 50
19 Ibid., p. 152
20 Ibid., p. 286
21 Ibid., p. 251
22 Dicey, *Law of the Constitution*, p. 19
23 Bagehot, *English Constitution*, p. 203
24 Johnson, *In Search of the Constitution*, p. 40. This seems to me to be one of the select handful of treatises published since Leo Amery's *Thoughts on the Constitution* (Oxford 1947) which gets close to the heart of the problem. Other works worth mentioning are: Geoffrey Marshall and Graeme C. Moodie, *Some Problems of the Constitution*(1959); R. F. V. Heuston, *Essays in Constitutional Law* (1964); and *Law, Legitimacy and the Constitution*, ed. Patrick McAuslan and John F. McEldowney (1985). In general, the political scientists tend to be less rewarding than the constitutional lawyers; for example, de Smith and Brazier's *Constitutional and Administrative Law*, 6th edn 1989, covers many of the most problematic points far more surely than most of the politics textbooks. For the most widely canvassed proposals for reform, see *Britain's Constitutional Future*, ed. Frank Vibert, IEA, 1991. Also the various publications of Charter 88 and the Institute for Public Policy Research.
25 R. S. Rait, *Memorials of Albert Venn Dicey*, 1925, p. 29
26 Richard Cosgrove, *The Rule of Law: Albert Venn Dicey, Victorian Jurist*, 1980, p. 8. Other works on Dicey are thin on the ground. Rait's *Memorials* is a hagiography from a devoted collaborator; Troubridge H. Ford, *Albert Venn Dicey: The Man and His Times*, Chichester 1985, is fanciful.
27 1 November 1882, James Viscount Bryce Papers, Box 2, Bodleian Library, Oxford. I am indebted to Mr Andrew Adonis for these surprising finds.
28 Ibid., 18 May 1886
29 *England's Case*, pp. 161, 169; *Leap in the Dark*, pp. 6, 167, 19–20
30 *England's Case*, p. 176
31 Ibid., p. 168
32 *Leap in the Dark*, p. 127

33 Ibid., p. 199
34 *Fool's Paradise*, p. 44
35 Jennings, *Cabinet Government*, p. 388
36 Ibid., p. 304
37 *Fool's Paradise*, p. 117
38 Ibid., p. 113
39 Ibid., p. 126
40 Ibid., p. 127
41 Sir William Anson, *The Law and Custom of the Constitution*, Oxford 1886 vol. I, p. 8
42 Heuston, *Essays in Constitutional Law*, p. 3
43 H. H. Henson, *Sir William Anson*, Oxford 1920, p. 148
44 *Hansard*, 18 June 1912, col. 1576. See also Asquith's great federalist speech on the Bill's Second Reading, *Hansard*, 9 May 1912, cols 691–701.
45 Dicey, *Law of the Constitution*, p. xcvii
46 Cosgrove, *The Rule of Law*, p. 221
47 Dicey, *Law of the Constitution*, p. lxv
48 Ibid., p. lxvi
49 Dicey, *Letters to a Friend on Votes for Women*, p. 82
50 Ibid., pp. 75–6
51 Jennings, *The Law and the Constitution*, p. 1
52 Ibid., p. xv
53 Ibid., p. 6
54 Ibid., p. xvii
55 Ibid., pp. 98–9
56 Ibid., p. 157
57 Ibid., p. 283
58 Ibid., p. 284
59 Ibid., p. 296
60 Quoted Jennings, *Cabinet Government*, p. 12
61 Jennings, *The Law and the Constitution*, pp. 295–6
62 Cmd 4060, Annex VI, p. 137
63 Laski, *Reflections on the Constitution*, p. 42
64 Ibid., p. 44
65 Ibid., p. 53
66 Laski, *The State in the New Social Order*, 1922, p. 12
67 Laski, *The Crisis in the Constitution*, 1931, p. 45
68 Ibid., p. 55
69 Ibid., p. 24
70 Ibid.
71 *Independent*, 11 July 1991
72 R. T. E. Latham, *The Law and the Commonwealth*, Oxford 1949, p. 523
73 John Dearlove and Peter Saunders, *Introduction to British Politics*,

Cambridge 1984, p. 113
74 Frederick Pollock and F. W. Maitland, *History of English Law*,
   Cambridge 1898, vol. I. pp. 182–3
75 Ibid., p. 182
76 Ibid., p. 188
77 Ibid., p. 175
78 7th edn, 1987, p. 21
79 Ibid., p. 13
80 Cmd 4060, pp. 8–9
81 Ibid., pp. 9–10
82 Jennings, *The Law and the Constitution*, p. 234
83 Amery, *Thoughts on the Constitution*, p. 11
84 Johnson, *In Search of the Constitution*, p. 220
85 Amery, *Thoughts on the Constitution*, p. 11
86 Wade and Phillips, *Constitutional Law*, 1931, 5th edn 1959, pp. 20–31
87 'The Vanishing Mandarins', BBC Radio 4, *Analysis*, 13 February 1985,
   quoted Peter Hennessy, *Whitehall*, 1989, p. 345. See Chapter Three,
   note 6, below.

3 The Present State

1 Bagehot, *English Constitution*, p. 67
2 Tony Benn, *Out of the Wilderness: Diaries 1963–67*, 1987, esp. pp. 334–9
3 Bagehot, *English Constitution*, p. 65
4 Geoffrey Marshall, *Constitutional Conventions*, Oxford 1984, pp. 21–3
5 *The Enchanted Glass* is a rough-cut, slightly chaotic piece of work, but
   there is no other sustained examination of the monarchy in modern
   times which repays attention. Kingsley Martin's *The Magic of The
   Monarchy* (1937) won't really do. More useful are the better royal
   biographies, such as Kenneth Rose's *King George V* (1983).
6 Quoted Hennessy, *Whitehall*, p. 345. Much of the pretended mystery
   surrounding the status of servants of the Crown looks suspiciously like
   humbug. For example, Mr Peter Hain, Labour MP for Neath, is not
   generally thought of as a fervent royalist. Yet he seems to have found
   no intellectual difficulty recently in calling on the Chancellor of the
   Exchequer to rebuke the Governor of the Bank of England for
   "staying into party political territory when he is supposed to be an
   independent servant of the Crown". (Evening Standard, 19 September,
   1991)
7 Ibid., p. 346
8 Northcote–Trevelyan Report, quoted as Appendix B to the Fulton
   Report, Cmnd 3638

9 Quoted Hennessy, *Whitehall*, p. 346
10 Ibid., p. 368
11 Ibid., p. 377
12 Ian Gilmour, *The Body Politic*, 1969, p. 370.
13 Jennings, *Cabinet Government*, pp. 219–21. Mackintosh, *The British Cabinet*, p. 446
14 David Butler and Uwe Kitzinger, *The 1975 Referendum*, 1976, pp. 48–52
15 Ibid., p. 164
16 Ibid., p. 286
17 Hugo Young, *One of Us*, 1989, p. 437
18 Ibid., p. 438
19 Letter to Beaverbrook, quoted Martin Gilbert, *The Challenge of War*, 1971 paperback, p. 25
20 Jennings, *Cabinet Government*, pp. 182–3
21 Mackintosh, *The British Cabinet*, p. 306
22 Young, *One of Us*, pp. 215–16
23 Ibid., pp. 475–6
24 Peter Jenkins, *Mrs Thatcher's Revolution*, 1987, pp. 211–12
25 J. Harvey and L. Bather, *The British Constitution and Politics*, 1963, p. 224
26 See Peter Hennessy, *Cabinet*, 1986, ch. 4 for a sparkling account. Also *Whitehall*, pp. 707–17
27 Barbara Castle, *Diaries 1974–76*, 1980, p. 227–18.
28 Denis Healey, *The Time of My Life*, 1989, p. 456
29 See Hennessy, *Whitehall*, pp. 648–9, for an outline of this bizarre incident.
30 Rodney Brazier, *Constitutional Practice*, pp. 101–11
31 Mackintosh, *British Cabinet*, p. 384
32 Ibid., p. 451
33 Ibid., p. 452
34 Fontana edition, 1963
35 Richard Crossman, *Inside View*, 1972, p. 8
36 Fontana edition, p. 51
37 Ibid., p. 8
38 Crossman, *Inside View*, p. 26
39 Hennessy, *Whitehall*, p. 298
40 Bernard Donoughue, *Prime Minister*, 1987, p. 101
41 Ibid., p. 106
42 Crossman, *Inside View*, p. 74
43 Fontana edition, p. 51
44 Trollope, *The Three Clerks*, New York, 1981, p. 60
45 *Constitutional Economics*, Oxford 1991, p. 38
46 *Civil Servants and Ministers: Duties and Responsibilities*, vol. I, HMSO, May 1986; *Top Jobs in Whitehall*, RIPA Report, 1986
47 *Guardian*, 15 June 1982

48 *Reflections*, Works, vol. V, p. 74
49 Ibid., p. 78
50 Dicey, *Law of the Constitution*, p. 46
51 See *Guardian*, 20 May 1991, for edited text. See also Rodney Brazier, *Constitutional Reform*, Oxford 1991, pp. 94–5 and 161–2
52 Quoted Amery, *Thoughts on the Constitution*, p. 47
53 *Hansard*, 14 August 1831, cols 1359–70; speech printed as a pamphlet by Roake and Vardy; quoted Derek Hudson, *A Poet in Parliament*, 1939, pp. 178–9
54 Joe Rogaly, *Parliament for the People*, 1976, p. 3
55 See also *Agenda for Change*, Hansard Society, September 1991
56 See William E. Paterson and David Southern, *Governing Germany*, Oxford 1991, pp. 81–9
57 2nd edn, 1953, p. 12
58 Brazier, *Constitutional Practice*, p. 183
59 A mixed chamber of this sort was also recommended by the Conservative Party Committee under Lord Home appointed by Mrs Thatcher, which reported in March 1978. For the 1960s proposals, see Joint Committee on House of Lords Reform, *Report* (HL 23, HC 38), December 1962; *House of Lords Reform* (Cmnd 3799), November 1968; Parliament (No. 2) Bill, 1968–9. Comparable proposals had been recommended as far back as the Bryce Conference Report of 1918 (Cmnd 9038), but other distractions always intervened, and all-party enthusiasm for the proposals lapsed.
60 Anson, *Law and Custom of the Constitution*, vol. I, p. 8
61 Heuston, *Essays in Constitutional Law*, p. 8.
62 Ibid.
63 O. Hood Phillips, *Constitutional and Administrative Law*, 1952, 7th edn 1987, pp. 83–92
64 [1974] AC 765; Hood Phillips, *Constitutional and Administrative Law*, pp. 52, 85
65 Hood Phillips, *Constitutional and Administrative Law*, p. 87
66 De Smith and Brazier, *Constitutional and Administrative Law*, p. 91
67 Hood Phillips, *Constitutional and Administrative Law*, p. 583
68 Crossman, *Inside View*, p. 113
69 Dicey, *Law of the Constitution*, pp. 27–30
70 Ibid., p. 24
71 Ibid., pp. 30–1
72 Ibid., p. 456
73 *Scruttons v. Midland Silicones* [1962] AC 446
74 *Liversidge v. Anderson* [1942] AC 206 at 244
75 *Hansard*, 24 June 1935, col. 799
76 Quoted Brazier, *Constitutional Texts*, pp. 595–6

77 7th edn 1987, p. 30
78 Gilmour, *Body Politic*, p. 371
79 Ibid., p. 379
80 Hewart, *New Despotism*, p. 11
81 See *Headmoor Productions* v. *Hamilton* [1981] 3 WLR 139, [1982] 2 WLR 322
82 8 Co. Rep., 113b, 118a
83 Lord Denning, *What Next in the Law*, 1982, p. 319
84 [1981] AC 303
85 *Schering Chemicals* v. *Falkman* [1982] QB 1.
86 *Trawnik* v. *Lennox* [1985] 1 WLR 532 at 541

4 The Incoming Tides

1 Burke, *Reflections, Works*, vol. V, p. 231
2 For a recent statement of the case, see Philip Norton, *The Constitution in Flux*, Oxford 1982, and Norton's own contributions to his collection of essays, *New Directions in British Politics*, Aldershot 1991
3 Crossman, *Inside View*, pp. 105–6
4 *Bulmer* v. *Bollinger*, [1974] 3 WLR 202
5 *The Times*, 21 June 1990
6 Leslie Zines, *Constitutional Change in the Commonwealth*, Cambridge 1991, p. 71
7 Ibid., pp. 71–2
8 Brazier, *Constitutional Reform*, p. 140
9 *The Times*, 26 June 1990
10 *The Times*, 7 July 1988
11 Norman Tebbit, *Unfinished Business*, 1991, passim
12 Ian Gow Lecture, 19 June 1991
13 In *Human Rights and U.S. Foreign Policy*, ed. P.G. Brown and D. Maclean, Lexington, Massachusetts, 1979
14 *Encounter*, December 1980
15 *Cambridge Journal*, May 1948. I am indebted to Mr Nevil Johnson for this quotation
16 *Spectator*, 21 July 1990
17 Bruges Group, 1990, p. 21. For alternative proposals, see *Europe's Constitutional Future*, James M. Buchanan and others, IEA, 1990
18 Article I:9 and 10.
19 Article IV:1. Of course, even the United States is not a perfectly free internal market. Dentists and lawyers face stiff barriers when moving to practise in a new state; some states refuse access to trucks with the wrong size of mudflaps; the banking system is fragmented by the federal law preventing a bank from opening branches in other states.

But the market remains infinitely freer than it would be if the
Constitution did not contain such provisions.

20 14 July 1990
21 *Daily Mail*, 29 October 1991
22 Speech in Edinburgh, 29 October 1991
23 *Guardian*, 24 June 1974

5 Shapes of Things to Come

1 Zines, *Constitutional Change*, p. 23
2 De Smith and Brazier, *Constitutional and Administrative Law*, p. 640
3 Cmnd 218, para. 40
4 Speech at Mansion House, 9 July 1991
5 Zines, *Constitutional Change*, p. 50
6 25 July 1991
7 Burke, *Reflections, Works*, vol. V, p. 175

INDEX